SIMPLIFYING
TIMESHARE

Mom,

Thank you for All
your support through
the years.. your drive
keeps me going.
Love always
Karen

SIMPLIFYING TIMESHARE

2ND EDITION

Vacation Ownership - How to Use it and How to Buy it!

by Karen Holden

authorHOUSE®

AuthorHouse™
1663 Liberty Drive
Bloomington, IN 47403
www.authorhouse.com
Phone: 1-800-839-8640

Published by AuthorHouse   10/01/2014

ISBN: 978-1-4969-4097-1 (sc)
ISBN: 978-1-4969-4098-8 (e)

Library of Congress Control Number: 2014917043

Contents

Acknowledgments xi

Author to Reader xiii

1. Defining the Vacation... 1
   ➢ What is a Vacation?
   ➢ So, why do we need to vacation?

2. Your Vacations... 5

3. A Little History... 10
   ➢ The concept of vacation ownership...
   ➢ Why do people buy vacation ownership?
   ➢ When did timeshare start?
   ➢ Where it is located?
   ➢ Who buys vacation ownership?
   ➢ What do they buy?
   ➢ How does it work?

4. Simplifying Timeshare... 20
   ➢ Myth or Misconception
   ➢ What do owners think?
   ➢ Now, what does the media think?
   ➢ What major hotel chains are involved in timeshare
   ➢ Where is the industry headed?

5. By Email, Telephone or Kidnapping... 33
   ➢ Understanding the marketing approach.
   ➢ What costs are involved?
   ➢ How is it marketed?
   ➢ The free stuff!
   ➢ Is there a better way to solicit prospects?

6. Attending a Sales Presentation... 45
   ➢ Understanding your fear
   ➢ The sales process
   ➢ Questions you should ask

7. *Making the Decision* 52
   - Is it fear?
   - Or is it the money?
   - The other nine excuses you give the salesperson

8. *Okay, I Already Own a Week* 58
   - Reconfirming your purchase
   - Ownership questionnaire

9. *Understanding what you Own?* 62
   - Deeded, right-to-use or leasehold
   - Fixed, floating, biennial, triennial and split weeks
   - Fractional interests & private residence clubs
   - The mystery words
   - Bonus time or bonus weeks or bonus points
   - Seasons and colors - is there a difference?
   - How are resorts qualified?

10. *Understanding Exchange & Member Benefits* 73
   - Overview
   - Who are the exchange companies?
     - Resort Condominiums International (RCI)
     - Interval International® (Interval)
   - Exchange Company Membership
   - The Resort Directory
   - Exchange Fees
   - How does the exchange work?
     - How Resorts are Rated?
     - What Weeks Should I Deposit?
     - What you must know before you go online or call
     - Determine what questions you want to ask
     - **Interval International Exchange Methods**
     - **RCI Exchange Methods**
     - Alternate Week Exchanges
     - Exchange Restrictions
     - Confirmation of Exchanges
     - Can I cancel an Exchange?
     - Internal Exchanges

- ➢ Membership Benefits
  - ◦ **Interval International**
    - • Regular Membership
    - • Interval Gold Membership
    - • Interval Platinum Membership
  - ◦ **RCI**
    - • Regular Membershi
    - • Platinum Membership
  - ◦ Exchange Company Websites
  - ◦ Vacation Travel Value Packages
  - ◦ All-Inclusive Resorts with RCI and Interval
  - ◦ Cruise Exchange Programs
    - • RCI Cruise
    - • Interval Travel Cruises
    - • ICE
  - ◦ Other Timeshare Exchange Options
    - • HSI
    - • Owner´s Link
    - • Others

11. The Price of Ownership... 117
- ➢ What are they really worth?
- ➢ What a week sells for
- ➢ Cash or financed?
- ➢ Paying it off by cashing it out?
- ➢ Annuity options
- ➢ Insurance programs
- ➢ Donating to charity and/or taking a tax deduction
- ➢ Maintenance & Other Fees
- ➢ Buyer's Remorse

12. For Rent, One Timeshare... 130
- ➢ Using your home owner's association or vacation club
- ➢ Using a rental company
- ➢ Renting it yourself
- ➢ Sample Rental forms

13. For Sale, One Timeshare... 141
- ➢ Why do you want to sell?
- ➢ How long will it take?

> What price should I ask?
> The truth about reselling your week
> What are my resale options?
> Should I buy a resale week?
> Resale checklist
> Resale questionnaire

14. Points, Coupons and/or Vacation Clubs? 157
> Points
  ◦ RCI points™
  ◦ Club Interval Gold
> Vacation clubs
> Coupons

15. What are My Rights? Am I Protected? 167
> Who is looking out for you?
  ◦ Home Owners Association (HOA)
  ◦ What does a Home Owner's Association do?
  ◦ The American Resort Development Association (ARDA)
  ◦ ARDA Resort Owners Coalition (ARDA-ROC)
  ◦ Federal Trade Commission (FTC)
  ◦ State Legislation
  ◦ The Canadian Resort Development Association (CRDA)
  ◦ Mexico
  ◦ Latin America
  ◦ South America
  ◦ GATE (Global Alliance For Timeshare Excellence)
  ◦ European Timeshare Federation
  ◦ RDO (Resort Development Organization)
  ◦ India
  ◦ Africa
  ◦ Australia, New Zealand And Asia
> Owning or buying a timeshare in a foreign country
> What if I/we die? - who gets our timeshare?

16. Now that You Have Had Time to Think About It... 189
> Recapping the benefits
> Ten tips on why ownership makes sense
> Ten tips for buying a week (or two)
> Trial memberships

17. *Buyer Beware - Timeshare Scams & Frauds*................194
   - ➢ Telephone Scams
   - ➢ Email Scams
   - ➢ What should you do?
   - ➢ Social media approaches

18. *Tips for the Savvy Traveler*.........................203
   - ➢ The Basics
   - ➢ Rental Cars
   - ➢ The Medical Stuff
   - ➢ Customs and Holidays
   - ➢ Currency
   - ➢ Tipping
   - ➢ Dates and Time and Electrical Power
   - ➢ Taxes and Other Fees

19. *Terms Used in the Industry*.........................217

20. *Timeshare Address Book*............................220

About the Author....................................241

Acknowledgments

First, I must once again thank David Fitzgerald for his longtime friendship, support and research assistance in the updating of this book. Again, thank you to my dear friends for their constant support and belief in me through everything. To my son Shayne, who travels to visit me wherever I may be living, a very special thanks.

In addition, I would like to thank ALL the people, companies, government agencies and corporations referred to in this book for their assistance in helping me research and put together this book. I dealt with many individuals in each company so to list everyone would be impossible, however I very much appreciated your time and knowledge - it was invaluable in helping me write this book, thank you again.

A group thank you to the following people because without them giving generously of their time and knowledge this updated version would not have been possible. I would also like to say that many of those mentioned were invaluable in the first writing of the book and I very much appreciate their continued support with this project. My thanks to Beatrice de Peyrecave, Christine Boesch and Jennifer West from Interval International, Catherine Reynolds from RCI, Richard Ragatz from Ragatz Associates for his updated statistical information, Darla Zanini and Peter Roth from ARDA and also Laurie Bowden from ICE for their continued assistance. In addition, I would like to thank the newcomers, Jared Nelson from HSI, John McDermott from Owners Link and the other folks for their invaluable help in helping me with the accuracy of their respective products and services used in the book. If I have overlooked anyone, I apologize.

As mentioned, this book would not have been possible if not for these companies who actively promote the timeshare industry. Their continued work in this industry is tireless and I am sure unappreciated by most. One last special thank you goes to Craig Nash, President of Interval International who provided me with the final ¨kick in the ass¨ I needed that sat me down to do this updated version - thanks Craig!

My use of Company and Industry names, copyrights and trademarks throughout this book was for providing reference and information. Any errors or omissions that occurred are mine, not theirs. All membership exchange and benefit information, along with the statistical information provided is source foot-noted when applicable and used with permissions.

Author to Reader

The original version of this book came from personal experience, both as a long time timeshare owner, two years of selling vacation ownership as well as twenty years of working directly with timeshare owners. Timeshare owners, and even a few non-owners, asked me, what originally prompted me to write this book? Well, for too many years I listened to too many people whom, for whatever reasons have a negative impression about the timeshare or vacation ownership industry. Then, when I worked in timeshare sales for a while, I kept hearing - it doesn´t work. As a result I starting asking them why they believed what they believe and the reasons varied from "they do not work", "they are a scam" to "we cannot afford it." For those folks this book will open your eyes, especially chapter 4. The second reason was for all those owners who honestly do not understand what they own. This book significantly updates the first version published in 2006.

Why did I choose to keep the title "Simplifying Timeshare?" Again, it was still the best title to get the message across by providing real information for those of you who do not own timeshare. This book is designed to give the straight goods on the industry in order to better familiarize you with the truth about timeshare rather than the negatives. This is especially true in this era of social media - bad things about people, places or things are posted or tweeted almost immediately, but anything positive - well it seems to take a little longer and is harder to find, especially in a web search. Since most people hear only what they want to hear, let us focus on hearing the truth for a change. Remember, knowledge is power.

For those of you who already own timeshare, this book will tell you more than you most likely wanted to know about timesharing. It will tell you when and where it started, what is in store for the future, which players are involved and much more. The book also focuses on how to make the most of what you own. If you do not own or felt that they ¨were not¨ for you, perhaps understanding what they are really about may give you a different perspective and opinion.

Throughout the book you will find questionnaires and little quizzes to help you understand your own vacationing habits. In addition, I also recant some personal travel experiences that you may find entertaining. After you have completed the last chapter, I hope you will realize that there are benefits to vacation ownership so you can now make an informed choice or better enjoy the vacations in your future.

Should you be planning to travel to any one of the over 100 plus countries where timeshare is located throughout the world, here is the first story I wish to retell - how I personally got involved with timesharing. For those of you who have been through this experience, you are welcome to have a laugh at my expense.

My timeshare journey started back in 1979, when I received a letter informing me I had won a "FREE" weekend stay. All I had to do was call the number shown to claim my prize. Well, at the time I was in the middle of a somewhat strained divorce and working in a rather intense job as an air traffic controller, so I called the number. I was informed that my "FREE" weekend was in Fairmont Hot Springs, Canada. The only condition of the trip was I would have to attend a short, ninety-minute, presentation at some point during the weekend. I agreed on two conditions. First, they would pay for two rounds of golf for a guest and me for each of the three days, and second, that I stayed in a suite facing the golf course. Arrangements were made, and a couple of weeks later, my friend and I drove to spend the weekend in a place I would never have otherwise chosen to visit.

Leaving after work, we arrived at the resort around midnight. We were pleased to find someone patiently waiting for us to guide us to our room. Surprisingly, it was a very well appointed two-bedroom, upstairs/downstairs condominium. After a quick look around we fell into an exhausted sleep. We were rudely awakened early the next morning by a feminine voice on the telephone, politely reminding me that I had a complimentary breakfast presentation to attend. So I dragged my friend out of bed and we had barely locked the condo door when the same woman, who was exceedingly too perky, arrived to take us to breakfast. What I really needed was coffee!!!

Now, I can honestly say that until this particular time, in my life timesharing was not something I had ever considered but I had travelled to a number of places and understood the costs, especially of travelling abroad. Like everyone else, I had heard some "stuff" about it, but did not know of no one who specifically owned, so I had no impression one way or the other. I think I had a vague recollection of some television program saying to avoid it at all costs, but I could not remember why. However, I had agreed to attend, and being a woman of my word, I thought I would give the presentation the benefit of the doubt. Nowadays, it is called keeping an open mind.

Forgive me, but I have strayed from the story. Getting back to the presentation - before we could help ourselves to the magnificent buffet and coffee, I (not my friend) had to confirm my age and show them a valid credit card. My guess was that I had to prove I could pay for a week. So one driver's license and an American Express card later I was asked to fill out a survey sheet.

The survey consisted of some basic questions: where did I live, did I own property, did I vacation, if so where, how much did I spend, etc., and of course, how much money did I earn. Now human nature is a wonderful thing. People will lie to avoid answering any of those questions because they believe they are going to be sold something, or they will tell the truth and hope they will not be sold anything. I took a few minutes to observe the room. I noted that it was full. There were around thirty couples, one or two families plus maybe six singles. I began to wonder what was going through their minds as they completed their survey forms.

During breakfast we had a "guest speaker" who extolled the virtues of Fairmont and why ownership there was a good thing. Our speaker went on to explain how we could travel anywhere in the world and save money on our future vacations for only a small investment. I watched the people around the room nodding their heads in agreement. It reminded me of those toy dogs that you used to see in rear car windows with the continuously nodding heads.

From the introductory speech we continued to sit with our "host" who then asked us more direct questions about our vacation habits. I think she believed we were a couple, and being the rebel I am, I did not dissuade her. Within fifteen minutes a very tall, somewhat portly gentleman came over to the table and introduced himself. The name Jim comes to mind, but again that was over thirty years ago. He did not have the appearance of a "used car salesman" but he talked like one. I was not sure what to expect, but I think he fit the part. First appearances are funny things. Standing in front of us was this good looking middle-aged man dressed in a nicely tailored suit. The only odd thing was that he was wearing far too much gold jewelry and white loafers. It was as if he had run out of flowered shirts and white pants that morning and all he had left to wear in his closet were suits. Now, I knew what he was expecting: A young, high income, divorced, well-traveled prospect: "the perfect shot." These days the term "gold ball" unit is used to describe what I was then.

My friend and I fell into his pitch, like sheep to the slaughter, with some exceptions. First, Jim did not have to convince me that timesharing was a good deal because I had already seen the value. Second, I knew I wanted to continue traveling the world and the possibility of doing it for the same money in twenty or thirty years appealed to me. So, we let Jim do his job and I became, what is now a common industry term, a "lay down." Oh do not get me wrong, we did dicker on the price and surprisingly seventy-five minutes later I owned my first timeshare. My final price was CAD$11,496. I was now the proud owner of an interval week, in a two-bedroom condominium for the rest of my life. By the way, my last bargaining tool was that I had insisted it be on a fairway of the golf course. The funniest part of this story is that I have never been back to Fairmont since that "free" weekend. For you golfers out there, playing the golf course twice was definitely worth the fourteen-hour drive there and back.

That purchase started what by far, has been the best vacation investment I ever made. Over the years I have traveled to five of the seven continents using both my exchange ability and the benefits that come with ownership. I have traveled alone, with family and friends and could not imagine a better way to see the world.

Since that first experience, I have subsequently bought many more weeks and now am considered a timeshare junkie. Statistically, I am not alone. It has been shown that once people buy their first week they will continue to buy weeks to enhance their vacation experiences. Everyone who owns a timeshare has most likely been through the process and shared similar experiences.

Vacation ownership is a wonderful alternative to the current packages available or continuing to travel independently. In addition, by buying your future vacations at today's dollar does eliminate inflation for your future vacations throughout the world.

In the industry there is a saying, "some do, some do not, so what." I do realize that timeshare is not for everyone, but if you see this as a benefit to your lifestyle, know you can use it, and it is affordable - just say yes. One last thing while reading this book - keep an open mind, and you might surprise yourself. The worst thing that can happen, you will be the most informed "prospect" who might be solicited, kidnapped or bribed for a presentation wherever your final destination.

Chapter 1

Defining the Vacation...

WHAT IS A VACATION?

If you look up the word **vacation** in the dictionary it means "an interval between terms." Terms are then defined as work, school or law courts. Oxford's second definition of **vacation** means to "spend a holiday".

The ancient Romans used to consider days that were holy days or sacred festivals, normal days. These days people rested from their routine daily activities. Days that were <u>not</u> considered sacred were called dies vacantes, or vacant days, days during which people worked and did not have any religious meaning. In more modern times, vacations are the periods of rest, renewal, rejuvenation or recreation away from everyday work. Whether they are known as mental health days, days off or short sabbaticals, they are to be periods of rest and spiritual renewal. Of course if the Romans only knew that we still take sacred festivals or holy days off along with dies vacantes they might have reconsidered their working hours.

Let´s face it; we ALL work very hard for our money. Each day we wake up with high hopes for a great day. Usually something happens to prevent that good day. Your smartphone battery is dead, the toast burns, there is no milk for our cereal, the kids are screaming and the dog is peeing on the carpet. However, we persevere and leave home ready to face another day of doing a job most of us do not like to do.

We travel on what seem to be, increasingly congested highways. We sit in traffic cursing our fellow commuters and trying to make all the green lights. We may be texting or talking on our cell phones (not recommended or legal in most places); slowing down to ¨looky loo¨ at accidents or whatever else

1

appears in our line of sight. We put up with bosses who do not understand us or how hard we work. We drink coffee left over from the last major oil spill. We remember, often too late, that we've forgotten our lunches on kitchen counters and then we try to find the time to grab a quick bite. At some point you look at your watch and realize that you should have been home or somewhere else a half an hour ago, then it's off to face the traffic again. Have you noticed that there is no longer a rush hour? Traffic goes all day, every day. Murphy´s Law: Wherever you are, the traffic reporter will say the other main road is moving well with no accidents. Meanwhile, your car is moving along at a snail's pace and you are texting your spouse or friends to say you are stuck in traffic!

Once your car has made it safely back into the garage, driveway or parking space, you consider yourself lucky to have again faced the enemy and won. Tired and hungry, you come home from your tough day looking for sympathy and a hot meal and a back rub to ease the days' stress. Only you discover these treats do not exist because your spouse, roommate, dog, cat, goldfish, etc. also had a bad day. Foraging for something edible or calling for take-out, you eat standing up at the counter or possibly make your way to the sofa to vegetate in front of the TV. The day then ends with you collapsing into bed with not so much as even a good night kiss from anyone - spouse, dog or cat!!

In addition, if you are a working mother, not only do you have to tend to yourself, you have to feed, clothe and raise your children. You do housework, laundry, shopping, and the other household chores and somewhere, in amongst all of that, find the time to keep any relationship you may have going. A famous comedienne once said: "Ladies, can we talk?" I agree. If anybody needs a vacation it's you. So guys, remember if the women are happy, then you are also happy, right?

SO, WHY DO WE NEED TO VACATION?

Foremost, vacations are critical to our well being. They provide an oasis in the desert of life. They rejuvenate our health, mind, body and soul. With so much that occurs in every day vacations are a way to put laughter, fun, romance, intrigue and happiness back into our lives. They provide an opportunity to fulfill childhood dreams of exotic lands and faraway places.

We need to take the time to re-acquaint ourselves with our spouses, partners, friends and family. We need to either establish or re-establish communications with our kids or with anyone else. Studies have shown that couples that spend time together will stay married longer and family time together strengthens the very essence of the family.

So, why is it that you're afraid to utter the words ¨I need to take a vacation¨ to your employer? Are we afraid that if we say the words out loud employers will send us to the unemployment line? Get over your fear by asking if you can take a longer vacation. Taking a vacation will provide you with the enthusiasm and energy you need to do your job more efficiently and effectively. Employers would rather you take a vacation and come back to work prepared to face new challenges, than continue to work when your mind is off drifting off elsewhere. Many companies throughout the world shutdown their operations for a time to insure that their employees take those well needed and well deserved vacations.

By the way, were you aware that Americans and Canadians take less vacation time that any other industrialized country in the world? I wonder why that is? Even a workaholic, like me, needs a vacation. Burnout does no one any good, least of all you.

Another important reason to vacation is to **learn**. It is amazing how you can turn otherwise boring history into a truly interactive experience. There is nothing like watching a young child's eyes grow wider at the sight of the Pyramids in Egypt. Learn about art by studying the great masters during a trip to the Louvre in Paris. Learn about music by strolling along the banks of the Danube in Budapest or Vienna and listening to the musicians, or by touring some of the world´s great Opera Houses. Perhaps, it is just simply learning about nature while walking around the mountains, deserts or valleys in your own back yard that is enough.

I knew a truly great lady, by the name of Aggie for many, many years. She was my surrogate Granny who once said to me: "**Travel is the best education in the world. Can you think of a better way to learn about art, history, language, mathematics, culture, politics, beauty, social skills, people and life than by seeing and experiencing the world? The world is your classroom so live long enough to experience it all, if you can.**" The world's boundaries have changed significantly in the last thirty plus years, so what better place to learn about life, and what living is all about.

Aggie spoke five languages, albeit her Italian was becoming rusty over time, but she relished every day as a new learning experience. We should all be so lucky to experience a tenth of what she saw in her lifetime. She had been on safari in Africa, walked with the spirits of the Czars in Russia and walked on the Great Wall in China. She visited Tiananmen Square in

Beijing and the Imperial Palace in Japan. She admired the Coliseum in Rome, the Parthenon in Greece and the Pyramids of Egypt. On the Rock of Gibraltar she saw the vistas of Morocco and Spain. She went from the Americas to India, Africa, Asia, Australia and Europe. I think she went to every corner of the globe - except maybe Antarctica, which I am sure she would have had she lived a little longer.

Growing up with her, I believe she had every copy of National Geographic ever printed, she always found a new place to go and experience. Sitting on her lap when I was a small child, I would listen to her describe the places she had seen and the things she had done. We would take out the map from the back of the magazine and plan a trip that we would want to take and for many years afterward she took those trips. She instilled in her children, grandchildren, great grandchildren and me, her thirst for life and travel. Granny died in 1994 while attending a family reunion near her birthplace in Switzerland. She was 97, at an age when most people would not even think of venturing too far from home. And until the day she died, she continued to travel the world visiting her family and friends. She touched all who came in contact with her. Those who knew her miss her very much, but with each new place we visit, we think of her and remember her words and vision.

The world has become a lot smaller than it used to be. Airplanes and ships now reach pretty much every corner of the globe. When I took my first trip there were only 79 countries on the world map but now borders have been redefined and as of today there are more than 200 countries to see and experience.

Vacationing, or traveling, also does three things to people subconsciously. One, it makes them more open-minded, two, it makes them less prejudiced and three, more flexible. It has been shown that children who travel will do better in school. They will also become self sufficient, independent and well-rounded adults.

So, what is a vacation? A vacation is time spent in a place that renews your mind, body and spirit. Where you go is your choice. Remember, life is about choices and you should choose to vacation. Who knows, you might even find the key to eternal life in your travels.

Chapter 2

Your Vacations...

Now that you know the reasons why you should vacation, let us find out a little about how you vacation? This chapter is going to involve some participation on your part. So, look through your purse, backpack, and fanny pack, carry on luggage, briefcase or whatever you use to transport pens and get one out because I am going to put you to work. If you cannot find a pen, borrow one, because these next few pages may just surprise you. Should you decide you do not want to participate in these little mental exercises, your choice, just remember what you do with your vacation is your choice.

What is your favorite vacation memory? Recreate the mental and emotional pictures by closing your eyes and letting your mind drift back to that special time and place. Remember how it made you feel.

Now that you have relaxed and are feeling good, are you ready to answer some questions? Some of these questions, though personal, may appear to have no relation to your vacations, but they will stimulate your thought process in a positive direction.

Where did you go on your last vacation? (Visiting relatives does not count.)

_____

The year of your last vacation?_____
How long was your last vacation?_____days/weeks/months
What did you enjoy the most about it?_____
What did you like the least?_____
Do you own an □ iPhone, □ iPad, □ Android, □ Blackberry □ Tablet □ Camera
Do you take the pictures with any of the electronics? □ Yes □ No
Do you take many pictures or videos? □ Yes □ No How Many
Any Selfies? □ Yes □ No

Are vacations important to you? □ Yes □ No
Why do you take them?_____
Do you have a dream vacation destination? □ Yes □ No
Where is it located?_____
Why (why not)?_____
What is your age? □ Under 25 □ 26-40   □ 41-55□ 56-65□ Over 65
What is your martial status? □ Single □ Married □ Divorced □ Separated
If married, how long?_____Where did you go on your honeymoon?
_____
Do you have children? □ Yes   □ No   In the future? □ Yes □ No
If yes, how many?_____ □ Preschool □ School Age □ Graduated □
Moved Out □ Living back at home
Do you travel with your children? □ Always □ Sometimes □ Never
Do you travel only when your children are out of school? □ Yes □ No
□ Sometimes

What is your job or profession?_____How many years?_____
Do you like your job? □ Yes □ No Annual Salary?_____
What would you change about your job if you could?
_____
Why?_____
Do you have investments? □ Stocks/Bonds/Commodities
        □ Property □ None
Do you have a retirement program? □ Yes □ No □ Thinking About it
If not, why not?_____
How many vacation weeks do you have per year? □ 1 □ 2 □ 3-4
        □ 5-6 □ More 6
Where do you normally go on vacation? (Choose as many that apply)
□ Beach Resorts□ Lake(s)   □ Mountains   □ Tropics □ Spas
□ Golf Courses □ Ski Areas □ Desert Areas □ Gambling Areas
□ Attraction Areas (Disney, Universal Studios, 6 Flags, etc.)
What do you like to do on vacation? (Choose as many that apply)
□ Golf □ Skiing (Water or Snow) □ Tennis □ Reading □ Shopping
□ Fishing (deep sea or lake) □ Hiking □ Biking □ Rafting □ Walking
□ Sightseeing or Historical Tours □ Sun Tanning □ Drinking □ Sleeping
□ Work around house or garden □ Safari □ Photography □ Camping
□ Other_____

Where would you like to go on your next vacation? (Choose as many that
apply) □ Mexico □ Canada □ USA □ Hawaii □ Caribbean □ Fiji/Tahiti
□ Latin America □ South America □ Australia or New Zealand □ Thailand
□ Indonesia/Bali □ Hong Kong/Singapore □ China □ Japan □ Eastern Europe
□ Western Europe □ Middle East □ India/Tibet/Nepal
□ North Africa □ South Africa □ Central Africa □ Former USSR States

□ England/Ireland/Scotland/Wales □ Norway/Sweden/Denmark
□ Antarctica □ Greenland/Iceland □ Cruise to anywhere mentioned above

How many people go with you? □ Spouse □ Children_____□ Other
How do you like to go on vacation? □ Fly □ Train □ Bus □ Drive □ Cruise
How far ahead do you plan? □ 1 Week □ 2-4 Weeks □ 1-3 Months
□ 3-6 Months □ 6-9 Months □ 9-12 Months □ 13-18 Months
□ Need more than 18 Months
Do you like to go to popular destinations during peak times? □ Yes □ No
□ Sometimes
Can you travel when it is not peak season? □ Yes □ No   □ Sometimes
Can you travel on short notice? □ Yes □ No □ Sometimes
Are you flexible on your vacation destinations? □ Yes □ No □ Sometimes
Means of vacationing? □ Pay by night □ Package Deals □ Timeshare
□ Mooch off friends/relatives
Do you save money for your vacation? □ Yes □ No □ Sometimes
How much per month?_____
Do you □ Charge it to a Credit Card? or □ Do you Borrow it?
How much?_____
Do you ¨shop¨ travel sites: □ Travelocity □ Orbitz □ Cheap Tickets
□ Other:_____
What is your total vacation cost? (including travel, food, entertainment, etc.)
□ Less than $1000 □ $1001-1999 □ $2000-2999 □ More than $3000

Do you own vacation or recreational property?   □ Yes   □ No
If yes, what? □ Ski condo □ Summer cabin or Cottage □ RV or trailer
□ Boat (Sail or Power) □ Timeshare/Vacation Ownership
How long have you owned it?_____□ Did you personally purchase? or
□ Inherit it?
How many days or nights per year do you use it? Days____Nights____
How much does it cost you to maintain this property per year?
Oh, one last question: How many additional nights per year do you
spend away from home? (Wild weekends, seminar or conventions, visiting
relatives, etc.)_____

Now, we are going to do some calculating. Just do your best, this is
not a test**.**

WHAT MY VACATIONS COST ME

How much do you spend per night on your vacation accommodations?
_____
How much do you spend on those extra night's accommodations?
_____

Take these numbers and average them: $_____(a)
How many weeks a year did you say you went on vacation per year?
_____

Convert those extra nights into weeks (if you can)_____
    NOW, Multiply weeks by total (a) = $_____
    (b) This is your yearly vacation accommodations cost.
Now, how many years will you continue to vacation?
_____(If you are having trouble with this, just take a realistic guess)
Then, multiply the years by total (b) = $_____

IS THIS A BIG SCARY NUMBER?

For an even more realistic number, consider that you did not include any percentage increase for inflation over those years. I could scare you more by saying that the average cost of inflation in the hospitality industry is 12% per year, but then I don't think that anyone would vacation ever again. Also not included is the cost of transportation to your vacation destination, eating, drinking or entertaining yourselves.

For the most part, most people do not think about the actual amount of money that they <u>do</u> spend on vacations. That's okay. The main objective, as I stated in Chapter 1, is to **rest, rejuvenate and recreate**. Any amount of money that you have spent on these three things is worth all the wonderful memories and great pictures.

To better illustrate my point on taking vacations, here is a little story:

One day, about 30 years ago, while walking towards the Parthenon in Athens I came across a fairly young man in a wheelchair. He was perspiring heavily under the hot September sun while trying to make his way, uphill, towards the funicular railway station to enjoy the view of Athens. I asked if he needed help. He was quick to accept and we walked for a number of blocks to his destination. He invited me to join him on the ride to the view, and I gladly accepted. We chatted about Athens for a few minutes and then I told him I admired his determination on choosing Greece as a vacation spot in spite of his obvious disability.

I will always remember his words. "I spent many years working like a dog, day and night, so that when I retired at 50, I could spend my money and see the world. Then one day I got hit by a drunk driver on my way home from work and lost the use of my legs and it shattered me to the core." As he went on, I noticed tears welling up in his eyes, "I believed that nothing could ever happen to me that would interfere with my dream, but I was wrong. So before the next drunk driver hits me and I lose my life, I am going to see the world." I found myself choking back tears as I remembered something that Aggie had said to me years before: "You only live once, so live each day to the fullest because it could be your last." That was exactly what this man was doing. Despite considerable obstacles he had managed to overcome his greatest one - the fear of not accomplishing his dream.

What have these first two Chapters, this little story and all those questions, do with vacation ownership? Not much at the moment, but a little later on all of your answers will help you decide if vacation ownership is the right thing for you. Give thought to taking back control of your life by owning your vacations, instead of renting them. Think seriously about doing something good for you and your family.

Remember you only live once.
If you wait until another day, it may never come.

Chapter 3

A Little History...

Let's face it, people all over the world like to vacation. What people want from their vacations varies from one end of the spectrum to the other. For example, you may live and breathe mountain climbing as the ultimate vacation experience, while, to someone else, it might be working on that perfect tan under a warm tropical sun. Whatever it is, it is a personal choice based on lifestyle. Are you a camping kind of person or do you want the "lifestyles of the rich and famous?" Are you looking for all the great diving locations around the globe or are you happiest walking around the Blue Ridge Mountains of Tennessee or trekking in Nepal. Whatever it is you like to do, or wherever you want to go, vacation ownership can do that for you.

THE CONCEPT OF VACATION OWNERSHIP...

In the first Chapter we learned that Oxford's definition of vacation is "an interval between terms." Well, Oxford defines **ownership** as "one who owns something." By deduction, and definition, vacation ownership means: owning one´s interval between work or owning one´s way to spend a holiday.

Technically, vacation ownership offers consumers the opportunity to buy prepaid vacations in fully furnished accommodations. It is sold in a number of manners, for specified lengths of time, for a percentage of the full cost of ownership. It is sold based on the size of accommodation, time and flexibility to suit the needs of any sized family. Owners then share the use and costs of the maintenance of not only their unit, but the property (common grounds) as well.

Simply, it means finding whatever means you use to vacation and owning it for use year after year, generation after generation. Whether your ideal vacations is a cabin by the lake, at a ski chalet on the hill, in a condo on the beach, a recreational vehicle, a houseboat, a sailboat or on a motor yacht. It is the pride of ownership for a fraction of the cost.

WHY DO PEOPLE BUY VACATION OWNERSHIP?

People buy vacation ownership to prepay for their future vacations thus eliminating inflation and guaranteeing a level of quality accommodations worldwide. In other words, by buying with today´s dollars the price of a vacation is stabilized, no matter how much the cost of hotel accommodations increases.

Up to, and including the early 1970's, air travel was non-existent or very expensive, so vacations were taken close to home. Families owned a summer cottage, cabin or home, usually by a lake and that is how, and where, they vacationed. The cabins were great, but for something that was only used, at most, four months of the year, were expensive to maintain. However, since they were owned, the cost of vacationing over the family's lifetime was considered a good investment. From the mid 1970's onward, air travel became a more viable option, so families began to look at something other than the cabin as their vacation destination.

Think of all the locations where you have vacationed over the years - Hawaii, Mexico, Florida, Disneyworld, Australia, Asia, Africa, Europe, India, Caribbean, South, Latin or North America? Now, think of how you vacationed. Were, or are you vacationing on that killer package deal from Expedia® or a similar travel site, or as a free independent traveler (FIT)? A FIT is one who makes their own arrangements and normally has resources to travel this way.

What type of accommodations were you renting? Yes, I said renting. That money you gave to your travel agent or paid for online through a travel site was passed along to a package wholesaler, which then passed it along to the hotel chain as rent. Alternatively, you may have given it to the owner of the condominium, house, chalet, boat or RV as rent. Anytime that you are paying someone else to use their accommodations you are renting. So again, I ask you, what types of accommodations were you renting?

Most likely, it is a typical hotel room. It comes with four walls, a bed (or two), a couple of bedside tables, three lamps... oh, let us not forget, a flat screen television bolted to the wall. If you were very lucky you get a mini-bar. How many of you want your kids in the same room as a mini-bar with that $25 tin of Macadamia Nuts? Why would you subject yourselves to staying in a room like that after working hard for fifty or fifty-one weeks a year? Your vacation, if you remember from the first chapter, is supposed to be designed for rest and relaxation, not crowding everyone into a space smaller than your living room.

The answer is the money. Money is the major factor that determines the type of accommodations in which we stay. Vacation ownership offers you the opportunity to buy fully furnished, one, two, three or more bedroom accommodations for the same or less money that you spent on that killer package deal from Travelocity® or a similar site. Resorts also provide all the same amenities that are offered at other top rated vacation destinations. There is no longer a requirement to spend large sums of money to stay at an expensive hotel resort.

If you could own, instead of rent, in any of those locations that I mentioned, would that interest you? Before, I show you how you can do that, let's learn a little bit more about the vacation ownership industry, shall we?

WHEN DID TIMESHARE START?

It is believed to have started in the French Alps, in a ski resort area known as "Superdevoluy," in the mid 1960's. Skiers wanted a place that would guarantee them a reservation for the "season" so a small hotel was converted to accommodate them. It became an immediate success. In 1966, a group of Japanese investors promoted a similar project what the Swiss company developed and called it the Japan Villa Club, its success was so resounding that company now has 300 resorts and 250,000 members.

The idea moved across the Atlantic to North America in 1969 when the first leasehold timeshare sold in the US was in Hawaii. The first deeded timeshare was offered in Lake Tahoe in 1973. By the mid 1970's, condominium projects, in the United States and Caribbean, that had been faltering now found a way to get out of the hole. They began converting themselves to the "timeshare" idea. Those first projects in St. Thomas, Puerto Rico and Fort Lauderdale enjoyed immediate success and timesharing was now a viable vacationing alternative for North Americans. By 1975, there were forty-five locations in the United States and boasted 10,000 owners. Today, there are more than 5,600 locations and over 6.7 million owners worldwide. Timeshare has become a major industry, reaching a high of $19.2 billion[1]

---

[1]   Statistics are from ARDA World Wide Vacation Ownership Report - 2012 Edition.

in 2008. Sales took a bit of a nosedive when the recession hit the US and Canada in late 2008 and 2009 by dropping almost 40%, but in 2011 sales started to come back and by the end of 2013, sales levels were steadily climbing above $6.5 billion. The last two years have seen sales increase and are forecasted to reach pre-recession levels by 2018.

WHERE IT IS LOCATED?

You can find timeshare projects on six of the seven continents - from Andorra to Zimbabwe. Timeshare resorts are located in more than 108 countries. What a great way to experience the world's cultural diversity. From a Chateau in the wine region of France, to an English Castle, a luxury yacht or climbing the ruins of Machu Picchu in Peru, vacation ownership can take you wherever you want to go.

Not surprisingly, the United States has the most timeshare resorts with 1,551. Mexico follows with almost 500 and Canada 168 respectively. Worldwide, Europe has 1,345, Central and South America 539, the Caribbean has 246, just slightly ahead of the African continent which now has 220 resorts. Australia has grown to 112 locations, but the biggest increase has been seen in Asia which now has 334 resorts and the Middle East with 53. All combine to make up the worldwide total of 5,300 resorts. Even as you read this, more projects are being developed and opened as continued growth occurs worldwide. Asia, Africa and Eastern Europe are some examples of areas experiencing major expansion. Rumor even has it that we may soon see vacation ownership in Russia, for those who wish to walk in the footsteps of Czars.

Regarding preferred locations, within the countries that offer timeshare, the beach is the number one location chosen. Following along in order are by lake areas, mountain regions, the tropics (including beach locations), golf course destinations, attraction areas, ski resorts and the desert. For Americans, Florida is the single-most preferred state, followed closely by California and South Carolina. For those thinking … what happened to Hawaii? It ranks fifth after Colorado. For you gamblers, Nevada ranks number seven.

WHO BUYS VACATION OWNERSHIP?

Now that we know where we can find it, who buys it? Today, the typical vacation owner is an upper-middle class, middle-aged, well-educated couple. They earn more than US$74,000 per year, are over the age of 50 and have at least a bachelor´s degree and 30 percent hold a graduate or professional degree. Since 1975, except for income, the general characteristics of the timeshare buyer have not changed. The baby boomer generation is getting older; they own their own homes, have considerably more disposable income and have been the staple of vacation ownership buyers for the past 10-15 years.

The new buyers of timeshare are now the Millennial's[2] who are tech and social media savvy using every one of growing list of social media options such as Twitter, Facebook, YouTube, Instagram, Pinterest, Yelp, Wikipedia and blogs, to name a few, before they purchase. They use their iPhones, iPads, Blackberry´s, Androids and Tablets to Google resorts during sales presentations just to make sure that what they hear is true, and to help them determine which option(s) they want and how much they willing to pay before they make their final decision - whether to buy or not. Millennial's now account for more than 50 percent of recent timeshare purchasers.

In addition to Millennial's, the past few years the industry has also seen single females become the next largest buyers of timeshare. This is due to the fact that more and more women travel, both for business and pleasure, and now timeshare provides them with a safe, secure alternative to hotels. This is particularly true in urban locations, such as New York City, where single women outrank couples as buyers in upscale, uptown condominium projects.

Buyers from eighteen to eighty, including all income levels, educational levels and nationalities, are purchasing vacation ownership. They are single, married, divorced, widowed or cohabiting. Despite the demographic that shows a higher income, more educated, middle-aged buyer, there is no real definition of a timeshare buyer.

Some other statistics[3] regarding the average owner,

> ➢ They have owned for 8 years.
> ➢ Average resort use is 1.9 weeks.
> ➢ 60% say they would purchase more weeks and already own in more than 1 resort.
> ➢ Average vacation time taken has increased to 22 days.
> ➢ 57% now use All-Inclusive programs (this number is up exponentially from 2006).
> ➢ 55.8% still use the units/suites kitchen facilities to prepare meals.

---

[2] Millennial's are people born between 1980 and 2000.

[3] Statistics from ARDA Worldwide Study of Timeshare Industry 2012

> ➤ Have made 3.7 exchange requests and taken a minimum of three exchanges.

One interesting statistic that stands out - globally 81% of timeshare owner's vacation each year compared to only 43% of non-owners. What does this mean? Owning a timeshare encourages people to take a vacation, which we learned in Chapter 2 was vital to your rest, recuperation and recreation, or in simple terms - maintain both good mental and physical health, create wonderful memories and enjoy life.

WHAT DO THEY BUY?

Both in 1978 and in 1998, the most favored size of unit bought was a two bedroom. Two bedroom units offered families the additional space they needed, as well as providing them with good value for their money. In 1978 a two-bedroom unit could be purchased from US$1,400 to $4,100 per week. That was a considerable sum in those days however it did entitle the purchaser to one week per year in perpetuity. Today, a two bedroom ranges from US$6,800 to $100,000+, on average per week, depending where you buy it and for what time period. For a unit that sleeps up to eight people, two bedroom units were always considered a good investment for your vacation dollar. It was believed that two bedroom units offered a much better exchange, rental and ultimately, resale value than the smaller studio and efficiency-sized units.

Today, there are no dramatic differences between one, two or three or more bedroom units, except in cost. All offer a better exchange and rental opportunity than the small hotel-like studios, but the initial purchase price usually ends up being the dictating factor in the buying decision. If you only have the money for a studio, buy a studio. You can always upgrade to a bigger unit later.

As of the end of 2012, 784,505 units were sold worldwide and the breakdown in percentage of units sold, based on size, are[2]:

Studio rooms, suites or efficiency type:	13 percent
One Bedroom	34 percent
Two Bedroom	63 percent
Three Bedroom	11 percent
Four Bedroom	Less 1 percent

Yes, this does equal more than 100 percent because owners do own more than one week. Due to this phenomenon, more developers are building a higher percentage of larger units.

In addition to the type of units sold, the increase in the number of different membership types has also increased substantially in the last 8 to 10 years. For example, purchases of fixed week programs are being replaced with points based programs and fractional ownership. To illustrate this, the sale of units in order of type of program sold as of the end of 2011[2]:

Points based programs	46 percent
Weeks (fixed or floating)	45 percent
Biennials (every other year)	8 percent
Triennials (every third year)	4 percent
Fractional Ownership (one month or more)	12 percent
Trial Programs	Less 1 percent

Another interesting report from that 2012 study reflects the increasing variety of timeshare options. It indicates that 88% of European properties and 86% of Caribbean properties offer weeks. In addition to weeks, properties are also offering new shared vacation ownership products in an effort to provide more options to potential buyers. In Australasia 42% of properties offer a points system, while 50% of resorts in Asia offer biennials.

The industry is also seeing a trend towards the length of ownership and owning larger units. In other words, the longer an owner owns, the more likely they are to own a larger unit, and more of them. For example, having personally been an owner for almost twenty years, I own weeks in both one bedroom and two bedroom units.

Okay, so far we have covered the - who, what, when, where, and why of vacation ownership. The only thing left is...

HOW DOES IT WORK?

Timeshare as defined in the Oxford dictionary. Yes, timeshare is in the dictionary, means "share in a property that allows use by several joint owners at agreed different times." Simplified, it is the shared cost of a vacation condominium divided into weeks, or intervals, and sold to cover the cost and maintenance for a specific time. The ownership can be done on a weekly, fractional or a point basis.

Timesharing is a means in which the total cost of the "condo" is shared amongst a group of owners. This makes it affordable for everyone to share in ownership of something that would otherwise not be affordable. An owner or developer takes each condo and divides it into fifty-two weeks. Fifty-one of these weeks are either sold on an individually or on a multiple week basis. People then buy either one, two, three or more weeks depending on their individual vacation requirements. One week is kept unsold to accommodate annual maintenance for the unit.

Today, you can also own in an old castle, chateau, or on a cruise ship. For nature lovers, campgrounds, recreational vehicles and houseboats abound. Anything that costs a substantial sum of money has the potential for timesharing - even business jets are timeshared by many successful worldwide corporations.

Specifically, a developer builds, or plans to build a condominium complex consisting of suites ranging from hotel-like studios with small kitchenettes to full size three, four or more bedroom homes. Sizes of units range from as little as 200 square feet up to 6000 square feet.

Along with new developments, old Chateau's, castles and similar historic homes are being converted into timeshare projects. Significant problem areas, such as back taxes, restorations or renovations to current standards in heating systems, water, electricity, makes upkeep cost prohibitive for old family homes to be kept, in the family. Arrangements are made to convert these "old or historic" places to timeshare to help defray the accrued costs. As such, average folk can then own a "share" of a castle and feel like royalty for a week or two.

Some basics about how timesharing works are as follows:

- The location where you make your original purchase is, for exchange purposes, known as your home resort.
- Maintenance fees are determined by the operating cost of the resort complex.
- Cost of a timeshare membership ranges from as little as US$1,500 to more than US$300,000 per week for a fractional interest when purchased from the resort or developer depending on the membership program offered.
- In the early years prices remained the same for each week bought so there was no advantage to buying multiple weeks. However,

to keep up with demands of today's more sophisticated buyers, more resorts are offering discounts for buyers for multiple weeks. A purchase of four or more weeks comes under the title of fractional interests or ownership.

- Pricing varies on location, week and/or season, size of unit, international rating, and amenities (on or near property) in addition to other programs that may be offered. However, location is the biggest determining factor in price. The higher the demand for the location, the higher the price asked. Just like the restaurant business, location is everything.

- Weeks purchased are allocated at time of sale. Traditional time-shares were sold as a **fixed** week or in recent years, as fixed week with a point's equivalent. Newer resorts sell **floating** weeks or points that can be used at any time during the year. Some resorts do offer both types. Usually a fixed week is assigned for in-House use, but trading can be done at any time of the year. Some resorts may still sell fixed weeks in fixed seasons. Fixed, fractional and floating weeks are further explained in Chapter 9. It should be noted that some older resorts are starting to convert their fixed or floating programs to point's equivalent based programs to offer their members more travelling flexibility.

- Check-in days for fixed week owners are usually Friday, Saturday or Sunday. This also applies to traded locations.

- With changing consumer needs, an increasing percentage of resorts do offer a flexible check-in day. Like that of a hotel, you can check-in whichever day you choose. This normally applies only to your home resort only, not to an exchanged location because for deposit purposes with RCI or Interval, the deposited week(s) will be limited to a Friday, Saturday or Sunday check-in day.

- Timeshare ownership is in increments of seven days. If you own a fixed week membership and cannot use all seven days, you forfeit the balance. Conversely, if you need ten days you will pay regular or "discounted or club" hotel rates for the remaining three days.

- In some fixed week timeshare locations, you may have to check-out of the unit you have been in for the seven-day period and relocate to a different unit for your remaining three days. This is due to the owner of the unit, or someone on exchange, coming in to use that unit.

- Resorts that are offering a split-week option have gained considerable popularity since 1992. More and more resorts now allow owners to break up their seven day ownership into three or four day use periods.

- In the past five years, points programs have increased exponentially in popularity and more resorts are now giving their membership

18

the option of staying a minimum of two consecutive days up to the full seven days depending on how many points they wish to use. If they use only two of the seven days for example, the remaining points/days can be used at a later time or in some cases, rolled over to the following year.

- Timeshare projects are usually affiliated with an exchange company, either Interval International® or RCI® (Resort Condominiums International) or sometimes both. Resorts may also offer their members alternative exchange options within their member base only. This is common among resorts with multiple locations and/ or sister resorts.
- Length of the ownership varies from country to country. Each country has their own rules regarding how long foreigners can own property. Terms can also vary from state to state or province to province, within each country.
- Ownership is conveyed (sold) either as **deeded, leasehold** or **right-to-use** for X number of years. Projects offer one or the other method of ownership. If a twenty-five or fifty-year lease is not a concern for you, then Right-to-use is an option. If security and peace of mind are a major concern, then Deeded ownership is your only option. Each has pros and cons. Choose whichever type of ownership makes you the most comfortable. Remember by whichever method you buy the ownership can be "willed" or bequeathed to anyone of your choosing.

The basics mentioned above are covered in more detailed Chapters later in this book.

In the next Chapter, I will continue to bring vacation ownership out of the closet. By examining the myths, the facts and realities of the timeshare industry - past, present and future - we can understand that there is nothing to fear.

Chapter 4

Simplifying Timeshare...

What are truths? What is just myth or fiction? This is the Chapter where timeshare truly comes out of the closet. The timeshare, or vacation ownership, industry has matured from its entrepreneurial beginnings in the Alps. Timesharing has seen exponential growth. In the past twenty-five years it has grown an overwhelming 1,000 percent. Why is it though, with sales of timeshares going through the roof, so to speak that so many people speak negatively about it?

I read once that the best way to be prepared for the future was to participate in its shaping. This is done first by educating everyone in the realities of the timeshare market: everybody, from the consumer to owners, as well as the media to the actual industry participants. Only then will industry credibility be gained and accepted.

The first group affecting the industry's image is you, the consumer. What you think and believe about the industry affects its future. Perception of a product is directly related to your exposure to that product. Unfortunately, we tend to believe what we hear, which in some cases, is really a...

MYTH OR MISCONCEPTION

What is a Myth? A myth is a belief about ancient times. **What is a Misconception?** A misconception is the wrong interpretation of events. These are both interesting definitions. **How do misconceptions and myths start?** In most cases, someone has a bad experience, tells someone else either in person, puts it on their Facebook page, Tweets about it, emails and so forth. Granted, it does take more than one person to generate a worldwide negative interpretation, but is the impression correct?

Below are eight myths, or misconceptions actually, that are still prevalent, or associated with timeshare, today. How many of them do you believe?

Myth number one: Owners must occupy the same unit at the same week or time each year.

>For some inexplicable reason, people felt that if they bought a fixed week of timeshare, that is exactly what it was, a fixed week. Timesharing was designed so that people could stay in the same place, during the same time, each year **IF** that was what they wanted to do. It is not a mandatory requirement of ownership.

Myth number two: If one year I do not use my week, I will automatically lose it. There are a number of ways to respond to this myth:

>(a) You will not lose it if you advise your home resort and make arrangements to carry it forward (or roll it over, bank it) into the next vacation year. Check with you home resort.
>(b) You will not lose it if you deposit (or bank) it with an exchange company. Exchange companies do allow you to bank your weeks for up to two years.
>(c) You will not lose it if you rent it out to someone.
>(d) You will not lose it if you give it to a friend or relative to use.
>(e) You will lose it, if you do not bank it, deposit it for exchange, pay your maintenance and/or assessment fees.

Myth number three: The exchange system does not really work.

>This myth started in the early years of the exchange programs. Initially, people did not understand that they could exchange to another location, and as such, did not deposit their week(s) into the exchange system. Because there were no weeks on deposit, people could not exchange their week (for example: from Florida trying to exchange to Hawaii). You can learn more on exchanging timeshare in Chapter 10.

Myth number four: Maintenance fees increase too much each year.

>Ownership contracts must state how much the maintenance fees can be raised from year to year. Some may show it as a maximum percentage, while others will state specifically. Although some resorts may stipulate no more than a 20 percent increase each year, the fees themselves may only increase from 3 to 10 percent. Maintenance and assessment fees are explained in Chapter 11.

Myth number five: Timeshares are not flexible.

Indirectly, this relates to myth number one. Should you choose to only stay at your resort, during your assigned or fixed week each year, then yes, there is no flexibility. With the arrival of more and more resorts offering flexible or floating time, points based systems and incredible exchange opportunities; this is no longer an area of concern within the industry. Timesharing today allows you to plan your vacations from twenty-four hours to two years in advance.

Myth number six: Timeshare is not a good investment.

Timeshares, as a personal investment, will provide many opportunities for yourself and your family to enrich the quality of your lives. As a financial investment, timeshares can be a good investment depending on the location you choose. Timeshare should be purchased as a personal investment, not as a financial investment.

Myth Number seven: Timeshares cannot be resold.

Everything can be resold. Everything has a price, including timeshares. Unfortunately, most people expect and want more than their timeshare is worth. Use good judgment and a common sense approach and you can and will resell your timeshare. Chapter 13 will explain everything that you will need to know about reselling your timeshare.

Myth number eight: Developers (or marketing companies) will just take your money and leave town.

In the early days of timesharing this was indeed a problem. Unscrupulous developers and marketing companies would set up shop, as it was, sell vacant land or properties located in the middle of nowhere, then take the money and run. Unfortunately, this held true for not just the timeshare market, but for other real estate sales as well as multi-level investment schemes. With all the regulations and legal recourse people have today, this type of sale is almost extinct. I say almost, because there are people who are not trustworthy. If you are ever in doubt, ask any one of the government or legislative bodies I mention in Chapter 15.

Hopefully I have been able to dispel these myths and misconceptions so that now you can begin see the positive side of the industry. I am not saying that all is now pure and clean, but as the industry continues to move forward in this new millennium, it would like to shed its "negative" image.

If we move from the consumer perception to owner perception let us look at:

WHAT DO OWNERS THINK?

Statistically speaking, 84 percent of timeshare owners are satisfied with their timeshare. Of that 55 percent are very satisfied. Yes, this section will reflect statistics[4]. I apologize for all these numbers, but they provide a summary about what owners think and feel about their ownership,

* ❖ 77.0 percent - now look forward to their vacations.
* ❖ 85.0 percent - have gotten good value for their money.
* ❖ 81.0 percent - amenities at resort locations.
* ❖ 74.6 percent - timeshare has met or exceeded their expectations.
* ❖ 70.0 percent - ability to fix future vacation costs
* ❖ 81.0 percent - full kitchen facilities.
* ❖ 73.0 percent - ability to exchange or trade to visit other destinations at various times.
* ❖ 78.0 percent - more overall space than hotel room.
* ❖ 64.0 percent - have increased their family vacation time.
* ❖ 88.8 percent - members extremely satisfied with their ownership.

This last statistic reflects what owners really feel, and believe, about owning a timeshare vacation interval. More than half have agreed that it has enhanced family relationships, facilitated family decision making, prevented work burn-out and improved their physical or mental health.

NOW, WHAT DOES THE MEDIA THINK?

If we go back to the beginning of timeshare not much was written about in, but starting in the mid 1970's, the magazine, U.S. News & World Report published a special report on timesharing. It read:

> "Time sharing is a new concept that could provide many middle income Americans with luxury vacations that they otherwise could not afford." It went on to say, "Time sharing can result in vacation saving of as much as 60 percent on hotel and restaurant bills, experts estimate. And by providing tomorrow´s vacations at today's prices, these arrangements can serve as a hedge against inflation."

---

[4]   Statistics are taken from Interval International Industry Insight Report 2010

In 1979, the Wall Street Journal stated:

> "TIME-SHARING CONCEPT of vacation resort ownership gains momentum .... The American Land Development Association says sales of such units this year will total $700 million, up from $300 million in 1978 and $150 million in 1977." John Steffans, director of Investor Services for Merrill Lynch, which made a recent study of time-sharing, says one of its main advantages is that it's inflation-proof. "Vacation ownership is like paying for tomorrow´s vacations with today's dollars."

In 1989, a New York newspaper article read:

> "The vacation time-share industry expects 1989's sales to reach $2 billion, up from $291 million in 1978, says the American Resort and Residential Development Association (ARRDA). ARRDA projects that sales will reach at least $30 billion within 12 years if the current pace continues. The industry has grown because timeshares offer affordable vacation options." It goes on to say, "There are also more exchange programs that allow time-share owners to trade their vacation week in a given year for a comparable vacation at one of the more than 1,200 resorts worldwide."

In the 1980´s and 1990´s, USA Today went to great length to publish objective and well research articles on both the positive and negative aspects of timeshare.

In 1996, the San Antonio Express-News published a lengthy story on the industry, entitled, "At last, some respect." Generally the article refers to a couple that bought weeks at a resort in Las Vegas and have "never done anything more right." It went on to state,

> "Rising from the muck of yesteryear's criticism, the time-share industry has grown exponentially." It continues with ... in a business riddled with dishonest developers, increased credibility has made cash registers sing a $5 billion chorus."

The list goes on and on...., regarding articles expounding the virtues and benefits of timesharing, however it has not always been that way. Between the years, 1984 and 1995, there was considerable negative press regarding the timeshare industry. Dishonest and unscrupulous developers and marketers were taking, what was a great product, and driving it down in a quagmire of uncertainty, fear and skepticism. Major television networks, in both Canada and the United States, were showing horror stories and documentaries about the industry and warning consumers to stay away. Large circulation newspapers were also lending their column inches to a complete array of negativity and warnings about the evils of timesharing. It was almost as though you needed a cross around your neck to keep away the timeshare devil.

Over the past decade there have also been in-depth investigative reports done by news programs looking at the misdeeds of the industry, but it is usually an isolated incident which is brought to light by disgruntled owners who felt cheated. I am not saying that there are not any unscrupulous companies out these and I would also be neglectful to mention that there is also a wide assortment of negative articles in the past three years regarding timeshare scams. Two groups, one the American Resort Association (ARDA) and the FTC (Federal Trade Commission) continually monitor and work with various state and federal law enforcement groups to clean up these scams. I will cover in more timeshare scams in detail in chapter 17.

However, in more recent years that those very same commercial television networks, major newspapers and magazines encourage people to consider timeshare an option to their present vacation, or lack thereof. Newspapers such as the Wall Street Journal, Los Angeles Times and Chicago Sun-Times to magazines such as Golf Digest, Skiing, Hotel & Motel Management and Good Housekeeping, even major Airline magazines encourage people to make a commitment to themselves to enjoy a better vacation lifestyle.

So what has happened to change the media perception of timesharing? The big guys entered the timeshare arena, with the premise, "if you can't beat them, join them." Who exactly are the big buys?

WHAT MAJOR HOTEL CHAINS ARE INVOLVED IN TIMESHARE

The hospitality resort luminaries such as Ritz-Carlton, Marriott, Sheraton, Westin, Hilton, Hyatt, Four Seasons and Disney have all helped to put timesharing back on the map. Their entry into the market has helped consumers regain credibility in the timeshare industry. When timesharing first started, it bailed out financially strapped condominium projects. Now these major hotel players are building projects strictly for timesharing. As timeshare sales skyrocketed, hotel companies realized that without "jumping on the bandwagon", they would be left behind. Timesharing was becoming the fastest growing segment of the travel and tourism industry and everybody wanted a piece. Today, all of them are selling high quality, first class vacations, one week, or one fraction, at a time.

Timeshare also did something else that none of the major hotel chains thought would happen. It found a way to increase their customer occupancy rates. More and more timeshare owners are extending their seven-day vacations, either before or after their use week, and staying in their hotels. Whether it is a hotel associated with their timeshare directly or indirectly, those extra days equivocate to more money in corporate coffers.

Starting off the list of luminary companies now participating in the timeshare or vacation ownership market is ...

RITZ-CARLTON

The Ritz-Carlton Destination Club® offers their members two exclusive memberships. The first is their Home Club, a deeded membership for those who enjoy returning to the same destination each year by purchasing a guaranteed minimum number of days or Fractions, with the option of using all of the other Ritz-Carlton Club Residences, resorts and estates in locations around the world. It is an equity based luxury travel program.

The other is a Portfolio Membership is a points based membership which gives members the option of experiencing different locations year after year. The membership offers more flexibility by permitting members to choose their time of year to travel, the length of their stay and the type and size of their accommodations. Memberships are sold in increments of 2,500 points, however a minimum of 5,000 points are required at time of purchase.

Founded in 1999, with over 3,000 owners, the Ritz-Carlton offers suites from one to four bedrooms and pricing starts at a conservative $100,000 and goes up significantly from there depending on the size of unit purchased, which range in size from 570^{sf} to 2,800^{sf}.

MARRIOTT

Marriott was the first major hotel resort developer to enter the timeshare market in 1984 and by doing so brought real credibility to the fledging industry. Marriott had studied the industry for years. They believed that if they combined their standards of excellence and philosophy, with the great idea of timeshare, they could supply the most flexible vacation program in the industry. They entered the market slowly and without much fanfare, but as the years went by they have developed a strong, loyal market share.

Marriott Vacation Club International© (MVCI), their timeshare ownership program, has approximately 400,000 owner families. Operating like a regular timeshare, you buy a specific interval, or season. Ownership options include floating time, split weeks and lock-off units providing flexible alternatives to fixed weeks and fixed seasons. Pricing for Marriott weeks or points range from US$15,000 to $50,000 with a minimum 1,500 points and may be upgraded in 500 point intervals.

Marriott operates, at present, 53 luxury resorts, in the United States, Caribbean, France, Spain and Thailand, for members to use within the MVCI program. As a MVCI owner you are also eligible to trade your week(s) for Marriott Rewards points that are redeemable towards other vacation and travel options. Marriott Rewards Program is the largest awards program in the hospitality industry and provides timeshare owners with access to fourteen additional vacation travel partners. In addition, Marriott is affiliated with Interval International (II) for exchange opportunities.

HILTON

Hilton Grand Vacations Company (HGVClub®) started off in the timeshare industry by managing small resorts in southern Florida in the early 1980's. Their direct entry into the timeshare market was the Hilton-Las Vegas, followed by the HGVClub at Seaworld^R International Centre in Orlando. They now have 59 Resorts in the USA, Canada, Mexico, Spain and Scotland.

HGVClub® was the first of its kind to introduce a point-based reservation and exchange system. A deeded week at a Hilton Grand Vacation Club Resort automatically converts into a set number of HGVClub® points each year. Owners may secure reservations within their home resort season at no charge. There are nominal fees to make reservations outside your use season or location. With more than 150,000 member owners, pricing for HGVClub® weeks or points runs between US$9,000 to $278,000 depending on the type of program purchased.

In addition, as an HGVClub^R member you automatically become a member in the Hilton HHonors^R Worldwide guest reward program. This entitles you to access to more than 400 participating Hilton, Conrad and Vista Hotels worldwide. HGVClub^R is affiliated with RCI (Resort Condominiums International) as their exchange partner.

HYATT

Hyatt Vacation Club entered the timeshare foray in 1994 with its first project in Key West, Florida. It is being marketed within the existing Hyatt Key West Resort to take advantage of the guest and visitor traffic. Hyatt Vacation Club has now 15 properties located in California, Hawaii, Florida, Arizona, Colorado, Texas, Nevada and Puerto Rico.

Today, Hyatt Vacation Club offers a point-based system and Hyatt Residence Club offers a deeded fractional week(s). Pricing for a week, ranges from US$10,000 to $330,000+, depending on the type of membership, location of property, the size of the unit and the season purchased.

Membership in either the Hyatt Vacation Club or Residence club provides members with a Hyatt Gold Passport to take advantage of using any of the 700 Hyatt and affiliated destinations around the world. Hyatt Vacation and Residence Club are affiliated with Interval International (II) for exchange options.

FOUR SEASONS

In 1997, Four Seasons opened its first timeshare property in Carlsbad, California. As a leading operator of luxury hotels, Four Seasons believes that they can set new standards of excellence in the timeshare industry. Four Seasons operates 3 properties in the US in addition to the Carlsbad property which are located in Vail, Scottsdale and Jackson Hole. Elsewhere, their other 3 properties are located in Florence Italy, Papagyo Costa Rica and Punta de Mita Mexico.

The Four Season blends resort style living with all access to all of the amenities and services offered by the Four Season group.

Ownership is offered as a fee-simple deeded fractional program, with floating usage. Four Seasons plans to retain, as fixed ownership, approximately 33 percent of their high, or platinum, season inventory. This is inventory for the buyer who wishes to secure a specific week during that season. Four Seasons also offers a lock-off capability and options to split weeks. Pricing in Carlsbad ranges from US$20,000 to $30,000 for a week but can be considerably higher at more exclusive locations. Four Seasons is affiliated with Interval International (II) for owner exchange.

STARWOOD

Starwood has been involved with timeshare market for 30 years and is one of the leaders in the industry. The Starwood Vacation Network[SM] consists of a deeded timeshare vacation weeks/points program (in US only) as well as fractional ownership. The Starwood group consists of 19 member resorts are situated in the USA, Mexico and the Caribbean.

Starwood Vacation Network members also have access to the 1,100 Starwood hotels and resorts in nearly 100 countries across nine distinctive brands through privileged status in the Starwood Preferred Guest® program. Starwood´s affiliated brands include Westin, Sheraton, St. Regis, and Le Meridian to name a few.

Starwood Resort accommodations consist of a 1 bedroom Hotel style unit to a 2 bedroom, 2 bath luxury villas, where the Westin and Sheraton properties have a slightly different variety of unit sizes. Pricing within the Starwood properties varies depending on the number of points, unit size and season purchased but a conservative starting point is approximately US$40,000. Affiliated Starwood properties such as Sheraton and Westin prices have a lower starting point, again depending on number of points, unit size and season.

WYNDHAM/FAIRFIELD

Club Wyndham® is part of the Wyndham Vacation Ownership group, which is the world´s largest vacation ownership company. Club Wyndham® boasts over 500,000 members as of December 2012 including their ownership which now includes Shell Properties and Asia Pacific in 185 resorts in the USA, Canada, and Mexico.

In addition to Club Wyndham®, Wyndham Worldwide brings together more than 190 vacation ownership resorts in over 100 countries. The variety and scope of these resorts are available to the almost 1,000,000 Wyndham Worldwide owner Members. Wyndham Worldwide also offers a successful Exchange and Rental program along with providing consumer financing in addition to other timeshare product offerings.

Membership packages vary with unit size, season and location but start from $15,000 and go up from there.

DISNEY VACATION CLUB®

Yes, Disney® sells timeshare. The very first Disney Vacation Club Resort opened in 1991, in Walt Disney World, Florida.

Disney Vacation Club® (DVC) is a point-based system on a right-to-use lease for a certain number of years. Members are allotted a certain number of points each year that can be used for stays of one night, a weekend, one week or longer. Owners can travel throughout the Disney® system or any one of the over 500 Member getaway destinations. Accommodations range from studios to three bedroom homes. Pricing for Disney Vacation Club points ranges from US$24,000 and go up from there depending on the number of points purchased.

Disney® operates 14 properties and in 2007, DVC passed a milestone with 350,000-members in over 100 countries. With locations from Florida, California to Hawaii and including France and Tokyo, DVC offers unprecedented flexibility. Besides Disney® property exchanges, members are offered Interval International (II) as an additional exchange option. In addition, DVC Members also receive discounts at all of the theme parks, golf courses and Disney cruises within their system.

And the OTHER HOTEL GUYS.

Hospitality industry involvement is not just limited to those names I mentioned above. Name brand firms from elsewhere in the world are entering the lucrative timeshare market. From the United States, Intercontinental Hotels, Preferred Equities Corp. (Ramada Properties), Promus Hotels (Embassy Vacation Resorts), Holiday Inns and Choice Hotels are involved with timesharing. Aston Hotels and De Vera Hotels in the United Kingdom are also involved. From Mexico - Sun Club Resorts, Meliá Group, Palace Resorts, Villa Group and Calinda Hotels to Malaysia and the Legend Hotel Group - just to name a few and more are responding to the tremendous growth in this aspect of the travel and tourism market. It is anticipated that in the coming years more hotel companies will surely be entering or affiliating into the timeshare market in order to keep their rooms occupied.

Remember that not all hotel groups or hotel locations will offer timeshare and for those that do, I do not foresee that the type of ownership would vary considerably from those mentioned above.

The world continues to shrink as timeshare circles the globe, emphasizing that a new generation of travelers are looking beyond their family cabins, Hawaii and Florida as a vacation destination.

WHERE IS THE INDUSTRY HEADED?

"The times they are a changing" this quote has never been truer. Consumers are traveling to more destinations, with greater frequency and are no longer limiting themselves to a one-week vacation. They are demanding quality and service, and are willing to pay a realistic price to achieve these goals. Between 1985 and 1998 the number of timeshare locations rose by 187 percent and the number of owners increased by over 500 percent which was seen as a huge increase but in each year since the millennium, these numbers increase even higher as more resorts are built and programs enhanced to today´s savvy purchasers.

Why is that? The timeshare industry is no longer market driven: it is consumer driven. What the consumer wants is what they will buy. Remember what I said earlier about the advent of social media? For the timeshare industry this is uncharted territory – especially learning to deal with prospects who Google them during a sales presentation and understanding why. It has taken a long time, but even developers are starting to realize that the traditional timeshare consumer no longer exists and that the old ideas are outdated at best, so now they take advantage of Facebook, Twitter, YouTube, websites and other internet options to reach members and prospects. On the other side, marketing companies are beginning to understand that being honest, ethical and forthright with prospective buyers gains them, not only gain greater respectability and credibility, but increased sales. Many developers now have social media consultants or departments within their organizations to ensure future long-term growth.

At the beginning of this chapter I mentioned that the industry has grown exponentially in the past fifteen years, so what can we expect in the next fifteen years? Despite the significant drop from the industry high in 2008 when the banking/mortgage industry collapsed, industry experts reflected that sales will bounce back and they are starting to climb again. The reasoning for the drop is more due to the external pressures of the recession and lack of credit/financing, not a declining interest in timeshare. I could quote an assortment of industry experts, statistics included, but what it boils down to is, they all say, "sure, no problem - the industry will to continue to grow as people become more concerned where their vacation dollars are going."

Are there any problems that stand in the way of the industry achieving US$20 billion in sales in the next twenty years? Possibly. Like any company experiencing growing pains, timeshare is no different. There are some issues that need to be addressed. High pressure sales and solicitation tactics, combined with the consumers need to make buying decisions immediately are just a few areas undergoing critical evaluation and change. Licensing, legislation, sanctions and monetary fines are being used to penalize, or eliminate, the unscrupulous and dishonest individuals or companies.

Has the arrival of social media - Facebook, Twitter, Linked In, YouTube, Instagram, Pinterest and others which are an internet click or text away on everyone's iPhone, Androids, Blackberry's, iPads, Tablets and computers, changed the face of the timeshare industry? Most definitely! Although timeshare developers and marketing companies will continue to entice prospective buyers into their sales rooms with "free" weekend stays, gifts and bottles of tequila, the social media age only serves to add credibility and respectability - but it can also take these things away as well. Social media is not taking away the traditional salesroom presentation, but have become invaluable tools for consumers to gain additional information about the industry.

Almost all salesrooms now provide some form of interactive, touch screen computer systems for prospective buyers to calculate their vacation costs and see resorts they might wish to visit on future vacations. Exchange companies now offer web site access to plan vacations, and DVD's now replace the once bulky directories or membership packages. Every resort now has not one, but various social media sites in addition to their website. Facebook pages, Twitter, YouTube, Blogs sites and other social media options have been added as new communication tools to their members.

Websites now provide immediate access for owners to their exchange companies, their vacation clubs, timeshare projects and related companies. Members are now paying their loans and maintenance fees online, making reservations, doing exchanges, finding answers to questions and making comments. Prospective buyers are surfing the net, and as such, more and more timeshare clubs, projects and companies have created informative and interactive web sites. Only by educating and informing consumers, will the industry move forward in the new millennium shedding its negative image.

So what is next on the horizon for the timeshare industry? Only time will tell. One thing that is for certain, timeshare is most definitely here to stay. It is most definitely a viable alternative to your present method of vacationing. So, the next time someone asks you to have a look ... Google it or take him or her up on it, you might surprise yourself.

Chapter 5

By Email, Telephone or Kidnapping

Now that you are aware of the industry as a whole, the next important aspect I will cover is how and why we are solicited the way we are. The vacation ownership market is maturing. From the high-pressure, "grab 'em, tie 'em and sign 'em" mentality of the 1960's and 1970's, to a more sophisticated, relationship sale, the way consumers are solicited must also change.

Today's consumer is much more conscious of "scams and hype" so marketers must use some form of enticement or motivation that is both credible and tangible. Due to this, marketing companies face a daily challenge of trying to recognize and deliver what the consumer is looking for without their costs skyrocketing. The consumer's desire for personal identification and recognition, something new and different, informative and most importantly, service and quality, have all but overshadowed the price concerns. Don't get me wrong, price, although not a predominant factor for enticing people, is still an issue at point of sale.

UNDERSTANDING THE MARKETING APPROACH.

In the early days it was off-premise solicitation. Today, direct e-mail, advertising on Facebook sites, the internet, telemarketing, radio, television, newspapers, magazines and even electronic billboards are all playing a role in getting the consumer in the door. The biggest questions for marketing companies are, do these methods really work and are they effective? The question for consumers is how much solicitation is effective and, for both, how much is too much?

In the introduction I mentioned that I had been solicited by a direct mail invitation. I called the telephone number listed on the invitation and set up my "free" weekend. I attended the presentation and bought a week, so, in that instance the marketing company's method was effective. Would I do that now, thirty-five years later? Maybe, maybe not, and <u>that</u> is the challenge the industry faces.

Today, timeshare is one of the fastest growing sectors of the travel and tourism industry. Timeshare´s contribution to the travel and tourism industry is exploding and no one wants to be left behind. In 2010 the timeshare industry worldwide generated slightly less than $14 billion, in sales as it continues to climb out of the recession which has affected global economies. As such, marketers and advertisers are constantly trying to find new ways in which to directly reach consumers, rather than have them go through major airlines websites or others like Travelocity© or Expedia©, Kayak, Trivago or use a travel agent. This is why all the major hotel chains have become an integral part of the timeshare industry.

Not only do marketers, developers and advertisers want to position themselves for well into this century, but they also have to remain competitive. Timeshare is timeshare the world over. There is no big secret to this industry and everyone uses the same methods to solicit potential buyers. It is the little distinctions or refinements that set one above the other. Refinements and distinctions, though, tend to cost money and unless they are effective, are unprofitable. There is one thing, however, all marketing companies agree on: the most effective way of lowering marketing costs is to increase the closing percentages of their sales operations. Sounds like a juggling act, doesn't it? This is a question all sales and marketing directors have been pulling their hair out over for centuries and will continue to do so in the future.

However, today's sophisticated consumer makes the "one size, fit's all" marketing techniques outdated. Consumers are looking for three things in products or services; they are unique and want those products or services to suit them individually. Second, they do not trust anyone anymore, especially advertisers. Third, they have more stress in their lives than they do time. As a result, timeshare marketers and developers, who want to bring consumers into their sales offices, must find a system that will meet all three concerns at a redeemable cost.

First, it is important that you understand that rarely does the developer market their own project. They either hire a marketing company or they will form an in-house marketing company staffed with experienced timeshare personnel. Since the developer's job is to develop, their focus is on the next project. They know they will get their money back plus a handsome profit. Marketing companies or departments are doing just that - marketing a product.

WHAT COSTS ARE INVOLVED?

Costs can be defined two ways. First, what is the percentage of marketing costs to sales? Second is on a cost per tour basis. Now, you as a consumer could care less about the costs either way. However, if the percentages are too high, then the price of the timeshare must go up to accommodate the increase. Conversely, if the cost per tour goes up, then the sales personnel are pressured to make more sales. If the sales personnel are forced to increase their closing percentages, then the old "high pressure" tactics will re-emerge.

In the industry as a whole, the percentage dedicated to the sales and marketing of a timeshare can run from 20-25% on the low end, up to 50% percent or more depending on the product offered. The average tour cost is US$385. Resort area tour costs can run up as high as US$700 or more per tour, depending on what is being offered as the "free gift" or motivation.

Where does the money go? To better explain this I will use the tour cost. First, you need to pay the personnel doing the solicitation. Second, you have to pay for the space occupied by the solicitor. Third, you have to pay for the handout materials given or sent. Fourth, you need to pay for the cost of the motivation or gifts used to you to come to a presentation. Fifth, is paying for the cost of any food or drinks consumed by you and the salesperson during the presentation. How this number calculated? Take the number of tours and divide it by the dollars spent in solicitation, for a specific fiscal period.

For those other folks, who want to know about the calculation of the percentage cost, see if you can follow along as I explain it. Take the total dollar amount of sales and divide it into the total dollars spent on sales and marketing. More simply put, for every $10,000 week sold, $3,850 may go towards selling it. From the person who solicited you to everyone else who works for the marketing company, including a profit margin, all make up the $3,850.

HOW IS IT MARKETED?

How many of you have ever received a flyer, postcard or envelope that said: "You have just won a free trip to Las Vegas" or, maybe, "You are the winner of an iPhone or Plasma TV." All you had to do to claim it was to call the listed number and attend a "quick" 75 minute sales presentation. Usually, you went because you wanted the trip or gift, right? Now, please do not say, "I would never be caught dead falling for one of those things," because you do. Human nature dictates that we are always intrigued by something free, even if it means giving up a little bit of our precious time.

Remember, there is no such thing as a free ride. If something can be had for nothing, then the lines become so long that they would probably go to Pluto and back. It is because humans are notoriously cheap and greedy and that is what the marketing companies do - appeal to that basic instinct. Now, before you decide if you have read enough or think I have insulted your intelligence, I apologize. But you should pay attention, because you might be next in line on someone's call sheet or email list.

Direct solicitation, social media, email, regular snail mail, telemarketing, radio, television, newspapers, magazines, billboards and the Internet all are means by which timeshare companies try to promote their product to the consumer. Are they effective? This depends mainly on geographic areas. What may work for one area does not necessarily work for another. Direct email and ¨prize¨ promotion options are very effective in Canada, but not so much in the United States where telemarketing works very well. Tourists on vacation tend not to watch local television or listen to the local radio station. They do not read local newspapers or magazines, so direct personal solicitation is used. Although direct personal solicitation is very predominant in tropical resort areas and Europe, it is against the law in some states and Canada.

Following is a quick look at each type of solicitation. In the next Chapter I do cover what occurs after you have agreed to attend a presentation.

Direct Email or Regular Snail Mail.

If you live within a few hundred miles of a timeshare location you will most likely be solicited through regular mail or email. Timeshare marketing companies will buy lists from vacation industry magazines or they have bought your name from a group that had "drawing boxes" in malls or stores. Remember, if you never, ever want to attend a timeshare presentation, never fill in one of those "WIN A JEEP CHEROKEE or WIN A TRIP TO HAWAII" draws.

Now, I'm not saying do not ever again enter a drawing! Instances where you pay money to buy a ticket are a wiser choice for two reasons. One, you are spending your money and second, you will have most likely helped contribute to a worthwhile charity in the process. Bonus: You might actually win the car or trip.

Direct mailing, whether by email or regular mail, programs allow timeshare projects to reach a large number of prospects quickly. An invitation, resembling either a gift or accommodation certificate is "mailed" to a prospective client asking them to call a specific number to redeem their "gift." You have a choice to either trash the invitation or accept. Should you call, you are told you are required to attend a short, usually seventy-five or ninety minute presentation. At the end of the presentation you will then receive your "gift." If you agree to attend the presentation you are then told where and when.

You are chosen based on certain demographics - such as age, occupation, income, education, vacation habits, etc. - that are requested by a specific resort. Most projects, or resorts, are targeting people whose profiles resemble the characteristics of their present owners. Some resorts, for example, may require a minimum yearly income of $100,000 due to the project being in an upscale location.

Beware if your chosen "gift" is an accommodation certificate. The accommodation cost is absorbed by the marketing company. To defray those costs, you as the prospect are required to pay any or all applicable sales and occupancy taxes. This is because vacation certificates cost the marketing companies a substantial amount of money each year, so beware of the fine print.

Although direct mail is relatively inexpensive, costs continue to increase each year. Direct mail is used by approximately 49 percent of active timeshare projects.

Telemarketing.

Yes, we are all familiar with telemarketing companies. These are the folks that call you during dinner or bedtime and want to sell you something or invite you to attend a presentation at their resort or off-site sales office. If you are not rude enough to hang up on them, you have a couple of options.

First is to listen to what they have to say and then chose to agree or not. The second option is to ask them to call back at a pre-arranged time. Either way, you should be polite they are just doing their job.

Most timeshare telemarketing companies will call back if you ask them. Over the years I have been contacted by many companies and all accept a polite "no, thank you right now, please call back later" response. Some presentations I have attended, some I have not. All depended on how interested I was in seeing, or hearing, what they had to offer.

There are also some projects where the first caller will make the offer and then explain the benefits and amenities of the resort. A second call is made to advise the prospect they will receive a letter verifying all the details. The letter also includes an 800 number, which the prospect is encouraged to call if they have any questions. A day before the presentation, a third caller will welcome the customer and re-explain the details in case the prospect has changed his or her mind about attending. This method is proving very effective, because the prospect then arrives for the presentation with no hesitations and misconceptions about why he or she is there. Yes, there is a "gift" or some form of motivation for you to attend. If you accept their invitation to attend a short, ninety-minute, presentation you will receive the "gift."

Again, you are selected based on the same methods as the direct mail prospect, i.e. names on entry forms in shopping malls, trade shows, catalogue lists, etc. Telemarketing is labor intensive, however relatively inexpensive and used by approximately 70 percent of active timeshare projects to solicit prospects either alone or to enhance a direct mail program.

More recently in Canada and the United States the introduction of the "do not call" programs and have begun to have an affect on the telemarketing programs for the industry.

Mini or Fly´n Buy vacations.

Mini-vacations or Fly´n Buy tours are where the prospect pays for a three day/two night or four day/three night stay to see the resort before making a buying decision. How many of you have seen the Vacation Break™ advertisements on television offering a cruise/hotel stay or a weekend stay at a resort for you and your family for $99, $199 or more? Possibly you have seen an ad in a travel magazine or heard one on the radio offering killer deals on weekend, or possibly weekday, stays. All list a toll free telephone number to call to take advantage of the special deal. When a date is chosen all the arrangements are made for you. Payment will be on a major credit card of your choosing. During your stay you attend the required presentation and from there make a buying decision, yes or no.

Mini-vacations or Fly´n Buy options are most effective marketing tools for a timeshare project. By having the prospect come to their respective resort it psychologically puts the buyer into a vacation state of mind. It is so much easier to be in a buying state of mind when you are surrounded by beauty and your happy family.

Owner Referrals.

Friends and family are the best source of referrals for any timeshare project. If the owner is happy they will tell everyone they know to consider buying a week or points in that particular location. When a referred prospect comes in the door there is a much better chance of getting them to purchase.

Costs for an owner referral are about the same as other marketing programs however closing ratios are 50 to 100 percent higher than for regular sales. Of all active timeshare projects, over 80 percent have some sort of owner referral program.

In-House Programs.

These are prospects solicited while they are staying at a particular resort. In other words, they target existing timeshare owners and exchanger's from other properties. For example, if you own a week in Las Vegas and have exchanged to Hawaii, you will be solicited to attend a presentation about that particular resort in Hawaii.

Costs for in-house programs are slightly lower than other marketing programs, depending on the incentives offered to attend. However, since 24 percent of timeshare owners own in more than one location, in-house programs are found in 79 percent of active timeshare projects.

Strategic Partnerships or Alliances.

The "you scratch my back, I'll scratch yours" marketing strategy: Strategic partnerships allow companies to share costs and benefits. For example, if you belong to a "frequent" guest, flyer, driver, etc. program, you can also experience the benefits of other services offered by other companies. As the timeshare market continues to mature, more strategic partnerships emerge. The exchange companies now work hand in hand with hotels, airlines, car rental companies, cruise lines, restaurants, etc., to provide their members with a full range of services and benefits.

Simply put, if you belong to a "frequent something" program, do not be surprised if you receive a solicitation to attend a timeshare presentation at some future date.

The Internet.

In a later Chapter I will explain what timeshare services are available on the Internet. Regarding soliciting for timeshare presentations, the Internet is very much in use and regulations are being introduced to ensure that consumers are protected.

And last, but certainly not the least...

Off-Premise Contacts (OPC's)

While I was writing this section, a good friend said to me, "don't even think about writing this if you are going to be sarcastic." My reply, "Okay then, I guess this part will never be written!" All sarcasm aside, this is my favorite solicitation topic and it is **the** single most controversial solicitation topic in the timeshare industry. So, let me tell you about OPC solicitation.

The off-premise contact (OPC) is a successful prospect generation tool however it is an area in need of considerable improvement. While the American Resort Development Association (ARDA), the industry's regulatory body, is playing a major role in changing OPC programs in the United States and Canada, the rest of the world falters. ARDA takes a very strong stand on total disclosure in marketing. Timeshare projects in the United States and Canada must tell the prospect exactly what they are going to attend and what they will be asked to buy. In other areas of the world, the OPC does whatever they can to "entice" people into a presentation. In the past ten years, AMEDTUR, Mexico's governing timeshare association also has been working to strictly enforce how consumers are approached by OPC's.

OPC solicitation process is the pretty much the same all over the world. Calling out to tourists who walk by their booths, either on the street, in the airport, or the hotel lobbies, with phrases such as:

"Hi, there, enjoying your vacation?"
"Hi, can I interest you in a tour (activity) to...?"
"Hello, have you been here in ... long?"
"Hi, have you seen our...? If not I can get you tickets to go."
"Hi, do you need any maps or directions?"
"Hi, you look hungry ... are you? Let me offer you some lunch..."
"Hi, do you need a taxi to your hotel?"

These are just a few of the questions used to try to get your attention. Have you heard any of these before while on vacation?

The OPC is trying to get you, the prospect, to stop and talk with them. Once they have captured your attention with a particular tour or activity, they will then try to talk you into going and seeing their hotel or resort. If their resort offers some type of buffet, they will use your hunger as the first step in getting you to the presentation or even something as simple as a "free taxi ride" to your hotel. Once you have stopped, you should be polite enough to listen to what the OPC has to say.

In the United States and Canada, the OPC must tell you that it is a timeshare presentation. In the rest of the world, well, you take your chance on the OPC being honest enough to tell you. I have attended presentations in more countries that I care to admit, and have had OPC's tell me the truth while others avoid the subject until asked. I have had OPC's follow me for blocks to try to sign me up and others, who, when I said "not interested," told me to have a great vacation.

It does not matter where you are in the world. By accepting the tour tickets, or gifts, you will be required to stay for at least the <u>minimum</u> time frame of the presentation – somewhere between forty-five and ninety minutes. In some countries the OPC will put you in a taxi and send you directly to their resort. Others may take you personally to their resort and check you in with the host. Alternatively, the OPC may "book" you for a presentation the following day and make arrangements to have you picked up at your hotel and taken to their resort.

If you have made arrangements to take some of the discounted tours or activities, you may be required to give them a deposit, usually US$10 or $20 or a local equivalent. The money deposit is a sign of good faith on your part and, if you decide not to take any tours, is refunded completely. At the end of the sales presentation the final arrangements for tours are made and any "gifts" are given.

If you are going on vacation and are approached by an OPC, please be polite to them and just say "no thanks," firmly. Yes, some are very persistent in their efforts but remember it is their way of earning a living. Wouldn't you be persistent if that was your only way of making money? If you are rude and try to ignore the OPC's, you will only become upset or angry but may ultimately not enjoy your vacation, so why bother with the aggravation.

THE FREE STUFF!

So we are going to attend a sales presentation for the free stuff. I always wondered why that is. What is it that gets people in the door? It is because we, as human beings, like free things or is it because we have nothing better to do with our precious time?

So what is your motivation? A free (or discounted) weekend, Blue Ray player, iPad, plasma television, dining certificates, Mexican blankets, and discounted tickets ... the list is endless. I know. I used and abused the free stuff system for many years. It started with the free weekend in Fairmont (where I bought my first week) to $100 in casino chips on the island of St. Maarten. Apart from those casino chips in St. Maarten, the Bahamas and Puerto Rico; the Walkman's (okay so I am dating myself!) and stereo system in Lake Tahoe; dining vouchers in Hawaii; Waterford crystal in Las Vegas and free golf most everywhere else, I had become very good at using, and abusing, the system.

Now I am **not** a proponent of doing this. During the two years I sold timeshare I came to dislike those tourists who used and abused the system like I did. This even included the way I had taken advantage of the system. Do you realize that each time you attend a presentation with NO intention of buying, you are practically taking away the only opportunity the salesperson has that day to make any money. I never realized that until I sat on the other side of the table. Just like a reformed smoker, I came to have no patience for prospects that wasted my time so that they could get a free ticket, or save $10 on a $50 boat trip.

Is the free stuff worth it? Remember, by whichever method you are solicited, for everyone to win, a delicate balance must exist. Between what is being offered as motivation and the costs involved, both prospects and marketers have to compromise. Unfortunately, OPC's, salespeople and marketing companies do not know which prospects are actual buyers and which are wasting their time, so they have to treat each prospect the same. So the next time that you feel the urge to attend a presentation because you are bored or just want the "free" stuff, remember, you may not only be wasting someone's time, you may also be wasting someone's money.

Free Money! Yes, there are also some OPC's which may offer you money to attend a sales presentation at their resort. You may think that this is a quick way to earn back your vacation costs, but remember that you still have to give up your precious vacation time (and sometime lots of it) to earn that money. Usually this type of incentive involves a higher pressure sales presentation because the resort wants to get their monies worth from you as well – so now, is there such a thing as free money?

IS THERE A BETTER WAY TO SOLICIT PROSPECTS?

If we lived in a perfect world prospects would walk into a resort, credit card in hand and say they want to buy a timeshare. Since we do not live in a perfect world, all we can ask for is that the person doing the soliciting, by whatever method, is being straightforward or honest about what they want. However, if you can think of a better solicitation method, contact any timeshare project and they may want to give it a try.

By the way, here are a few statistics[5] for you to ponder:

- ❖ The average prospect receives six mail, email or telemarketing solicitations per month.
- ❖ Of prospects who attended a presentation, more than sixty percent have attended more than one.
- ❖ Prospects attend approximately four presentations before they buy a timeshare.
- ❖ Sixty-five percent of prospects go to receive the free gift!
- ❖ Sixty-One percent of buyers have a very positive view of the timeshare company.
- ❖ Forty-Four percent of prospects felt some form of extremely high or high pressure.
- ❖ Approximately 40 percent of all prospects know people who already own a timeshare purchased a timeshare.
- ❖ Almost 60 percent who did not buy would attend another presentation.
- ❖ Over eighty-five percent of buyers, who intend to make an additional purchase at the resort they toured, stated their interest in purchasing from a developer.

---

[5] Statistics quoted from ARDA Shared Vacation Ownership: Non-Buyer Study 2013

One last piece of advice: Do not tell the salesperson you "did not know this was a timeshare presentation or you would not have come." They are not that naive. Next Chapter, why...

A little side note on solicitation:

On an exchange trip to Hungary about sixteen years ago, I was not solicited once to attend a sales presentation. Since working on my first book, I now go in search of the sales department to gather information regarding the resort, pricing and other details. When I finally found it, I was politely informed that I was not solicited because they only invited European prospects, and even then, only by direct mail to attend a presentation. Being on an exchange disqualified me from the presentation. Incidentally they would not provide me any information either, as they felt it was not important since I could not buy anyway. In this case, I could not have purchased even if I had wanted to.

Chapter 6

Attending a Sales Presentation...

Whether it is skepticism, industry credibility, or the confusion of what it really is, ignorance or "it's a rip off." These are a few, and the most common, reasons why you are afraid to attend a timeshare presentation.

I remember back in the "old days" when the saying, "it's a rip off" was true because people did not really know what timeshare was or how it worked. From this ignorance came the skepticism. It is hard to believe in, or understand something that you do not know anything about. This generally leads to skepticism. Specifically, in the past ten years the industry has done remarkable things to try to improve their image and credibility, as well as continuing to find ways and means of eliminating the "rip off" stereotype. In a later chapter I do cover the ways that the consumers can protect themselves against the "rip off" salesperson.

However, the single biggest reason that most people do not want to attend a sales presentation is fear. Fear manifests itself in a variety of logical reasons, like those mentioned above; however it is usually the more emotional reasons that frighten us. Why are we afraid? Whether it is being sold something we "do not want", buying something "against your will" or the fear of making a mistake, we all justify our reasons with logic. It makes us feel better and stay in control.

Unfortunately, fear stems from something we cannot control - the unknown. If we all knew what was going to happen when we went into a sales presentation, we would go in with confidence and assurance. The confidence coming when the salesperson asks you to buy, you could say yes, or no. An analogy would be similar to being told to open to the door to a very dark room, then cross it to turn on the lights. Would you do it? Maybe - by taking small, uncertain steps you try to avoid any danger that maybe in front of you. Walking with your arms extended, you eventually reach the other side to turn on the light. Now, if you were told that there was nothing in front of you and it was just twelve paces to the light switch, which was at arm length height, you would walk confidently through the darkness and turn on the light. Fear of the unknown.

This Chapter is going to help you eliminate the fear of walking across that dark room. So, when you turn on the light, you will feel confident, self assured and ready to tackle anything put in front of you.

THE SALES PROCESS

In the last chapter you learned how and why you are invited or kidnapped off the street, now we will look at what happens when you get there. To understand the sales process a little better I will break it down into those who were invited and for those of you who were unwittingly solicited while on vacation.

By Invitation (Off Site)

As previously mentioned, in the United States and Canada you can be invited by email, regular mail or telephone. If you are interested enough you will willingly attend without too many reservations or pre-conceived ideas. These sales presentations, usually close to your home, are made in off-site offices of the resort or hotel banquet rooms and require only your "motivation" to attend. Your motivation may range from a free trip, iPhone, Blue-Ray player, iPads, dinner certificates or plasma televisions. However the most important thing is you have chosen to attend.

Before the presentation starts you can walk around and chat freely with others or with salespeople who may be milling around. There will be drinks and possibly, pastries or snacks. While you are waiting for the presentation to begin, you will be asked to complete a survey form of minor questions about the way you vacation. It can, and may be, be similar to the one you completed in Chapter 2.

The presentation will begin with someone who will speak for approximately fifteen to twenty minutes. Some resort presentations show you a ten-minute video on the resort and exchange company. After the speaker or video you will then be assigned to a salesperson. They will ask you more about the answers you put on the survey and for more information about yourself, family, occupation and what you like to do for recreation. All this helps the salesperson determine which type of vacation program they will want to show you.

All through the "pitch" the salesperson will encourage you to ask questions and you should ask as many as you can. **Do not be afraid to ask anything of the salesperson**. It is their job to know their product and if they do not know the answer, have them ask someone who does. Because you are not physically present at the resort, you will be shown pictures or a scale model of it, including the room accommodations, and any other literature that helps you to visualize the property.

If, after listening to the sales pitch, you want to become an owner at that particular resort, you will be asked to complete a credit application and provide some means of making the down payment. The presentation ends after you have signed contracts and any other paperwork necessary to complete the sale.

Should you not be interested, just say no thank you and leave. I will let you know that before leaving the table you might have an assistant manager or supervisor come to the table to find out why you are not interested in their program. Explain your reasons or not, that is your choice. Usually in off-site sales presentations there are no direct "high pressure" tactics because the companies do not wish to have complaints registered against them with the Better Business Bureaus within their communities.

By Invitation (On Site)

Again, either a verbal or written invitation has been offered and accepted by you, but this time you attend the presentation at the resort itself. Your initial motivation may have been the "free" weekend in the mountains by a lake or maybe in the desert playing a couple of rounds of golf. Whichever your choice, you have given up a weekend of your time and driven or flown there. If you have any reservations or pre-conceived ideas, they are pushed into the back of your mind because you are willingly attending a presentation to take advantage of the "free" vacation.

You may be greeted at the entrance to the resort by a "representative," who will assist you with checking in and confirm the arrangements for your "free" weekend. They will also confirm the time of your attendance at the ninety-minute sales presentation. There are some projects where the representative will call you on the telephone, after you have checked in, to confirm your weekend plans.

The sales presentations in most cases, usually involves breakfast or a brunch with the "representative" before being handed over to a salesperson for the balance of the presentation. The format from then on follows the off site scenario.

By "Kidnapping" or Direct Solicitation

If you are in a tropical resort location the sales presentation process is not altogether that much different. However, it is the way in which you are solicited, that immediately brings fear into the minds of otherwise intelligent human beings. Why does a person's whole mentality or demeanor change when they are directly solicited? It is the confrontation? It does not matter whether you are in your home town being asked to give money to the poor or buying raffle tickets, even all the way through to being confronted on the street by a religious group - people do not like confrontation or being put in an uncomfortable situation. These scenarios are no different from being approached while walking down the street in Puerto Vallarta or St. Thomas and asked to attend a timeshare presentation. Your first instinct is to get the hell out of there. Why? It is that fear of the unknown.

In a direct "mail or email" or telephone solicitation you can toss the invitation into the trash or hang up on the caller. However, when asked face to face, we panic because we do not immediately know why people are confronting us. Due to this fact of human nature, the job of the OPC is made very difficult and that ultimately leads to an unpleasant experience for both.

Your motivation to attend a presentation may the "free stuff" that we discussed in the last chapter. In agreeing to attend a presentation, the OPC will either take you immediately to their resort, or make arrangements to meet you the next day.

When you first arrive at the resort you are escorted by the OPC to a check-in counter. Then a host or hostess will ask to see some identification and a major credit card to ensure that you are a qualified prospect. Qualifications vary from resort to resort, country to country. On average they are looking for you to be between the ages of 25 and 65, married, employed and own at least one major credit card. Singles are also welcome but the age qualification is normally 30 or 35 to 65. Some resorts require you to own a home to qualify.

After check-in you will be handed over to either one of two individuals, a liner or the actual salesperson. A liner is someone who will help you complete the vacation survey sheet, eat with you and explain the basic agenda of what will happen during the sales presentation. Very large resorts use liners to help prepare the prospect to be turned over to a closer. Closers will then do their presentation and ask you to become a member of their club or resort. If you really want to know if you are with a liner or the salesperson, just ask.

After you have eaten and completed the survey form, one of two things will happen. The first, you may be required to listen to a short, usually 10 minutes, speech or given a tour of the property on your way to the salesroom. When, during the presentation, you tour the resort or property, varies from resort to resort. The second option is you will go to somewhere to eat and then go to the sales room or just directly go inside the sales room for the balance of the presentation.

The rest of the sales process is very similar to those I have mentioned above. Resorts do vary their formats depending on the tourist, or prospect flow, otherwise it is pretty much the same all over the world. An important thing to remember, this is the resorts only chance to sell you on their idea. Expect a "takes no prisoner" attitude or approach. If, at any time, you feel overtly pressured you <u>do</u> have the option of getting up and leaving. The days of "tying people to chairs and then locking them in the salesroom" have long gone.

The difference between an invited prospect and a solicited prospect - the invited one has an open mind. The hardest thing for the liner or salesperson to do is to open the mind of a prospect so they listen to what is being said. **Do not let fear close your mind**. Listen to what the salesperson has to say. Remember they are trying to help you enjoy YOUR vacations, not theirs.

The time taken to do the sales presentation is then determined by your interest, your questions and your participation level. Remember the time taken is entirely up to you. I have known presentations to take as little as twenty minutes or as long as twelve hours.

QUESTIONS YOU SHOULD ASK

Remember, all through the "presentation" the salesperson will be asking you a variety of questions to help understand your vacationing habits, but they will also encourage you to ask questions. **Do not be afraid to ask anything of the salesperson**. It is their job to know their product and if they do not know the answers then have the salesperson ask someone who does.

Sound familiar? I should hope so. It is important for you to have all of your questions answered before you buy anything. Ask questions, it does not matter whether you are buying a smart phone, iPad, car, house, boat, life insurance, roller blades, vitamins or Blue-Ray player. Asking questions eliminates any doubt or misconception that you may have regarding the product. No question is too silly or frivolous when it comes to spending your hard earned money. Never be afraid to ask that "silly" question. I cannot think of one question that has ever been asked of a salesperson that has not had a valid reason behind it.

In most sales presentations the salesperson will cover all the information that you need to make a good, sound decision. However, the following questions should be asked **if** they are not addressed during the presentation.

1) How long have you been in business?
2) How long has the resort been here?
3) Does it have any liens or encumbrances on it?
4) Who owns the resort? Is it the Developer, Marketing Company or a Vacation Club?
5) Does it have a Home Owner´s Association and is it active?
6) How much have maintenance fees gone up in the last five years?
7) Can I pay cash or get outside financing?
8) If I finance with you, can I pay if off at any time without additional cost?
9) Can I upgrade or downgrade my membership as my vacation needs change in future?
10) Can I leave it to someone in my will?
11) How would I contact the member services people?
12) What exchange value does this program have to trade with your exchange company?
13) Will you continue to service my needs after I have bought?

The last question is the most important. The others deal more with credibility and financial issues, but the last question is personal. If you like and trust the salesperson, believe they are sincere in their desire to continue to look after you, join the club or resort. To this day I still keep in touch with most of my clients.

The number one reason that people do not buy timeshare is they did not believe the salesperson, or resort, will continue to service their needs after the sale is completed. Trust and belief are important in any purchase, but none more so than in buying timeshare. Trust in your salesperson and belief in the product will bring you many, many years of great vacations.

Remember: Never be afraid to try anything, the worst thing that can happen is that you do not like it. The best thing that can happen - is you do!

Chapter 7

Making the Decision...

Okay, so now I have walked you through your initial fear of attending a sales presentation. You have kept and open mind and sat willingly through it. You listened to everything the salesperson had to say and now have to decide yes or no and, if you are thinking of saying no.

IS IT FEAR?

I mentioned earlier that most people fear making a decision because they do not want to make a mistake. Is it a mistake to want to have more for yourself and your family? Do we really want to deprive ourselves and our loved ones of an opportunity to explore the world and experience life to the fullest? Only you can answer those questions, but just do not let the fear of the unknown prevent you from experiencing something wonderful. Aggie once said to me, regarding fear, "never be afraid to try anything once. It is the only way you will find out whether or not you like something. The worst thing that will happen is you won't like it and the best thing is that you will." She was right. Every time I am afraid to try something new, I remember her words and go for it. Even if you find out you don't like what you try, at the very least you have learned and experienced something you did not know before.

Life is too short to deprive ourselves, or our families from living life to the fullest. In the American Constitution does it not say, "... life, liberty and the pursuit of happiness?" How can one pursue life, liberty or happiness if fear holds us back?

If it is pure, unadulterated fear, I am afraid that neither I, nor anyone else (except maybe a good therapist) can do anything to overcome that for you.

OR IS IT THE MONEY?

Normally there are only two main reasons people do not own. One, you have more money than god. Two, you have no money or believe you have no money to purchase. For the average, middle class family owning a week of timeshare is a good investment in your future. In Chapter 12, "The Price of Ownership," I cover what they are worth and how much you should pay for one.

The 2nd most common excuse that all salespeople hear is "I (we) cannot afford it." My question is "cannot afford what?" If you say you cannot afford "the time," shame on you, because you most likely take vacations and this answer just sounds ridiculous.

If it is the money, let us look at some comparisons shall we?

<u>Here is simple example (based on a hotel option - worldwide average):</u>

Average cost of accommodation (Hotel)	$ 300 (per night - 2 people)
Average Timeshare maintenance cost	$ (112) (per night - 4 people)
Hotel Savings (Timeshare vs. Hotel)	$ 188 (average per night)
x 7 Day Savings in Timeshare	$ 1,316
Investment figure from above	
(at real return rate <u>3.5</u> percent)	(350)
Adjusted savings per annum	$ 966
X 18 Years	$ 17,388
1 Week purchase timeshare	$ 18,200 (average price - worldwide)

Second, from an investment standpoint, and my personal favorite, "I would make more money on my IRA's, CD's, RRSP's, Stock, Mutual Funds, etc." So, if you have any financial investments, get out your pen to do this little quiz on the next page.

	EXAMPLE	YOUR $
1. If you invest	$ 10,000	
2. At	10 % *	
3. Interest earned (Line 1 x Line 2)	$ 1,000	

4. Marginal Federal Tax Bracket	33%	
5. Return after taxes (Line 3 x .33 - Line 4)	$ 670	
6. Net Value of investment after taxes (Line 1 + Line 5)	$ 10,670	
7. Inflation rate (Use today's rate)	3%	
8. Inflation's effect on after tax value (Line 6 x Line 7)	$ 320	
9. Value of investment after inflation and taxes (Line 6 - Line 8)	$ 10,350	
10. **Real rate of return** (Line 9 - Line 1) Line 1	3.5%	

*Calculation at a generous Interest rate of 10%

What happened to the other 6.5 percent?

The above examples show how a timeshare purchase can be paid for in as little as eighteen years and after that, it is money in your pocket. In my 2006 edition, it took about nine years to break even, so to speak, but as investment return rates remain low, timeshare is still an investment to seriously consider. Also, depending on which country you own in, your timeshare can still be paid off in less than ten years.

The most important thing to realize, if you are using savings or investments to vacation with, the average person's savings will be gone in five years. By the way, most maintenance fee increases are offset against hotel industry inflation rates.

If you still believe that your money is better off in your investment portfolio, leave it there and enjoy your vacations on the after tax interest.

One last comparison I will leave you with is a "then and now" review of the hotel industry. Prices are quoted from the hotel websites, per night average for a week in April 2014 (lowest rate available), in US$ for double occupancy in a regular room. Pricing will be higher for larger suites and at other times of the year.

HOTELS: Averaged Prices	1971	1991	2004	2013
Plaza - New York City	$ 45	$ 245	$ 660	$695
Fairmont - San Francisco	$ 32	$ 180	$ 340	$359
Peninsula - Hong Kong	$ 23	$ 205	$ 399	$810
Breakers - Palm Beach	$ 20	$ 95	$ 425	$695
Okura - Tokyo	$ 15	$ 241	$ 550	$388
Caesars Palace -Las Vegas	$ 21	$ 95	$ 189	$340
George V - Paris	$ 50	$ 460	$ 1700	$1450
Cipriani - Venice	$ 43	$ 468	$ 1389	$1650
Ritz - London	$ 28	$ 315	$ 946	$625
Motel 6 - USA	$ 6	$ 29	$ 56	$62
Hilton Hotel - USA (average)	$ 21	$ 79	$ 179	$180
Holiday Inn - USA (average)	$ 12	$ 45	$ 137	$162

You will notice by the chart above that some hotels have seen very little increase or even a decrease, but other locations which have become more popular have shown increased rates. Also, I have reflected pricing for a non-holiday week in April which is traditionally not a big vacation travel month.

If the investment quiz and the hotel comparisons still have not shown or convinced you enough to re-consider owning a timeshare then certainly continue to vacation the way you have in the past.

THE OTHER NINE EXCUSES YOU GIVE THE SALESPERSON

Thinking about it is the number one excuse that salespeople commonly hear when they ask a prospect to buy. Again, it does not matter what you are buying, you will say, at one point or another, "I need to think about it." Fair enough. Salespeople do understand that, but they really want to understand the reasons behind the "think about it." So think about <u>that</u> the next time you use "I need to think about it."

The following excuses, listed in no particular order, are heard by salespeople the world over. To really appreciate these excuses, imagine yourself as the salesperson and think about how you would respond after hearing them.

1. I/We don't vacation this way
2. Vacations are not a priority
3. I am (we are) buying a home, condo, boat....
4. We are saving to put our kids through college
5. I/we need to talk to my/our attorney, father, brother-in-law, etc.
6. I/we need to talk to my/our accountant, financial advisor, etc.
7. I/we need to shop around
8. I want it but my spouse does not
9. I/we cannot possibly make a decision today

At some point or another we are all guilty of using these excuses when making a purchase. Whether you have sat through a timeshare presentation before or even when you were out "kicking the tires" in a car showroom or looking for a smart phone or iPad, these excuses were there. If you are not in a frame of mind to consider a purchase, you will always find a reason not to buy.

Realistically, people always have reasons for hesitating when making a purchase and timeshare is no exception. In a study done a few years ago, the following were cited as reasons why people hesitated in buying a timeshare. Some are valid as they were not addressed during the sales presentation, however <u>all</u> the reasons reflect a lack of knowledge about the industry.

1. Disliked the idea of a maintenance fee
2. Concept was new or unfamiliar
3. Were not sure that it would be used enough
4. Had heard or read something negative about the industry
5. It cost too much
6. Wondered if it was "too good to be true"

7. Sales presentation was too high-pressured
8. Did not want to be tied down to a fixed annual use period
9. Travel to unit too expensive or inconvenient
10. Did not want to be "tied down" to one location
11. Concept too complicated to understand
12. Would have to share with others

Before I leave this chapter and move on, I would like to point out that the actual sales process is the least favorite aspects of attending a timeshare presentation. Whether it is because of the perception of being "too high pressured" or having to make a decision at that moment, people continue to believe both. The elimination of the high pressure and the first visit incentives to buy ¨that day¨, are constantly being addressed and evaluated by the industry to improve the overall image of vacation ownership.

Primarily, the reasons that prevent people from buying are personal. Whether it is the lack of income, the lack of interest per se, or the manner in which timeshare is marketed and sold. Until more people understand the benefits of ownership, gain more knowledge about the industry and willingly participate in its improvement, things will not change.

So, before you say no to the salesperson, you should have a very good reason for wanting to deprive your family of a lifetime worth of quality time together.

If you said, yes... Congratulations, if you said no – perhaps the next resort (or salesperson) is more to your liking and you will say yes!

Chapter 8

Okay, I Already Own a Week...

Congratulations, you are the proud owner of years, or perhaps a lifetime worth of vacations. Yes, you probably thought that you made a huge mistake in buying one and are now trying to find a way to get out of it, am I right? Rather than that, let's go over the reasons why you chose to buy one.

Ownership has:

- ❖ Ensured that you take a vacation at least once a year AND you look forward to them
- ❖ Guaranteed you a certain quality of accommodations on your vacations
- ❖ Allowed you to enjoy your vacations more
- ❖ Provided you an opportunity for greater vacation experiences
- ❖ Provided you with more restful and revitalizing vacations
- ❖ Given you quality time with your family and/or friends
- ❖ Saved you money on your vacations
- ❖ Generally made a positive impact on the quality of your life

These eight reasons were the most popular responses when asked of existing timeshare owners.

Statistically speaking, an astounding 85 percent of owners felt that since they bought their timeshare they have enjoyed their vacations more. Another 73 percent felt that they have experienced and traveled to more destinations because of their ownership. In addition, almost 78 percent believe that timesharing has had a positive impact on their lives and look forward to vacationing. My favorite statistic, from all the statistics I read, was that people who owned a timeshare increased their vacation time from 11.8 to 16.1 days per year. Not only are you, as an owner, looking forward to you vacations, you are taking longer ones. Congratulations. By the way, one other number, over 95 percent of owners who made the decision to buy, did so based on the ability to exchange worldwide.

Another area of positive encouragement for continued vacation ownership is that more that 17 percent of owners are looking to buy additional weeks. For example, in the U.S. alone, this would equate to more than 250,000 households. Because owners are looking to buy more time, the number of weeks owned continues to climb. Seventy-two percent of owners who bought their first week more than eight years ago, bought additional weeks. This is due to the increased flexibility of exchange and the desire to own in more than one location, providing for a "home resort" for use and a second location for exchange opportunities.

There also appears to be a direct connection between the time you own and the more positive an impact ownership has on your life. Anything that can improve the quality of your life should be treasured.

To refresh your memory about what you own, try to answer the following ownership information questions. If you can't answer all of these questions that is okay, you just might however, not be using your ownership to its full potential.

OWNERSHIP QUESTIONNAIRE

Name of Resort(s):_____

Where is it located?_____

Year(s) Purchased?_____

Do you have □ Deeded Ownership □ Right-to-use -

How long?_____years

Number of Weeks Owned: □ 1 □ 2 □ 3 □ 4 □ 5-8 □ 8 or more

    Fixed □ Week(s) Number (s):_____

    Floating □ Season(s):_____

    •   Do you have Split Week Usage? □ Yes □ No

      □ Don't know

Do you own a Biennial or Triennial Membership?

    □ Yes □No □ Can't Remember

Are you a Fractional owner? □ No □ Yes,

How many weeks?_____Summer_____Winter

What size of unit or points equivalent unit do you own?

    □ Hotel Studio/Efficiency □ 1 Bedroom □ 2 Bedroom

    □ 3 Bedroom □ Other_____

Does it have a lock off/lock out unit? □ Yes □ No □ Can't Remember

Check in Day: □ Friday □ Saturday   □ Sunday □ Any Day

Do you own a Points or a Coupon Based Program: □ Yes □ No

If yes, how many points (coupons) do you own?_____

How long?_____years

Do you, or did you have, some type of Bonus weeks, Points?

    □ Yes □ No □ Don't Know

Have you ever used them? □ Yes □ No

Does your Resort have a Vacation Club? □ Yes   □ No

Maintenance Fee$:_____

Name of HOA or Vacation Club?

Have you ever exchanged your week(s)?   □ Yes □ No □
Sometimes

How Often? □ 1 □ 2-5 □ 6-10 □ 11-20 □ More 20 times

Where have you exchanged?_____

Exchange Company Affiliations: □ RCI □ II

Alternative Affiliations □ ICE □ HSI □ Owners Link □ Other:_____

Membership or Contract Number(s):_____

In the next few Chapters I will be answering those questions you were afraid to ask when you bought and show you how you can get the most out of what you own.

Vacation ownership works great when used properly.

Chapter 9

Understanding what you Own?

Were you able to answer the ownership questions at the end of the previous Chapter? My heartfelt congratulations if you could. You have most likely been an owner for many years and enjoy using what you own. If you were not able to, do not feel too bad as I have met many owners over the years that can barely remember the name of the resort they own in, let alone anything else.

Some of the questions on that information sheet, as you may have noticed, asked about what you owned specifically. Is it deeded or right-to-use? Do you have points, split weeks or floating weeks? To what exchange companies do you belong? Did you get bonus weeks? You may have been able to check them off, but do you really know or understand exactly what you own?

This Chapter will examine the different types of ownership, explain industry terms and take a brief look at the exchange companies. By the time you have read this Chapter, and the next one, you should know everything about your membership and how to use it too its fullest potential.

DEEDED, RIGHT-TO-USE OR LEASEHOLD

To refresh your memory from Chapter 3, timesharing or vacation ownership simply describes a method by which you own exclusive use of accommodations for a set number of days each year. Timeshare is normally sold by the week, but your ownership can be conveyed in one or more of the following methods.

Deeded

Deeded ownership interest provides a title, or the use, of a specific condominium at a particular time of the year, forever. For example, if you own a home you will receive a deed as the owner of the property. For many years, in the United States and Canada, more than 75 percent of timeshare projects are sold through a deed-in-perpetuity. This type of ownership gave people the security of having a deed to the property, which gave them options rent, sell, have exchange opportunities and bequeath your ownership to whomever they choose.

Right-to-use

This is where you have the right to occupy the property for a specified number of years, but you do not have any ownership interest in the property. Ownership ranges generally from ten to ninety-nine years, after which all the rights return to the developer or the property owner.

Most of the timeshare projects worldwide are sold as right-to-use due to government ownership restrictions, whereas in Canada and United States only 11 percent are sold that way. Right-to-use ownership also allows you to rent, sell, exchange and bequeath to whomever you choose.

Leaseholds

This is quite simply that the resort property is located on leased land. You can still own a deeded or right-to-use timeshare, but the land on which it sits has been leased from another party. This is quite common on native Indian lands and countries that do not allow for foreign ownership of land.

FIXED, FLOATING, BIENNIAL, TRIENNIAL AND SPLIT WEEKS

Now, I will break down memberships into five additional options, any, all, or a combination of which can be offered by a resort. Deeded, Leasehold and Right-to-use ownership is sold in one or more of the following ways.

Fixed Week(s)

Fixed ownership is ownership of a **same unit** during the **same week**, or dates, each year. For example, I own fixed weeks in Las Vegas that are always the second week in November, or week 45. Yes, you computer folks, this also happened to be during the world computer show back in the days of COMDEX, which is why I bought that specific week. The benefit is that you are guaranteed a well-deserved vacation (or rentals in my case) each year with no hassle. Your unit is reserved for you each year and if you do not want to use it that is your choice.

Fixed week ownership was first type of timeshare program sold and is most commonly conveyed as a deed-in-perpetuity. Although 70 percent of projects still have them, there is a decline in fixed week ownership. In tropical resort locations, fixed weeks are sold under right-to-use ownership and are not as popular as the floating week or points based membership programs. Even fractional programs are no longer sold as fixed weeks, but on a floating week basis.

Floating Week(s) or Points Based

Ownership is defined by a **certain season** of the year rather than a specified week. Season length can vary from as little as three or four months, to as many as seven or eight months. You, as the owner, have the right-to-use a week within that specified season. No exact week or unit is promised. The owner is guaranteed a week in the size or type of unit that was agreed to at the time of purchase. Under this method, however, the owner must reserve their vacation time before their use season. Confirmation of reservations is on a first-come, first-served, availability basis.

For example, if you own floating time in a one-bedroom unit, winter season in Puerto Vallarta. As long as you call your vacation club, by the required date, you are able to make a reservation for your one bedroom, in any building on the resort, at any time of the year (except holidays). Generally if you own the highest point program in your unit size category you have the ability to come at any time of the year, however if you own a summer, low point program you may be limited to staying during peak season or holiday periods. Points based programs vary dramatically and are explained in more detail in Chapter 14.

Floating ownership, especially point's based floating ownership, provides tremendous flexibility for those people who wish to take their vacations at different times of the year. Floating time, especially points programs, have become so popular that 70 percent of timeshares sold in the United States now are being sold as floating time. This is an increase of 29 percent in the last four years. In addition, more timeshare projects are offering both fixed and floating time to cater to a wider buying public. Floating time can be sold as deeded, leasehold or right-to-use. Again the right-to-use conveyance is the most popular type of ownership outside of Canada and the United States.

Biennials

Just as the name infers, biennial ownership is an **every-other-year** purchase or use option. You have the use of the resort every other year for a specified time. Biennials are normally conveyed as right-to-use, although a small percentage of projects deed biennial membership. This type of membership is much less expensive at the time of purchase and, as such, maintenance fees are only due in use years only. Florida and the Western United States offer the greatest number of biennial memberships with almost 50 percent. Worldwide this type of ownership is not as common although it is becoming more popular.

Triennials

Just as the name infers, triennial ownership is an **every-third-year** purchase or use option. You have the use of the resort every third year for a specified time. Triennials are normally conveyed as right-to-use, although a small percentage of projects deed biennial membership. This type of membership is much less expensive at the time of purchase and, as such, maintenance fees are only due in use years only. Florida and the Western United States offer the greatest number of triennial memberships with almost 50 percent. Worldwide this type of ownership is not as common although it is becoming more popular.

Split Week(s)

Not specifically a conveyed method of ownership, split weeks are offered as a subset to weekly ownership. What that means, in English, is that you can take your week of ownership and break it down into two, three or four day segments for short, mini-vacations each year. Split week membership is very popular within urban or high demand recreational areas. Reservations are on a first-come, first-served, availability basis. Due to the flexibility of split weeks, you can usually call a week or two in advance and secure a unit without too much trouble. It is easier for a resort to provide you with a couple of days on short notice than a week.

65

Again, those weeks I own in Las Vegas and Puerto Vallarta provide me with a split week option. I can go and play golf over a four day weekend in May, and take the other three days in October, all on my one week of ownership, if I so chose.

From the beginning of timeshare and owning a fixed week to today's full flexibly, split, floating, fractional, biennial memberships, the options are yours. If you have one type of ownership and would like to upgrade or change to another, contact your home resort. Possibly visit a different resort and see what they have to offer you. Variety is the spice of life.

FRACTIONAL INTERESTS & PRIVATE RESIDENCE CLUBS

Fractional or **Fractional Interest Ownership** is the purchase of a larger share of a vacation ownership unit, usually from five to twenty-six weeks. Some timeshare projects do classify a fractional as four (4) weeks, but the majority consider fractional to be five or more weeks. This type of ownership is very popular due to the prime resort locations - on a golf course, ski slope or next to an ocean.

Fractional ownership is becoming increasingly popular with busy professionals looking to maximize their family vacation time. Families prefer this type of ownership as it provides the amenities of a luxury home, such as granite kitchen countertops, whirlpool baths and roomy closets along with the benefits of a first-class hotel - such as concierge services, housekeeping and grocery shopping services. Depending upon the design of the property, residences may be hotel suites, cabins, townhouses or detached homes.

The industry reached a sales volume peak in 2007 of $2.3 billion, then declined due to the mortgage crisis and financing in the US but in 2013, gained 10% over 2012, reaching $517 million. Although overall this is a decrease of 78% from the peak in 2007, fractional and residence club membership is once again gaining ground as the US economy has showed improvement as well as the availability of more home equity funds.

Owners purchase a deeded share (or long term right to use depending on country) in a residence (1/15, 1/12, 1/10, 1/8 and 1/4) that gives them a certain number of weeks per year at the property and use of all amenities. There are resorts where you can own as little as four consecutive weeks to qualify as a fractional however most are sold in blocks of three to six months. Fractional ownership then becomes a much more cost-effective way to stay in desirable locations such as Vail, Colo., or Pinehurst, N.C.

where prices range widely from $40,000 to more than $1 million, depending on the location, number of weeks, number of bedrooms and level of luxury. Most fractional interests are either two or three-bedroom units averaging about 1,640 square feet with the average price about $115,000 per share or $19,500 per week.

In addition to Fractional ownership properties there are also "**Private Residence Clubs**" and can be found at some of the most exclusive resorts in the world — the St. Regis, Ritz-Carlton, and Fairmont hotels, to name a few, all have fractional residence club programs. The average price for private residence clubs is much higher at $300,000 per share or $67,600 per week. Since the market peak in 2007, pricing has decreased by 32 percent which now makes them a more affordable option for purchasers.

Fractional or Private Residence Clubs also participate in an exchange program that gives owners the ability to reserve time with other properties that have a similar level of luxury and service. With four or more weeks to enjoy, owners can choose to spend part of their time at a different property in another part of the country or the world. For example, if you do not feel like visiting your Vail property for your whole time period, you may want trade part of it for two weeks in a Tuscan Villa or relax on the sand of a Bahamian beach. Although planning ahead is essential, the flexibility of this type of ownership is one of the exciting aspects of fractional ownership.

Yearly maintenance fees for Fractional Interests run from $6,000 and Private Residence Clubs, $11,625 for the term of membership, which breaks down to approximately $1,045 and $2,656 per week, respectively.

Destination Clubs

I would be remiss if I did not mention destination clubs. In addition to fractional interests and private residence clubs, these are a third option for some buyers who are looking for exclusivity. Destination Clubs, typically sell a thirty year membership on a non-equity basis into a wide network of vacation clubs. Some clubs are equity-based, however. This concept also is characterized by a refundability policy when members leave the club. The average price is $280,000 and unit sizes run about 3,355 square feet. There are approximately 9,000 members in the seven destination clubs.

THE MYSTERY WORDS

These are the terms that crop up during a sales presentation, or after you have signed on the dotted line, that you may not have remembered.

Lock Off or Lock Out Units

You bought a "three bedroom lock off," and are not sure what that means? Simply put, you can occupy a portion of the unit and offer the remaining portion for exchange or rental. It is like buying two weeks for the price of one. To help you better understand I will use a three bedroom lock off, or lock out, as an example:

> Option 1 -- Use or exchange as a three bedroom for personal use or rental (1 week)
>
> Option 2 -- Use or exchange the two-bedroom portion personally and rent or exchange the third bedroom and bath (Equivalent of 2 weeks)
>
> Option 3 -- Use or exchange the one bedroom and bath and exchange or rent out the two-bedroom/two bath side (Equivalent of 2 weeks)
>
> Option 4 -- Use or exchange the studio portion personally and rent or exchange out remaining unit a one or two bedroom and bath (Equivalent of 2 or 3 weeks)

Premier, Gold, Platinum, Elite Memberships, etc...

Premier, Gold, Platinum, Elite or other similarly named memberships are based on enhanced or distinct benefits offered by your resort only. In resorts with multiple locations this may mean that you have no internal exchange fees. It could also mean you do not have to pay for on-site amenities where an exchange owner or guest might.

Elite Memberships are normally defined by the purchased of large blocks of weeks or points depending on your program. In some cases, there are different levels of Elite Programs and what benefits are attributed to these levels varies, with obviously, the most benefits or perks being given to the highest elite level. For example, perks can run from complimentary transportation to and from airports, wine or flowers in your room on arrival, reserved pool and beach areas to private dinners with the resort Chef.

Exchange companies also offer enhanced membership options which may use similar names so you need to make sure when referring to your

Platinum program for example, you should define whether it is your resort membership or from your exchange company.

Founding Membership

This is a privilege extended to owners who bought in an original development and continue to buy in succeeding projects owned by the same developer. Founding members usually have a financial advantage over a non-owner by buying additional weeks at a substantially reduced price.

This is more of an ego recognition membership as the only other benefit may be a brass plaque in the lobby and the ongoing personal attention from the resort staff. [I do however wish that they would polish my brass plaque more in the lobby of the Polo Towers in Las Vegas a little more often than they do - just kidding!]

Dual or Multiple Destination Membership

In the case of resorts with multiple locations this form of membership allows an owner to use one or more of the resort locations at little or no charge. For example my ownership in Puerto Vallarta allows use of the sister resorts in Cabo San Lucas, Loreto or Cancun at no additional charge.

BONUS TIME OR BONUS WEEKS OR BONUS POINTS

These are usually a **bonus** or **incentive** offered by the salesperson at time of purchase. Bonus time, points and/or weeks provide a timeshare owner with the opportunity to pay for either additional nights or weeks beyond their purchased time at a maintenance fee or a discounted rate. Bonus time or weeks are normally only valid in your home resort. There are some projects that do allow for bonus time to be used at sister locations.

Bonus time, usually referred to additional nights, can be used as often as the owner chooses. These can be bought on a single night basis or up to, and including, six nights. The resort will normally charge anywhere from 35 to 50 percent of their "hotel" rate, depending on season and location.

Bonus weeks are just what they imply, a full week use at your home resort. Reservations need to be made and are on a first-come, first-served availability basis. Cost for using a bonus week is usually the maintenance fee for the unit size you choose.

Bonus points are just what they imply; the equivalent number of points needed for a full week use at your home resort and some resorts do not allow these points be upgraded to a larger unit or accumulated. Reservations need to be made and are on a first-come, first-served availability basis. Cost for using a bonus week is usually the maintenance fee for the unit size you choose.

There is normally a time limit set on how long you can use bonus time, points or weeks. There are presently some resorts which limit use of bonus weeks or points to one per year, but the average tends to run from three to five years. At present over two-thirds of timeshare projects offer some form of bonus weeks, points or time to their members.

By the way, you should not buy timeshare just for the bonus weeks. While being a great perk, prices and programs are subject to change without notice. Contact your Home Owner's Association or Vacation Club for current Bonus information. Oh, and one last thing, you cannot deposit Bonus time for exchange with either exchange company...

Some resorts do offer different bonus week programs so it is best to check with your home resort.

SEASONS AND COLORS - IS THERE A DIFFERENCE?

Seasons, or the color-coding system, was implemented in the beginning so that the exchange companies could determine the value of your timeshare against what they have available. Season, unit sizes and sleeping capacity are the three elements important in determining your exchange value. In other words, you want to exchange your South Carolina, three bedroom summer week to Hawaii in January. Is what you are offering equivalent to what the exchange company has on deposit for you? If it is, off you go -- if not, why not?

Now, not only do developers and marketing companies define seasons differently, so do the exchange companies. Why? That is one of the timeshare mystery questions that may never be resolved. In past years, before you deposited your week for exchange, you had to tell the exchange company what week would be exchanging and they will tell you what season, or what color it is or what trading power value it has. Because it is ultimately the exchange company's season, color code or trading power value that determines what you get, not what you think you own. Although Interval´s new Travel Demand Index and RCI´s Deposit Trading Power (both explained in the next chapter) have incorporated these specific color and seasonal designations into their new format, it will still help you understand how the week you own reflects your ability to exchange.

If you own a red week, during prime time or a holiday in a tropical or skiing location consider yourself fortunate as you will never have an exchange valuation problem. When you own the best, and usually most expensive, you will always exchange to the best accommodations available. Customer demands for locations change as more people vacation every year. This directly affects the starting and ending dates of the season designations. Below are some examples of seasonal membership designations offered by resorts around the world. Consider this a little quiz on what you think you own. Ownership during the Christmas/New Year/Easter holiday periods are generally referred to as Holiday and Platinum ownership.

Holiday	High	Mid	Low
Platinum	Gold	Silver	Bronze
Diamond	Gold	Silver	
Red	White	Blue	
Red	Yellow	Green	
Premium or Prime	High	Mid	Low
High	Shoulder	Low	
Winter	Summer		
Winter	Summer	Spring	Fall
Holiday	Winter	Summer	Spring/Fall
Winter	Spring/Fall	Summer	
Winter/Summer	Spring/Fall		
Winter/Spring	Summer/Fall		
Winter/Spring/Fall	Summer		
Summer	Winter	Spring	Fall
Summer	Winter/Fall	Spring	
Summer/Spring	Winter/Fall		

So, how did you do? Were you able to determine what season you own? Remember, although no longer used for exchange purposes, seasons are still important within your resort ownership.

HOW ARE RESORTS QUALIFIED?

Resorts are rated much in the same way that hotels and non-timeshare properties, condominiums and other similar products are rated with some variations. Generally speaking resorts must reach at least the minimum based on US Travel, Hospitality and Leisure Practices. Exchange companies have their own criteria that they look for when making a decision on a resort that they will include in their programs and these resorts must maintain these criteria in order to maintain their affiliations.

The following criteria are taken into consideration:

- ❖ the location and its desirability with respect to it being a travel destination (beach, ski areas, etc)
- ❖ the condition and appearance of the property, including all public and common areas
- ❖ the availability and variety of on-site and in-room amenities
- ❖ the proximity and variety to recreational facilities, tourist attractions, gaming etc
- ❖ the size of units, style and decor of the accommodations (is it current or dated for example)
- ❖ any recent trends which may be coming to, or affecting, the timeshare industry
- ❖ overall guest experiences (based on surveys, internet and social media posts/comments)

All affiliated resorts are inspected and reviewed annually and should they fail to meet the criteria may be subject to lowering their recognition levels or removed as an affiliated property. Some resorts may be given warning reviews and if improvements are made with the time frames given, can keep their designations.

As a timeshare owner, it is up to you provide feedback on your stay, whether at your home resort or an exchange resort is so very important. Post-stay phone and online surveys, done by independent companies hired by home owner associations (HOA) are becoming increasingly more popular. HOA´s are using them as a thermometer on how the resort is doing, based on all the criteria listed above so that they can keep their property at a level of excellence so there is no reason to lose their affiliations.

In the next chapter I will cover everything you possibly wanted to know about exchanging your week(s).

Chapter 10

Understanding Exchange & Member Benefits

One of the most popular features of vacation ownership is the opportunity, and flexibility, to exchange one week for another week. Most buyers buy timeshare for that very reason.

Whether your travels take you to St. Tropez to sun bathe or explore the Mayan ruins of the Yucatan. Maybe you want to learn to surf in Hawaii or deep sea dive in the Cayman Islands. Quite possibly, you may wish to experience the sights and sounds of the Middle East and Africa, or just visit Mickey Mouse[R] - the exchange opportunities will astound you. Timeshare owners all over the world are reaping the benefits from exchanging to any one of the over 100 countries worldwide. Imagine the possibilities of exchanging what you own and going to places you have only previously dreamed.

In 2013, RCI and Interval made almost 4 million personal vacation dreams became a reality. Between the two exchange companies, owners have the opportunity to exchange to more than 5,200 resorts worldwide.

Are owners satisfied with their exchanges? There are an overwhelming 80 percent of owners who are satisfied and will continue to exchange. Considering that more than 30 percent of owners have exchanged more than six times, that figure is not surprising. Amazingly, fewer than 10 percent of owners are dissatisfied with their exchanges and have plans to drop their membership with their exchange company.

Does everyone exchange? No. There are approximately half of owners who are very happy to stay in their home resort. This is not to say that the other half dislike their resorts, it is just that they would rather exchange to another location. Of those exchange owners, a very small percentage alternate their usage – one year they stay in their home resort, the next they exchange.

So, how does the exchange work? The process of exchanging is very simple. Interval and RCI offer you a choice of exchange methods. To select a destination where you would like to go you look through their printed or online resort directories. After that, you can then either call RCI or Interval, or use their web sites, and request your exchange location(s), pay your exchange fee, wait for your confirmation and then off you go. Sound easy? It is easy, however the process can be confusing and I will be explaining that a little later on in this Chapter.

First, let us start with the simple things.

WHO ARE THE EXCHANGE COMPANIES?

There are two major exchange companies that handle approximately 90 percent of the timeshare exchanges. The larger of the two is RCI (Resort Condominiums International, LLC) with nearly 4,500 affiliated resorts followed by Interval International (Interval) with nearly 2,900 affiliated resorts.

RCI®

RCI recently celebrated its 40th Anniversary!! Originally founded in 1974 as Resort Condominiums International they pioneered the vacation exchange business. Their innovative idea of allowing people to take their timeshare week and exchange it for another location was instrumental in shaping the future of the timeshare industry. Since those first exchanges in 1974, RCI is the industry leader and has been implemental in creating the first global points-based exchange system, - RCI Points, the world´s first luxury exchange program, RCI TV and the unveiling of Trading Power transparency which has revolutionized vacation exchange with added flexibility and choice, as well as the first mobile version of an exchange website. More important for members though, is that over the past several years RCI has confirmed nearly 1.8 million exchanges each year.

With nearly 4,500 RCI resorts located in more than 100 countries, RCI recognizes more than 2,000 of their resorts as **RCI Gold Crown**, **RCI Silver Crown** or **RCI Hospitality Crown**. These resorts have attained high levels of excellence in resort accommodations, hospitality and member experiences ratings as measure by RCI. Should any of these standards fall, the status is reduced or taken away.

Depending on what affiliation your resort has with RCI, RCI members can be part of the RCI Weeks program, the RCI Points program or, owners at certain resorts can be a part of The Registry Collection, the world's largest luxury exchange program with nearly 30,000 members in approximately 200 affiliated resorts, in 40 countries, spanning six continents.

RCI has approximately 3.7 million families and along with exchanging weeks for their Members, RCI also offers an assortment of other membership and travel benefits which will be covered in more detail later in the chapter under the heading "Membership Benefits."

The benefits of membership are covered in more detail later in the chapter under the heading "Membership Benefits:"

Interval International® (Interval)

Interval International® entered the exchange market in 1976. It boasts, and maintains, the industry's highest standards for resort affiliation. Resorts that surpass these criteria are awarded the Interval International **Select Resort®** distinction or their highest level of recognition, the Interval International **Premier Resort®** designation. Within each of the distinctions the Interval International Select Boutique Resort® and Interval International Premier Boutique Resort® awards commend those that offer differing vacation experiences, with accommodations in desirable locations and limited on-site amenities.

Interval's network consists of nearly 2,900 affiliated resorts in more than 80 countries, with almost 2 million families enrolled in various membership programs. Interval also has offices in 16 countries and produces membership information in 29 market-specific versions and languages.

Interval has three different membership options, which may be dependent on what affiliation your resort has with them. There is Interval International membership, Interval Gold® and Interval Platinum®. Members may upgrade to Interval Gold or Interval Platinum for an additional fee. Also, some resorts participate in Club Interval, which is a points based exchange service that gives buyers of fixed or floating-week timeshares the flexibility of a points-based program.

The benefits of membership are covered in more detail later in the chapter under the heading "Membership Benefits:"

Dual Affiliation

There are a small percentage of resorts that are affiliated with both exchange companies. Dual affiliation normally involves different phases within the same project or resorts that are not in active sales and are controlled by owners associations. There are also less than one percent of resorts that have no exchange affiliations with either exchange company.

Both Interval and RCI also participate actively with the American Resort Development Association to promote consumer awareness and support government legislation around the world.

IMPORTANT NOTE:

> **Interval International® and RCI® are separate and distinct entities from any developers or marketers of any affiliated member resort. They only provide exchange services for timeshare products that are sold by, or on behalf of, affiliated resorts.**

> Should affiliated resorts fail to honor commitments and agreements with the exchange companies, membership in that exchange company may be terminated. If a member's home resort loses its membership affiliation, the member may also lose membership rights and privileges. If the member owns in another resort affiliated with that exchange company, the member has an option to renew through that property.

EXCHANGE COMPANY MEMBERSHIP

At the time of purchase, the purchaser is typically enrolled in either Interval International® (Interval) or RCI for one or more years. Often this is done for you as part of your sales agreement and covers all enrollment fees. If the resort that you purchase with offers both exchange companies, they will enroll you in both.

After you have purchased your timeshare, you will receive your membership package generally from thirty to sixty days later after receipt and approval of an application. A typical membership package includes a welcome letter, benefit brochures, the current membership magazines, your membership card and in some cases a printed resort directory. The card shows your membership number, resort code of the resort where you own, the renewal date and, of course, your name.

At, or near the end of your first (or second) year you may get a notice from either Interval or RCI advising you that it is time to renew your membership. At this point you can decide if you want to keep up your membership(s) or not. If you do, you have the option of renewing for one, two, three, five or ten years depending on the exchange company. Membership fees do vary so you should check on either RCI or Interval's web sites for their current fee structure.

Should ownership of a timeshare interval be a corporation, partnership or trust, the exchange membership will be under the name of an individual. This individual may be a director, officer or owner of the corporation, a partner of the partnerships or the trustee of a trust.

IMPORTANT NOTE:

> **Remember that membership benefits and privileges will be provided as long as you, the member, and your home resort is in good standing. If your resort is suspended or cancelled you may lose your membership benefits, including any exchange privileges.**

Included with your membership package in some cases is a:

THE RESORT DIRECTORY

The resort directory is a catalogue of resorts that have been accepted to be affiliated with that exchange company. In many cases, members may receive a hard copy of the directory. The respective Resort Directories can be found on the Interval and RCI Web sites.

Each of the directories contains Exchange and Membership information, a Listing of resorts by Region, Special Programs, Contact Information and the Terms and Conditions of each membership and exchange. In addition, the directories are divided into world regions and color coded by region for easier use. Each regional area is then broken down by city or town within the regions. Each resort within that region is then listed. Resort information about the affiliated resort includes:

- ❖ Name of Resort + Resort Code or ID Number
- ❖ Exchange Demand Indexes, Color Codes or Seasonal Designations
- ❖ Resort address, Telephone number & Web Site
- ❖ Closest major airport
- ❖ Check in/Check out day(s)
- ❖ On site and nearby amenities
- ❖ Unit Types plus max/min. occupancy
- ❖ Map reference
- ❖ Golf Resort and All-Inclusive designation icons
- ❖ Resort Photos

Okay, so we found a resort we want to exchange to, what is next? We need to pay our...

EXCHANGE FEES

When you go online or call if you are not very internet savvy to make an exchange you will be asked to pay an exchange fee.

Fees are payable up front upon the placement of a valid exchange request. This is due to two reasons:

(1) To initiate an ongoing search for a location in the Weeks program, it shows that you are interested in your request and;
(2) If your request is matched the exchange fee must be paid to hold or confirm the unit.

Exchange fees do vary so you should contact either RCI or II or go to their websites for their current fee structure.

Fees may be paid to the exchange companies by (1) credit card, (2) check or (3) money order. If you are paying by check or money order, confirmations will not occur until the checks, or money orders, have been processed by the exchange company. You may also pay by credit card directly on line through the web site.

Guest Certificates can be obtained for use by another individual upon request. There is a Guest Certificate fee (free for Interval Platinum members), besides the exchange fee.

Cancellation of an exchange request will be explained following the exchange process section. RCI will, however, refund the exchange fee upon request if it cannot confirm an exchange within nine (9) months of your request.

IMPORTANT NOTE:

> **Interval International**® **Terms and Conditions** provide that it may assess an administration fee, should the member, rent, sell, assign or exchange the member's week to a third party after it has been deposited for exchange. The member will also be responsible for all liabilities incurred by Interval associated with a double booking.

> **Neither RCI nor Interval International**® **will allow members to use their host accommodations for commercial purposes. If this is discovered, members forfeit their deposited week and will not receive any refunds in connection with the transaction.**

HOW DOES THE EXCHANGE WORK?

Well, we are finally here. The section that we have all been eagerly awaiting: how do we exchange? If you remember, at the beginning of the chapter I said the exchange process was quite simple. The first thing that you need to do is to either request or deposit your interval or week, with the exchange company affiliated with your resort. Then you look through the resort directory and you pick the location(s) that you would like to go. After that, you can go online with Interval or RCI and request your location(s), pay your exchange fee, receive your confirmation and then pack your bags. You can also call, however the online process provides a much faster option.

However, before I get into the nuts and bolts of the actual exchange process, I want to cover a couple more important things that you should know.

How Resorts are Rated for Exchange.

This is very important. Both exchange company's work on a comparable rating system of determining exchange value. It is designed to match the value of the week deposited within the exchange system with the value of the week from the exchange system that you request. Trading Power is based on the following criteria, not necessary in their order of importance.

1. **Supply, demand and utilization**
   A high demand location or week is one that is the most sought after. If you give up a high demand location or week or exchange, you will have a greater opportunity to receive one or the other. For example: major holidays, prime ski locations in winter, golf locations in summer are usually in high demand.

   Each exchange company identifies its resorts by their times or seasons and these are based on historical demand. Remember, there are many instances where demand for a location far outweighs supply.

   It is also important to understand that timeshare owners in locations, that are highly sought after may not necessarily deposit their weeks with an exchange company. For example, if you cannot get an exchange to Key West or Paris, it might be because owners are not depositing their weeks which results in no availability – this is supply.

2. **Travel Demand Index (Interval only)**
   The Travel Demand Index consists of seasonal indexes presented on each of the region introduction pages in the Resort Directory or online at IntervalWorld.com. Each area in a region is assigned a numerical index for every week of the year, with 100 representing the average inbound leisure travel demand. The higher the number over 100, the greater the relative demand for the area during that week. Numbers below 100 indicate weeks when it might be easier to confirm exchange accommodations and less expensive to reserve other travel services. The Travel Demand Index runs from 50 to a maximum of 150.

   This feature is designed to assist you in planning and determining when the best opportunities for travel are likely to be available in the area you want to visit.

3. **The location of ownership**
   Location, location, location!! Just like a restaurant, or home, location is everything. If you own in a high demand location, in a high demand area, your chances of a better exchange increase dramatically. Local culture, lifestyles, attractions and amenities also affect the locations and type of accommodations. For example accommodations in northern Thailand will differ tremendously from Orlando.

4. **Resort Quality**

   RCI's **Crown** properties are considered first. Resorts are valued within an exchange system on their individual ratings given by RCI. Interval considers how the quality, facilities, and overall experience offered by the home resort compare to these characteristics of the resort being requested in exchange.

5. **Size of unit or sleeping capacity**

   Unit occupancy or sleeping capacity is derived from the number of people that can be accommodated per private sleeping area.

6. **When you deposit your week for exchange (Deposit Anticipation)**

   How far in advance you deposit your week or make an exchange request also can be a determining factor in your trading value, or power. To ensure maximum trading power deposit your week(s) as far in advance as permitted by your exchange company. If you wait until the last minute you probably will not get your most preferred exchange no matter how well qualified your resort may be.

What Week(s) Should I Deposit?

This seems straight forward enough if you own one fixed week. Unfortunately, for other owners it may not be that simple. They may own a floating week, in a floating season or belong to a point based program.

If you own a floating week, floating season or in a point based system, the process is ALL the same. You **MUST** call your home resort and **request a specific week and unit** assignment. If your resort allows you to choose a specific week and/or unit(s) during a floating season, obviously choose the one that will give you the best value for an exchange. For exchange purposes, should your home resort not be able to give you a "prime" week or unit, chose the best one available, at the time.

Remember, if you know you are going to exchange your week(s) for the following year, get your assignment(s) as early as you possibly can. At a resort a friend of mine owns a timeshare, she calls the same day she pays her maintenance fees and always gets a prime week and unit. Check with your resort for the best time to make your assignments.

It is also important to note that some resorts which have floating or points based systems will deposit owners weeks for them as a method of keeping better control of deposits and ensuring that there is no possible duplication of either units or weeks deposited.

What you MUST know BEFORE you go ONLINE (or call).

Okay, you have gone through the directory and picked a location and you are on your way to the computer or telephone. STOP! Do you have everything that you will need to go online or again call if necessary and deposit your week for exchange?

The one thing that never changes when you chose to call is the questions asked. If you have the answers ready, then the questions are easy.

- ❖ First, you should know the correct **name** of your resort. For example you may own at the Hollywood Beach Tower, but tell the person on the phone the Hollywood Beach Hotel. Both are in the same location but are different buildings. Second, you should know the **resort code or number**. Next, you should know exactly what it is you are exchanging (**week, unit number and size**).
- ❖ You should also know **how many people** you will be traveling with and the **dates** that you want to travel. The first thing that you must do when making an exchange request with Interval is provide the vacation advisor with a combination of four different resorts and travel dates. If you only want to go to one location, then provide at least three dates – preferably as many as possible.
- ❖ Also, another important thing to remember is that if you are travelling with someone who has a **physical disability**; please make sure that you choose a resort which can accommodate them. Speak with an exchange advisor to select a unit that will meet your specific needs. Each of the exchange companies reflects the resorts that are handicapped accessible by placing the wheelchair accessible symbol with the other amenities offered by the resort. It is normal for handicapped units to have at least one of the following attributes:
  - o access via a ramp or elevator for wheelchairs
  - o extra wide entrance ways and/or doorways to allow access for a wheelchair
  - o Handrails in the shower, toilet area and bathtub.

If your unit is a **lock-off** (lock-out) ask the vacation advisor which portion of the unit is eligible for exchange purposes and its sleeping capacity. If you decide to exchange only the lock-off unit, be prepared to stay in a lock-off unit with that same sleeping capacity when you exchange.

To ensure that you get the correct size of unit when you exchange, keep in mind the following:

With RCI, when you deposit your week, you get a deposit trading power assigned to that week. You can use that trading power to exchange for another week of equal or lesser trading power. For example, if your deposit trading power is 15, you can exchange for any other week that has an exchange trading power of 15 or less. The trading power is not based solely on unit size so you can deposit a studio that sleeps 4 and exchange it for a 2 bedroom that sleeps 8, or vice versa. That's the benefit of a transparent exchange system, only available through RCI.

Last, but not least, **your credit card**. Both exchange companies take Visa, MasterCard and American Express.

An exchange story:

Many, many years ago, I exchanged to a resort in Orlando. I had deposited a RED, two-bedroom unit at a Five Star resort, and when we arrived, the resort tried to put us into a very (and I do mean very) small lock-off unit. The unit had no cooking facilities, not even a mini-bar. When we first opened the door, you found yourself in the bathroom. I immediately went to the front desk to complain and they were not the least bit cooperative. So, I called the exchange company from the check-in desk, and they promptly moved me to an appropriate sized unit, in another nearby resort.

The moral of this story - Be careful when exchanging, read your confirmation carefully. If you are put into the wrong size unit, immediately complain to the resort and request the promised unit size. There are times when resorts do overbook their units and will do their utmost to accommodate you, even if it means sending you to another location. By the way, the exchange company also gave me a free bonus week for my being inconvenienced.

By having all of this information handy, it will make your deposit go quickly and smoothly. One more little reminder that needs mentioning before you pick up the telephone is:

Determine what QUESTIONS you WANT to ASK if you Call

Okay, we are getting there, I promise. Now you have gone through the resort directory and picked out a couple of places where you wish to go on vacation. You have all the information about your resort handy and are finally on your way to the telephone. Stop, hold it right there. There is something else you have forgotten. Do you know what you want to ask the vacation guide or advisor when you call, or are you just going to wing it as you go along? Just like a Boy Scout, be prepared.

Just like answering the questions to deposit a week, you should have questions about the locations that you are requesting. Do you plan on more people traveling than just yourself? Ask about any accommodations restrictions that may apply. If someone in your party has a physical disability, ask about handicapped facilities. If you are traveling with your 97 year old grandmother who cannot climb stairs ask about being located on a first floor or if the resort has elevators. Keep in mind that exchange companies cannot guarantee unit location; only the resort can do that. **Ask questions**. Sometimes what is shown in the resort directories may not be available. The more questions you ask, the more satisfied you will be when you get your exchange.

By the way, write all the answers down on a piece of paper and then slip it into the section of your requested location. That way you have a bookmark and the information at your fingertips.

By this time you should have also decided which method of exchange you would like to use.

Gotcha!! This is the meat and potatoes, or nuts and bolts section of exchanging. Before you pick up the telephone or go online, you should know which exchange company you use and you should decide if you are going to deposit first or request first. Do not panic, your options will be explained in these next few pages. These options will be covered separately by Exchange Company, so skip the one that does not apply to your membership, and read the one that does.

Interval International® (Interval)

Interval provides you with different exchange methods depending on which type of program you have with them. With their regular membership program you have two options - **DEPOSIT FIRST and REQUEST FIRST**.

Club Interval Gold, Interval's points-based program, is explained in Chapter 14.

Let´s review the exchange options shall we[6]?

1. **DEPOSIT FIRST** gives you a flexible four year travel window. It allows you place an exchange request from **up to two years before to two years after** your home resort check-in date. However, if you do not travel by the end of that two-year period after your deposited week's check-in date, you will no longer be able to travel using that deposited week.

   You may also deposit your week for **two years up to and including 14 days** before your start date but realizing that your options become limited if you deposit as you get closer to your check-in date. If you make a deposit between 59 and 14 days prior to the travel date, you must use the Flexchange® short-notice service when you place a request.

2. **REQUESTFIRST** offers you only the ability to place a request and travel on an exchange from **up to two years before the week you offer in exchange up until the dates of that week**, or travel to your home resort if no match is found. You cannot travel **after your week's start date**. You must have an eligible week available for deposit at the time of the call or a week already deposited.

   Once a deposit is made, it may not be withdrawn.

   When requesting a week, a minimum of four alternative resorts and dates must be specified.

I will now cover the **Club Interval[7] exchange options:**

Club Interval is a points-based exchange service that allows participating members to deposit their fixed time and/or floating time home resort accommodations in exchange for Club Interval Points. To be eligible to participate in Club Interval, members must own or purchase a ¨Eligible¨ vacation interest in a resort or development that is enrolled in the Club Interval program.

---

[6]   All Interval Deposit format information provided is from Interval International Membership Guides, Program brochures and website.

[7]   Club Interval Gold® exchange information if provide from Interval International´s ¨Exchanging with Club Interval Gold¨ membership materials.

Club Interval Gold® members have a number of options for exchange. The first is using **Shop for an Instant Confirmation**. They can go to the Exchange tab and then click on My Units. Their available points will appear in the Available Points Tool, including their expiration date. From their members can then click Vacation Exchange to continue choosing any of the options below:

1. **Request First:** As a Club Interval Gold member you can also use Request First. All you have to do is place your request and keep your points until Interval confirms that you have enough points to make the exchange that you have chosen. Please remember that some points based members will be able to exchange online while others may have to contact the resort from which they purchased.

2. **Deposit First:** Members have the ability to redeem their points for full weeks of vacation time across the entire Interval resort network. Members just select the week they want to deposit, making sure that the check-in date, check-out date and expiration date of their points is correct, and then click deposit.

   The sooner you deposit your week, the longer you will have to use your allotted points. If you deposit at least 120 days before your check-in date, you will receive the maximum number of points available for your particular week. See the table below for the percentage of points aware for deposits inside of 120 days.

   You do have the flexibility of up to a four-year travel window - exchange anytime from two years before to two years after the first day of your deposited week.

Deposit Lead Time (Before Check in Date)	Percentage of Points Allotted
Less than 14 days	Not Accepted
14 - 29 days	25%
30 - 59 days	50%
60 - 119 days	75%
120 days or more	100%

From this point members can then check on availability using the online search function that meet the criteria that you entered. If you find something that you want, and have enough points to make the exchange, you will see an Exchange button next to the required point's value. Click on the Exchange button to start booking. If you do not have enough points to make the desired exchange, scroll over to the More Info button and you will be prompted to add more points to your account. Just follow the instructions from there to access more points.

The following applies to ALL Members:

If you do not find what you are looking for you can place a request and let Interval search for you. If your choice becomes available, you will be confirmed automatically. As availability changes daily, and the week(s) that you want may become available at any time. If you do not place a request, the vacation week you are specifically searching for could be confirmed to someone else who has also put in a similar request.

As with any exchange request, be sure to select a minimum of three different resorts and at least one time period OR one time period, three resorts OR two resorts and two time periods. Also remember to select the smallest unit that can accommodate you and/or your party. Many resorts have more small units than large ones, and this tip can go a long way towards helping you with a match.

If you can´t get away for a week and are looking for a shorter vacation, you may want to take a....

3. **ShortStay® Exchange vacations: Also for Interval Gold and Interval Platinum members.** This option gives you the freedom to trade your week for vacations from one to six nights. Club Interval Gold members can redeem their points for as many shorter vacations as their available points allow. To use ShortStay Exchanges, click on ShortStay Exchange under Exchange actions. Select where you want to go and for how long. Availability and the required points will show instantly. After you click Exchange, the booking process will continue.

4. **Interval Options®: Also for Interval Gold and Interval Platinum members.** With Interval Options, Club Interval Gold members may use their points toward the purchase of a cruise, golf, spa, or tour vacation. You need to be aware that Interval Options exchanges do require the payment of the Options transaction fee, plus a supplemental fee. The supplemental fee will vary based on the scope of the vacation, the value of the week relinquished, and other factors.

For example, if you want to book a cruise exchange. Click on Cruise Exchange under Exchange Options on the website. Then select how many of your available points that you would like to use and then click continue. Search availability, then select a cabin and take note of the supplemental fee per person.

Whichever option you chose - regular week, ShortStay or Interval Options, you will receive a vacation confirmation (via email, telephone, or regular mail) that includes the details about the unit, resort, and surrounding area.

For more information contact Interval directly, refer to your membership documents or use the members' section on their website.

If you are someone who likes to plan very far in advance, I would suggest that you deposit early and request early. If you like to live dangerously and can travel impulsively like me, and are not particular about where you go, be brave and deposit on or near the deadlines but remember your options do become limited and you should then not complain if the resort does not meet with ¨your¨ standards.

RCI®

Both RCI Weeks members MUST first have a deposit of a week before they can request an exchange. As I mentioned earlier in this chapter and before I cover the specifics of depositing, I will explain how to determine the value of your week for exchange using RCI´s transparent Deposit Trading Power.

RCI Deposit TRADING POWER[8] – Transparency is a new feature implemented by RCI in 2010. As mentioned above on page 65, this means that each week within the RCI exchange system has a trading power value established by RCI based on its rating system and is dependent on location, unit sizes, season, weeks deposited and demand.

What are Deposit Credits? Deposit Credits are kind of like getting change back! Your unused trading power is placed on your account as a Deposit Credit to use toward another vacation(s). So essentially, you used

---

[8]   ALL RCI Deposit Trading Power information is excerpted from RCI Member Directory and RCI Website from Deposit Tools and Resources. Receiving two vacations for one week under Exchanging for another vacation is based specifically on booking based on a lesser value property. Always refer to www. rci.com/DepositCredits for current information on Deposit Trading Power.

one week and can potentially take two weeks or more of vacation! You receive a Deposit Credit when you exchange your Deposit for an exchange with lower Exchange Trading Power. The difference in trading power is put back on your account in the form of a Deposit Credit, to use toward future exchanges.

Days in Advance of Deposit Start Date	Percentage Retained
< 14 days	45%
15 - 30 days	60%
31 - 90 days	80%
91 - 180 days	90%
181 - 270 days	95%
271 + days	100%

Remember, your Deposit Trading Power varies based on when you deposit! Depositing from 2 years to 9 months in advance will maximize your Deposit Trading Power. In addition, upon depositing, you can take advantage of searching and exchanging your week for another vacation. You don't need to know where or when you want to travel as long as you're not planning to return to your home resort unit on your next vacation. And best of all, depositing is FREE!

A Deposit Credit takes on the same expiration dates of the original deposit it was created from. For example, if you Exchange using a Deposit that has a travel through date of December 31, 2015, and receive a Deposit Credit, you will be able to use that Deposit Credit toward another exchange through December 31, 2015.

You can use your Deposit Credit in one of two ways:

1. **Exchange it for Another Vacation**[4]
    You can use your Deposit Credit on its own to book a second vacation of equal or lesser value than the credit. So, essentially you can get two vacations for using just one week!

2. **Combine it with another Deposit**
    You can combine you Deposit Credit with another Deposit, including a Combined Deposit or another Deposit Credit, to increase that Deposit's Trading Power. With higher Deposit Trading Power you will have access to an exchange vacation with higher Exchange

Trading Power. This can give you access to more exchange options than you had previously.

Deposit Credits give you more options than ever before and can get you on even more vacations! When searching for an exchange, consider looking for what you need, not necessarily something identical to what you own.

For example, if you own a two bedroom unit but there are only two of you traveling, you may be comfortable in a one bedroom or studio unit. By trading-down into what you need, you may be more likely to receive a Deposit Credit and increase your vacation options for the future.

Choose two or more Deposits to combine into one week with a higher Deposit Trading Power. You will be charged USD$109 to combine your Deposits.

Now that you understand your Deposit Trading power, let´s look at what comes next:

1. **Depositing your Week**: Depositing gives you a three year travel window. It allows you to travel ***one year before*** and ***up to two years after*** your start date of your week. To maximize your vacation options and to receive 100% Deposit Trading Power you should deposit two (2) years before your start date. You will still receive 100% Deposit Trading Power up to nine (9) months prior to your check-in date. As you can see by the chart on the previous page, your Deposit Trading Power will decrease after that date.

   However, if you do not travel by the end of that two year period after your deposited week's check-in date, the deposit will expire and you will no longer be able to travel using that deposited week. You can extend the time period for one more year, however there is a charge for this option and you should contact RCI directly if you feel that you need an extension and they can review your options with you.

2. **Searching** for your exchange is as simple as going to the RCI website and then choosing the Search for a Vacation pull down and make your choice of vacation options. Then you can narrow or filter down your search by filling in the applicable blanks by location, vacation types and/or dates requested. You can also filter by resort activities and amenities if you want to get very specific. Once you

select Enter all your available options at that time will appear. If you find the one you are looking for then you can...

3. **Book** your vacation. This is where you can use your Deposit Trading Power to book your vacation. Your options here include:
    a) If your exchange requires less trading power than your deposit is worth, you will receive a Deposit Credit for the difference;
    b) If your exchange requires more trading power than any one of your deposits or Deposit Credits, you may want to consider a Combined Deposit. For a fee, you can combine multiple deposits or Deposit Credits into one combined ¨week¨ with a higher trading power than anyone of your deposits or Deposit Credits.

RCI Points, their Deposits and Exchange procedures are explained in Chapter 14. For more information, please contact RCI directly**.**

So go online or dial already! You should now have:

❖   Your exchange membership number
❖   All the information about what you own in front of you
❖   A combination of four resorts and travel dates
❖   Should you chose to call - the questions you want to ask about your requests
❖   Decided on which method of exchange you want to use

So, what is the problem now? Let me guess, you forgot your credit card to pay your exchange fees. For those who cannot wait to go online or call from the United States or Canada, the websites and telephone numbers for the exchange companies are:

Interval International:
800-828-8200 or 305-666-1884
www.intervalworld.com
RCI:
800- 338-7777 Or 877-968-7476
www.rci.com

In the **Timeshare Address Book** at the end of this book you will find all the international telephone numbers for RCI and Interval.

When requesting a week with Interval, remember a <u>minimum</u> of four alternative resorts and travel dates must be specified. This can be a combination of: 3 resorts + 1 travel date; 2 resorts + 2 travel dates; 1 resort + 3 travel dates.

All exchanges are on a space-available basis and take into consideration the comparable exchange concept mentioned earlier. **No one can guarantee you a specific week**. Neither Interval, RCI, the developer, the marketing company nor your home resort or vacation club can guarantee you will receive a specific interval on exchange.

If your home resort offers **both** Interval and RCI as exchange companies, use the one that you believe will provide the best exchange options for the location or area you want to go. For example, RCI offers six resorts for exchange purposes in the Banff Rocky Mountain area in Canada, Interval currently offers three. In this example, your chances are likely better with RCI. You **cannot deposit the same week** with both exchange companies and wait to see which one comes through first. If you are caught doing this you could lose your membership in both exchange companies.

Exchange Restrictions

You may be restricted from exchanging within your home area. What does this mean? For example, if you own at one resort in Puerto Vallarta, Mexico, you may not be able exchange to another resort within that area. Why is that? There are some member resorts that restrict exchanges within a specific geographic area.

Please check with your host resort or exchange company to see if your resort choice is restricted or not.

Confirmation of Exchanges

If a resort or area is not immediately available to fulfill your request, ask your vacation guide or advisor to enter it as an **ongoing search or you can do so online**. Until a match is available, both companies will continue to search for you or suggest alternative destinations. Bear in mind that not everyone deposits their weeks in the same manner that you might so the week, or location, that you are requesting might come available a few hours, weeks or months, down the road from your original request. Remember, patience is a virtue if you really want a specific location and/ or week.

When a match is made, you **will be notified** by telephone or email that a match has been found and be given the option to confirm your request. You will then be sent an exchange confirmation, by email or regular mail, seven to ten days after verbal confirmation. If you are confirmed for an Interval Flexchange week within forty-eight hours before check-in, you will only receive an oral confirmation, not a written one.

The **Exchange Confirmation** contains:

- ❖ The resort name, address and telephone numbers
- ❖ Date the confirmation was processed
- ❖ Check-in and check-out dates and times
- ❖ Unit information
- ❖ Sleeping capacity of the unit, including minimum and maximum number of persons
- ❖ Number of bedrooms in the unit
- ❖ The type of kitchen facilities (if applicable)
- ❖ Terms and conditions that should be read and followed

Included with the exchange confirmation is the following information:

- ❖ Resort facilities, including amenities and facilities that are available at the resort itself
- ❖ A listing of amenities and facilities available nearby
- ❖ A description of the resort and the surrounding area
- ❖ How to Get There: These are directions from the nearest major airport and highways
- ❖ Unit amenities: These areas list what is available in the unit, from coffee makers to ironing boards. Whether the unit has air-conditioning and if there is housekeeping services available are also shown on the information sheet. What types of fees or deposits are required (if any) down to the type of voltage used at the resort.

READ OVER, very carefully, the confirmation of exchange and resort information sheets when they arrive by mail or via regular mail. Make sure that all the exchange information is correct: the check-in date(s), location and even make sure that it is the correct week. This is particularly true if you have deposited more than one week for exchange.

If you have asked for consecutive weeks in the same location or resort, make sure the dates are consecutive. On more than one occasion I have failed to do that and arrived in a location only to discover that when I check out on Friday, I cannot check into the next place until Sunday. I had failed to read my confirmations and now found myself with an unplanned expense – a two-night stay in a hotel. Thank God for member benefits, but more on those benefits later.

Can I cancel an exchange?

If, for some reason you change your mind about exchanging your week, your options may be limited. Following is just a quick summary of the exchange companies cancellation terms. RCI also offers a product called Trading Power Protection which if added to an exchange, allows you to protect your full trading power used to book that exchange if you decide to cancel. For more information please read the Terms and Conditions section of the Resort Directory, go online to your exchange company website or call and ask your exchange company directly.

Cancellation Conditions for **RCI** are as follows: RCI´s Cancellation Policy can be found in your membership documents, their resort directory, online at www.rci.com or you can call one of their representatives.

❖ RCI reserves the right to cancel a confirmation if the members credit card payment is rejected, their check is returned or they have failed to pay their home resort maintenance and/or assessment fees.

❖ You may cancel an exchange confirmation by notifying RCI either in writing or by telephone. RCI may refund all, or a portion, of the exchange fee and trading power, according to the cancellation policy.

❖ You may make a new exchange request if cancellation occurs before the start date of the exchange without making another deposit, however all applicable exchange fees will apply. Unless you purchased trading power protection, some or all of your trading power may have been lost. Please see RCI's terms and conditions for more information.

If you find you need to cancel an **Interval exchange:** Before you consider canceling your Interval exchange, you may want to use their E-Plus Program. E-Plus allows Interval members to "retrade" their original confirmation up to a total of three times for different host accommodations and/or alternative vacation periods upon the payment of an additional fee paid at the time of the original confirmation.

If you still need to cancel and decide not to use E-Plus as an option, here are some important things you should know about cancelling your Interval exchange. Interval's Exchange Cancellation Policy can be found in their

Resort Directory, online at www.intervalworld.com or you can call one of their vacation advisors.

❖ Interval reserves the right to cancel a confirmation if the members credit card payment is rejected, their check is returned or they have failed to pay their home resort maintenance and/or assessment fees.

❖ You may cancel an exchange confirmation by notifying Interval either in writing or by telephone. Interval may refund all, or a portion, of the exchange fee, depending on certain conditions.

> (1) You will receive a full refund if you advise Interval within the first 24 hours after the exchange confirmation has been received.
> (2) Any other cancellation aside from the first 24 hours will result in Interval keeping the exchange fee. Please refer to Interval´s Cancellation Policy for specific time intervals as well as options for accommodation and exchanges.
> (3) Club Interval cancellation policies are slightly different than for other members, so please refer to Interval´s Cancellation Policy for specifics, however should a member using their Club Interval Points cancel within the first 24 hours after the exchange confirmation has been received, they will receive a refund of any exchange fee associated with the cancelled confirmation. Members will also be credited back the applicable Club Interval Points used for that exchange.

❖ You may make a new exchange request if cancellation occurs before the start date of the exchange without making another deposit, however all applicable exchange fees will apply.

Remember, if you have any concerns regarding cancellation, contact RCI or Interval directly.

Internal exchanges

Internal exchanges are exchanges which are done either between sister resorts or within your own resort.

Almost all resorts will offer some type of internal exchange program. In most instances you will be restricted to exchanging within your ownership season (for example going from early summer to late summer). If you own a summer week you may not be able to exchange to a winter week or a holiday week. There are some resorts that do allow members to go from one season to another however there is usually an up-charge by the resort for this privilege and is always subject to availability in the requested season.

Internal exchanges are always subject to availability and if you have any questions contact your vacation club or member services office.

Well, that about does it for exchanging. I told you it was easy. I have been exchanging weeks for so long, I can honestly say it is something I can do in my sleep. All it takes is doing it two or three times and you will also become an expert at it. One last thing before I move on to Membership Benefits, if you have any questions, or concerns, about exchanging, both RCI and Interval will be more than pleased to answer them. Remember, they are in the exchange business.

One last thing, find a vacation guide that you like and ask for them every time you call - you will be amazed at what benefits and rewards your new friendship could bring you.

EXCHANGE MEMBERSHIP BENEFITS

Quite accurately, RCI and Interval offer you the world. Not only is the ability to exchange throughout the world a great advantage, but also the other benefits and privileges offered by RCI and Interval provide the icing on the cake. Both exchange companies do offer guest certificates, travel services, resort directories, magazines and other membership benefits. I have included brief descriptions of the respective benefits below, however due to the continual updating of Membership benefits; you should also refer to either the RCI or Interval International Web sites listed at the end of the benefit section.

Interval International® Benefits[9]

Interval offers a number of benefits and programs to their Interval, Interval Gold, Interval Platinum, and Club Interval Gold® members. Again, Club Interval Gold is explained in more detail in Chapter 14, as it is Interval´s

---

[9]   All Interval membership, Interval Gold Benefits, including Interval Platinum Benefits that are summarized from Interval Program Summary´s Membership brochures as well as the Interval Resort Directory and Interval World website.

points-based program and additional Interval Gold and Interval Platinum benefits are covered at the end of the overall benefits.

Interval Membership

- ❖ **Getaways**
  One of the most popular benefits of having an Interval membership that offers week-long vacations with affordable prices, without exchanging. Interval Gold members automatically receive US$25 off, and Interval Platinum members take US$50 off the prices. These vacations may include accommodations at any of their resorts, condos, cottages, and villas around the world. These can be booked anywhere from 24 hours to 365 days in advance either by visiting www.intervalworld.com or calling Interval directly. Getaways currently start at US$224 per week.

- ❖ **FLEXCHANGE** offers short-notice exchange opportunities.
  You can request travel from 59 days up to 24 hours prior to your check-in date. Locations offered under the Flexchange service may be limited and holiday, summer, and high demand weeks are usually not available. If your desired location is not available, Interval will place you on a waiting list. When your desired area or resort becomes available, Interval will call to advise you and confirm a reservation.

- ❖ **E-PLUS**[10] - Interval´s exciting new vacation exchange feature!
  E-Plus is an attractive option for those who like to plan in advance yet like to keep their options option. Through this exchange option members can continue to keep their comfort level in having an exchange confirmation as well as the opportunity to continue searching online 24/7 for other accommodations or destination preferences. It definitely puts the ´change´ in exchange. E-Plus is available for purchase online through www.intervalworld.com or by calling any Member Services Center. Fees do vary by country and may not be available to all vacation owners.

- ❖ **Interval Guest Certificates**
  Interval permits its members to assign the use of their exchange accommodations to a friend or family member by purchasing a Guest Certificate. Cost of the Guest Certificates is USD$59.00 All guests must be at least 21 years of age.

---

[10]   E-Plus features are quoted from an Interval Press Release on August 22, 2013.

❖ **Offers & Extras**
If you are tired of fighting the crowds at malls, you can check out Offers & Extras at www.intervalworld.com and buy everything you need right from home. You can shop for clothes, as well as deals on shoebuy.com, outletbuy.com, Fodor´s travel guides and more. This benefit offers discounts on movie theatre ticket purchases go to Offers & Extras for more information and other offers.

❖ **Interval Travel®**
Interval offers members a full-service travel agency that can arrange and book cruises, hotels, rental cars, vacation activities, airline flights, and more. Members can also extend their vacation experience by accessing Hotels.com form the Interval website. Interval members can find special rates not available to the general public on their website www.intervalworld.com

❖ **Interval International Visa Signature® Credit Card with WorldPoints® Rewards**
Interval members can receive more great rewards faster by using their Interval International Visa Signature card with WorldPoints rewards. Use the card to earn points on travel expenses and on all of your other purchases. You will earn one points for every retail dollar you spend. Points can be redeemed for cash, merchandise, gift cards, travel with no blackout dates, and payment of your Interval membership fees and/or Interval Gold or Interval Platinum upgrades. Go to www.intervalworld.com for more details, terms and conditions, and to apply.

❖ **Golf Resort Program and Golf Access®**
Interval´s Golf Resorts can be identified in the Resort Directory by looking for the symbol of the green golf club. This symbol signifies resorts which participate in the program and have an on-site 18-hole golf course, or are located near one. These resorts offer members special privileges, such as discounted green fees and lessons, advance tee times, and more.

The Golf Access program is a directory of golf related deals providing discounts of up to 50% on various fees at more than 2,000 courses, driving ranges, and resorts throughout the U.S. and certain international destinations. It is available to Interval members for US$19.95 or $14.95 for Interval Gold, Club Interval Gold, and Interval Platinum members. To purchase members can go to www.intervalworld.com or call 800-843-8843.

❖ **Interval Community**
Interval Community is an online forum that members can log onto through www.intervalworld.com and share exchange tips, resort details, and travel recommendations all in real time. Just click on the Community tab, create a screen name and begin exploring.

❖ **Interval Magazines and Subscriptions**
Interval World® magazine keeps members informed about the latest exchange and Getaway hotspots, membership benefits, new member resorts, and travel bargains. The magazine can also be accessed through www.intervalworld.com, on your smart phone or tablet.

Members also can receive an email newsletter which delivers travel updates and other special offers. You will need to sign up for them under the My Account section of www.intervalworld.com.

In addition to the regular Interval World magazine and newsletter, Interval also partners with Conde Nast publications to bring members very special offers. When you do a qualifying transaction with Interval (exchange your week, purchase a Getaway, renew your membership, or upgrade to Interval Gold or Interval Platinum), a one-year subscription is offered to your choice of either: Conde Nast Traveler, Allure, Glamour, Gold Digest, Bon Appétit, Architectural Digest, GQ, Vanity Fair or Vogue. Conde Nast also offers Interval members exclusive discounts on all of its magazines given as gifts or on additional subscriptions. You can find this option under Offers & Extras on the IntervalWorld.com website.

❖ **Emergency Travel Services**
Last, but certainly not the least of Interval´s membership benefits is that for one low price, you can receive a year´s worth of emergency medical-evacuation protection for you and your family whether you book through Interval or someone else. You also receive 25 other vital travel benefits, including lost travel documents or luggage assistance, emergency care for your pet, medical and dental referrals, and more. Go to the Benefits tab on www.intervalworld.com to learn more about this program and to enroll.

Interval Gold Membership

Interval´s second membership level is Interval Gold. Regular Interval members can chose to upgrade to Interval Gold at any time by paying the applicable fee. As an Interval Gold member you receive the following benefits <u>in addition</u> to the all of the membership benefits listed above.

- ❖ **ShortStay Exchange**
  ShortStay Exchanges allow you to turn your regular week vacation into two shorter vacations, either for six nights or fewer. If you are a Club Interval Gold® Points member, you can take as many as your points allow.

- ❖ **Interval Options®**
  Interval Options allows you to trade your week towards the purchase of a cruise, golf, spa, or tour vacation.

- ❖ **Hertz Gold Plus Rewards®**
  Members have the option to enroll at IntervalWorld.com to earn bonus points on qualifying rentals. These points can be used for up to two free weekend rental days. Members will also be able to bypass the counter and have the opportunity to change your rental car or type, enjoy express returns, and much more.

- ❖ **VIP Concierge℠**
  This benefit gives members access to personal assistance 24/7 that can assist with dining reservations, directions, attraction booking, and other travel planning needs.

- ❖ **$25 Getaway Discounts**
  Each time you want to use a Getaway, take USD$25 off the already low-priced weeklong resort stays. The discount applies to each and every time.

- ❖ **Cash Back on Selected Cruises**
  This program gives all Interval members the opportunity to receive up to USD$100 cash back on selected cruises when you book through Interval Travel.

- ❖ **Attractions, Sightseeing, and More!**
  For those members who love to plan ahead this could be the benefit you use the most. You can reserve, book, and/or pay online many of your vacation activities before you leave home to help you avoid those long ticket lines or any sold-out attractions after

you arrive. Sign in to www.intervalworld.com and browse through hundreds of sightseeing tours, activity outfitters, attraction tickets, and other recreational pursuits that are available in more than 80 countries.

Interval Platinum Membership

Interval or Interval Gold members can upgrade to an Interval Platinum membership at any time for a fee. In addition to receiving all of the above Interval and Interval Gold membership benefits, Interval Platinum members will receive these additional benefits:

- ❖ **Platinum Escapes**
  These are the same as the regular Getaways, however Platinum members can take advantage of deeply discounted last-minute Getaways that are available from time to time and sent to them by special email invitation.

- ❖ **Guest Certificates**
  Interval permits its members to assign the use of their exchange accommodations to a friend or family member by purchasing a Guest Certificate. There is no cost for Guest Certificates as a Platinum member. All guests must be at least 21 years of age.

- ❖ **$50 Getaway Discounts**
  Take USD$50 off the already low-priced weeklong resort stays every time you book.

- ❖ **Priority Getaway Viewing**
  Priority Getaway Viewing gives Platinum members exclusive access to the Getaway inventory before other members.

- ❖ **Companion Airline Travel Program**
  Platinum members receive a discounted rate on a companion airline ticket when you purchase one adult round-trip coach-class ticket with the same itinerary to participating cities.

- ❖ **Airport Lounge Membership**
  Only available to Platinum members, the Airport Lounge Membership provides complimentary enrollment in the standard Priority Pass™ program. This gives Platinum members access to more than 600 airport VIP lounges in more than 300 cities in over 100 countries.

Please note that some benefits may vary depending on country of residence and a per-person fee is required at some airport lounges. For more information on Interval´s membership programs go to their website and click on the Member Benefits tab and click on the membership that you think would be right for you - Interval, Interval Gold or Interval Platinum.

Interval and Social Media

All Interval members can access the website, including Getaways, through their iPhone, iPad, or Android by using the Interval International App. You can find the App at http://www.intervalworld.com/web/cs?a=60&p=mobile-app. This App also features Getaway Alerts. It's easy to customize your search and create a Getaway Alert. Get instant notifications when your desired Getaway vacation becomes available. It's that simple!

Also, new to the Interval app is Interval World® magazine. This exclusive, members-only   publication is packed with articles on vacation destinations, travel tips, updated membership information, and new resort listings.

In addition to the Interval International App, you can also find Interval on the following social media sites:

- o   Facebook (https://www.facebook.com/intervalintl)
- o   Instagram (https://www.facebook.com/intervalintl/app_151858328287166)
- o   YouTube (https://www.youtube.com/user/IntervalsWorld)
- o   Pinterest (http://www.pinterest.com/intervalworld/)
- o   Google+ (https://plus.google.com/+intervalinternational/about)

All social media sites are found at the bottom of the Interval website homepage. Interval World magazine is also available by barcode scan.

RCI Regular Membership Benefits[11]

In addition to being an RCI member and having access to nearly 4,500 affiliated resorts, there are other travel related benefits and services available. A few of the benefits of membership include:

---

[11]   All RCI Regular and Platinum Membership Benefits explained are summarized and/or excerpted from RCI Weeks Membership brochures as well as the RCI Resort Directory as well as the RCI website.

❖ **Extra Vacations**^{SM}**Getaways**
These are resort vacations available to RCI subscribing members at resort locations without having to deposit or exchange your week. These can be booked at any time, subject to availability and you do not need to use your week. They are offered at member-only pricing. This is a great way to book all of your vacations with your exchange company. These can be booked by calling RCI directly or visiting www.RCI.com.

❖ **Last Call**^{SM} **Vacations**
For the best deals on last-minute vacation opportunities members can go to Last Call vacations online at RCI.com. You can get extraordinary prices on full-week vacations based on availability regardless of the resort, season or destination. This inventory is updated frequently so you need to check regularly if you are looking for something specific. I always suggest that if you find an option that works for you to book it right away because if you come back to it, someone else may have ¨scooped it up.¨ Last Call Vacations are available less than 45 days before the check-in date.

❖ **Guest Certificates**
As an RCI member you can share your passion for travel with the ones you love by purchasing a Guest Certificate. These Certificates allow you to give your exchange vacation as a gift so that the recipient can vacation at any of the available affiliated resorts. There is a small fee for the certificate, there may be age restrictions and the certificates cannot be sold or used for any commercial purposes.

❖ **RCI Cruise Vacations** - See cruise options below.

❖ **RCI Elite Rewards® Credit Card**
The RCI Elite Rewards® credit card is designed exclusively for RCI members in the United States and lets you earn Rewards on everyday purchases as outlined by the Elite Rewards Program. You can redeem Rewards for everything from the latest electronic gadget to gift certificates for shopping, dining and entertainment. The RCI Elite Rewards® card also lets you redeem your Rewards for items that you can use on your RCI vacation or toward your RCI membership fees. For more information you can go to www. RCIEliteRwards.RCI.com or call RCI.

❖ **Endless Vacation® Magazine and Website** <u>www.Endlessvacation.com</u>
This is a member-only magazine and iPad magazine that provides special offers, a wealth of information to help you plan and enjoy your vacations, including useful information on great places to eat, shop and not-to-be missed sightseeing excursions, exciting cultural events and popular outdoor activities. There is also an ¨app¨ so that you can also receive the Endless Vacation magazine on your iPad.

❖ **RCI Travel**
RCI Travel provides the assistance of a knowledgeable travel agent for travel arrangements to complement your resort vacation. RCI travel also offers discounted rates on airfare, hotels, car rentals and much more! You can find information at <u>RCI.com/RCITravel</u> or Call RCI.

❖ **RCI Perks^{SM} Program**
As a subscribing member of RCI this is yet another great way to get even more from your membership. RCI has negotiated special deals with select companies on behalf of RCI members. Next time you shop, don´t just spend, enjoy savings and earn rewards when you shop for qualified purchases online through the RCI Perks program. You can find more information at RCI.com and then go to the Members Perks section.

❖ **RCI TV**
RCI TV explains through online video, how members make the most of their membership. RCI Members can click on the RCI TV link under the Explore RCI tab on the RCI website home page or go to (http://www.rci.com/rci-tv).

RCI Platinum Membership

RCI offers its members the opportunity to upgrade their regular membership to a RCI Platinum membership which not only gives them access to the benefits listed above, but also the following enhanced benefits.

❖ **Priority Access**
RCI Platinum members will receive Priority Access to specially acquired exchange vacations at select hotels and resort accommodations in destinations such as New York, Chicago and

San Diego. Plus, receive (1) day advance notice of Extra Vacations getaways sales and access to a dedicated toll-free phone line.

❖ **Unit Upgrades**
RCI Platinum members with a confirmed exchange vacation can receive a complimentary unit upgrade if a larger unit comes available within two weeks of check-in. There is no additional RCI fee for this upgrade.

❖ **Vacation Packages**
RCI Platinum members can book vacations at world-class resorts with a Best Rate Guarantee. Terms and conditions for the best rate guarantee can be found on www.rci.com/BRG. The Best Rate Guarantee is available to all RCI members.

❖ **Platinum Rebates**
RCI Platinum members can receive rebates on various RCI transactions. Rebates are automatically credited to your RCI Platinum membership account. These would include select RCI transactions like RCI Guest Certificates toward accommodations, Extra Vacations getaways confirmations, or combining multiple Deposits or Deposit Credits.

❖ **Platinum Cruise Exchange & Experimental Vacation Exchange**
Platinum members may book an exchange vacation with RCI Platinum Cruise and receive an additional USD$25 off per cabin towards the purchase on select sailings, up to a maximum of 8 cabins.

OR, you can save USD$500 per couple when you exchange a Deposit trading Power of just 7 toward the purchase of select Experiential Vacation exchange tours. For more information on Experiential Vacation tours go to www.cruiserci.com/experiential l/terms.

❖ **Travel Rewards**
RCI Platinum members earn valuable Travel Rewards on select RCI Platinum transactions which can be redeemed toward future RCI Platinum Lifestyle Benefits and RCI Travel transaction. One Travel Reward is equivalent to USD$1.00. Travel Rewards can be earned and redeemed through select Golf green fees, purchasing selected wines from the on-line wine store, shopping RCI.com on-line shopping sotre through a selection of luxury retailers or by

using their Box Office programs for tickets to concerts, sporting events, movies and more.

- ❖ **Restaurant.com Certificate**
  Every month, RCI Platinum® tier members receive a complimentary $25USD Restaurant.com dining certificate, redeemable at more than 18,000 restaurants across the United States. At a $300USD yearly value, the dining certificate benefit alone can more than pay for the RCI Platinum membership tier fee.

For RCI Platinum Membership Rules go to www.RCI.com/platinumrules

RCI and Social Media

You can also find RCI on
Facebook (www.facebook.com/RCITimeshare)
Twitter   (@RCI_Timeshare
YouTube (http://www.youtube.com/rcitimeshare)

In addition to the sites above, RCI offers a members blog. All social media sites are found at the bottom of the RCI website home page, including a link to the Endless Vacation Magazine.

RCI also has an APP available for members through mobile phones and the iPad. You can find it from the Apple Store - https://itunes.apple.com/ us/app/rci/id356769392?mt=8

Exchange Company Websites

On both Web sites you will find many helpful features. You can check their up-to-the-minute resort listing section, or find out what vacations are available. You can also deposit your week(s) and request an exchange(s) or renew your membership.

Interval Online -- www.intervalworld.com
RCI Online -- www.rci.com

In the Address Book section of this book you will find all the telephone and facsimile numbers you will need for both Interval and RCI. Please contact either Interval International or RCI if you

have ANY questions, concerns or require further clarification on anything I have covered.

Before I move onto other exchange options I specifically want to mention that both exchange companies offer discounted vacations. These are my favorite way to vacation. Seriously, for an incredibly low weekly or daily rate you can travel anywhere in the world.

Why are these weeks so popular? You do not have to give up your ownership week to use them. Members also like the fact that they can stay in full resort type accommodation for either a week or a long weekend.

These vacations can start as low as $199 and go up from there for a three or four night stay up to a one week's accommodation. Pricing depends on location and the number of people traveling. I mean, where else could you take nine of your best friends and each only pay $70 for a week in a luxury condo in Lake Tahoe.

I think it is time for **another timeshare story**:

> When I was selling timeshare for a bit, I met a young couple and the husband had been a recipient of an Interval Getaway as a prenuptial gift. His friends, truly believing in the idea of a memorable bachelor party, had taken it one step further they took the party to Paris, France. A friend, and timeshare owner, had thought that a weeklong bachelor party was just as good a reason as any to "Getaway" as the impending honeymoon. What happened in Paris? Well that, they say, is another story.

Since Interval first introduced Getaways many years ago, I have traveled from Canada to Mexico and from Asia to Greece. Before I decided to move to Mexico, I called Interval on a Tuesday morning and was in Puerto Vallarta that Thursday afternoon for a seven-week vacation. Even back then (early 90's) those seven Getaways were, not only a great way to vacation in Mexico, but inexpensive as well - just over $800. Please note that Getaways pricing has increased from when I travelled in the early 1990´s but they are still are a great price and value for a quick vacation.

Yes, I did say seven weeks. Ask your vacation advisor to **try to do their best** if you want to stay consecutively at the same location, or resort.

Okay, so now that we have decided our exchange location **or** are taking a quick vacation, how do we do it? To find out what is available log onto either the Interval or RCI web site or call their 800 numbers.

Before I move on to some additional exchanging options, I would like to mention one last thing offered by RCI and Interval.

Vacation travel value packages

In **both** of their member magazines, **RCI and Interval** and their respective resort affiliates offer incredible vacation destinations throughout the world at <u>substantial discounts</u>. These packages include accommodations and a rental car for three, four, or seven night stays. With some packages, airfare is included from selected locations. All rates are subject to availability and change without notice. Even cruises on major cruise lines are offered. They are a great value.

So, are your bags packed yet?

All-Inclusive Resorts with RCI and Interval

As the name implies, all-inclusive resorts include everything - meals, beverages, accommodations and on-site amenities. RCI and Interval International affiliated resorts introduced their all-inclusive resort programs to provide members with a hassle free vacation.

Whether you are using Interval or RCI, affiliated resorts exchange companies offer two types of all-inclusive programs. There are All-Inclusive resorts that REQUIRE purchase of the all-inclusive package and those that offer an OPTIONAL all-inclusive meal and beverage program. Optional programs are just that - optional, for those who do not wish to have the worry about finding a restaurant or a grocery store. All-inclusive programs vary from resort to resort and some may charge for certain activities or special events. Most all-inclusive resorts do offer a variety of restaurant choices within their properties to avoid the all too familiar "one buffet all day" syndrome of days past.

All exchange company members must also be aware that if you check into a mandatory all-inclusive resort you may have to purchase an all-inclusive package for every member of your family or traveling party. Costs do vary from resort to resort so please call the resort for more detailed information.

At present RCI has 440 All-Inclusive resort properties, of which 360 are mandatory all-inclusive and the balance are optional. RCI´s all-inclusive resorts are designated with **Ai** or **M** (mandatory) in the resort directory or on the website. Interval´s required all-inclusive resorts are indicated with the symbol of a circle with a cross inside in both their printed and online Resort Directories.

Cruise exchange programs

The first cruise I took in 1978 was pre-Love Boat and was mainly for the wealthy and older generation. I say that because, at the time, I swear I was the youngest, and poorest, person on the ship but I did not care. I had a great time and since then I have been hooked on cruising.

Cruises are an excellent value for the money. Where else can you have your accommodation, meals and entertainment included while watching some of the world's best scenery pass you by. You can have a massage, work out, read, gamble in onboard casinos, shop, practice your golf swing, learn how to cook or you can just relax on deck while sipping an exotic drink. The list of ship board activities is lengthy and more and more even offer programs for children and teenagers, so cruising has now become a family affair.

The television show The Love Boat introduced cruising to everyone by bringing out the romance of cruising and then the glamour of the movie Titanic hooked almost everyone on cruising, or the idea of cruising. Approximately 80 percent of the population never haven taken a cruise, so timeshare developers are "jumping aboard" to offer owners an alternative to land based exchanges. Resorts around the world are now becoming affiliated with RCI or Ice Gallery to bring affordable, fun, intriguing ports of call and, of course, romance to their members.

Which Cruise lines are participating?

Carnival was the first cruise line to participate and now includes Costa Cruises, Holland America, Princess Cruise, Royal Caribbean, Norwegian Cruise Line, Celebrity, Disney Cruise Line, Windstar Cruises, Cunard, Seabourn and more. This all-star line up can sail you to more destinations than ever before.

RCI Cruise

RCI was not the first to enter the cruise exchange market but it has now become one of the leading ways for RCI owners to take a cruise that they might not have considered previously. RCI's cruise options let you purchase by RCI® Members only (i) at a reduced price with an exchange of a qualified Deposit or applicable Points or (ii) without exchange (sometimes referred to as "Cruise Extra Vacations℠ getaways)."

A qualified Deposit, including Combined Deposits and/or Deposit Credits with a Deposit Trading Power of 14 (Standard RCI Weeks® Exchange Rate) or 7 (Reduced RCI Weeks Exchange Rate) is required, or an exchange of 40,000 Points (Standard RCI Points® Exchange Rate) or 20,000 Points (Reduced RCI Points Exchange Rate) is required, subject to change without notice by RCI Cruise. Fuel supplement, port fees, and if applicable, the Combined Deposit fee are additional. Certain restrictions may apply. Prices and offers are subject to availability, are accurate at the time of publication and may change at any time thereafter.

RCI members can either call 1-877-RCI-BOAT or log onto the RCI web site and chose ´Cruise´ from the Air/Car/Cruise pull down and start planning their cruise. Once you have found that perfect cruise you will be required to answer a variety of questions, so be prepared, and then pay your exchange fee. The price of the cruise covers most onboard meals, activities and entertainment while onboard the ship. Prices vary due to length of sailing, dates, as well as itinerary and cabin type.

RCI Cruise is provided by a third-party provider under agreement with RCI. Therefore, RCI disclaims all responsibility in connection with any third-party travel savings. For RCI Cruise Terms and Conditions, go to CruiseRCI.com/terms

Interval Travel Cruises

Interval Travel offers fabulous cruise options to all of their members. Members can go to www.intervalworld.com, click on Member Benefits and then Special Offers to look for which itinerary will work for them, research deck plans, ports, short excursions, and dining options. You can reserve your cruise online or call any of Interval´s cruise specialists at 800-622-1540.

Private Travel & Lifestyle Club

International Cruise & Excursions, Inc., (ICE) launched its Cruise Exchange Program for timeshare resorts in 1997. They pioneered a way for timeshare owners to see the world in an affordable manner instead of Titanic prices. ICE's mission was to be the leading international market maker in the travel and leisure industry through the introduction and management of private travel-based membership clubs in key markets worldwide.

ICE's primary objective was to partner with specific affinity groups to provide high-quality cruise, resort and hotel vacations, as well as other desirable travel and leisure opportunities. ICE soon attained affiliation and support from the world's most popular cruise line, Carnival Cruise Lines. Carnival's support, paired with ICE's unique product ideas, opened doors to multiple business alliances with high quality resort developers in the United States, Southeast Asia, Mexico and the Caribbean. Resort developers partnered with ICE to provide their owners cruise and resort vacations, including the opportunity to exchange a timeshare week toward a cruise.

Today, ICE works with all major cruise lines and is recognized as one of the largest cruise and travel providers in the world. Serving more than 55 million consumers worldwide, ICE now provides innovative cruise, travel and lifestyle programs, as well as unique membership reward and loyalty based programs to leading corporate brands as well as resort developers, cruise lines, and leisure travel providers.

ICE's newest innovation is the "Lifestyle Collection"— a fully branded leisure & lifestyle benefits program that provides valuable discounts on travel and lifestyle activities, exclusive offers and an integrated Cash Back Rewards account, which can be utilized for payment of maintenance or membership fees within a program or toward savings on future travel or activities. The Lifestyle Collection includes cruise, golf, ski, resorts, airlines, car rentals, hotels, tour/experiential vacations, spa, wine, online shopping, concert or theater tickets, and much more. From the comfort of home, members can experience 24-hour online shopping, view high-definition virtual tours of cruise lines, resorts and popular vacation destinations. Members can also choose to call ICE's experienced and knowledgeable Vacation Consultants to assist and help guide their planning.

ICE is a membership based company and does not sell travel to the general public. The only way to take advantage of ICE's valuable savings on travel and leisure activities is through your timeshare purchase. A resort must be affiliated with ICE for its owners to have access to the benefits and savings ICE offers. Resorts may offer ICE benefits either under their own brand or as an ICE Rewards membership.

ICE **Rewards** offers members all the benefits of Lifestyle Collection with the addition of allowing the member to deposit their timeshare week in exchange for savings across all travel and leisure activities – not just cruise. ICE Rewards offers members a Best Price Guarantee, Exclusive Member Deals and Member Concierge Services. ICE Rewards is offered as part of a resort's timeshare sales presentation, and at the time of purchase new owners may receive either a one or two year membership included with their purchase. After this initial membership period expires members are offered the option to purchase an extension of their membership benefits and access.

To see if your resort is affiliated with ICE or to use your benefits, contact your home resort or Home Owners Association.

By the way, I do apologize for all the cruise puns. However, now that we are back on dry land, let us explore the last few exchange options for timeshare owners. They are:

Other timeshare exchange options

In addition to the two major exchange companies - RCI, Interval and ICE mentioned covered above, the following is a list of just a few of the other companies which do offer timeshare owners and members exchange opportunities. **Membership in each, or any, of the following is only offered through resort properties and not all resorts offer all options**. If you wish to participate in any one of the programs listed below check with your home resort to see if it is an option for you.

HSI. (Holiday Systems International®)

Founded in 1993, HSI was built on a business model of customer value, and uses exclusive and comprehensive products, services and benefits not available anywhere else in the world. There are many timeshare resorts and properties which offer HSI, which give their members an alternative to either RCI or Interval. HSI members enjoy an exclusive Vacation Ownership program which enhances their membership by offering the following travel benefits and/or programs:

1. **Converting weeks to Travel** – Member can submit any Vacation Ownership owned, even if it is not an HIS affiliated resort, in exchange for:

- ❖ 500,000+ of the world's finest Hotels
- ❖ 27+ Cruise Lines and every itinerary
- ❖ 8,000+ Tour Packages (every major)
- ❖ 60,000+ condos, apartments, castles, bed &breakfasts, etc.
- ❖ 400,000+ destination activities in over 5,000 cities
- ❖ 5,000+ Sports Travel Packages (Olympics, World Cup, NFL, NHL, etc.)
- ❖ 4,000+ Golf course specials
- ❖ Unlimited Custom Vacations
- ❖ Airfares, over 250 carriers to and from virtually every country in the world.
- ❖ Rental cars, spa services, event ticketing, and much more

This is great news to vacation owners as you are now able to exchange your weeks/points for a 3, 4 or 5 star hotels in every imaginable destination. Imagine exchanging into an amazing hotel in London's city center, or having the flexibility to exchange for tickets to the Olympics. With HSI, your weeks/ points are worth a whole lot more than what you are used to.

2. **Converting weeks to Cash**
   - ❖ Members can submit their weeks and receive cash!
     Whether you are unable to use your week or points one year, or have fallen on hard times, HSI's Maintenance Fee Payment Program is the best option available!
3. **Vacation Exchange**
   - ❖ $99 fee for exchanges both domestic and international (Lowest in the industry!)
4. **Cash for Travel** – Guaranteed <u>lowest</u> rate or HSI pays <u>double the difference in cash</u> on:

- ❖ 500,000+ of the world's finest Hotels
- ❖ 27+ Cruise Lines and every itinerary
- ❖ 8,000+ Tour Packages (every major)
- ❖ 60,000+ condos, apartments, castles, bed &breakfasts, etc.
- ❖ 5,000+ Sports Travel Packages (Olympics, World Cup, NFL, NHL, etc.)
- ❖ Custom Vacations

HSI offers services to over 4 million private clients worldwide in seven languages (English, Spanish, German, French, Italian, Portuguese, and Russian)

HSI, a privately held company, as well, they are a member and sponsor of virtually every leading industry organization, including the American Resort Development Association (ARDA), the Canadian Resort Development Association (CRDA), the Global Networking Expo (GNEX) and the Mexican Association of Tourist Developers (AMDETUR), among others.

You should contact your resort to see if they offer HSI as a membership benefit.

Owners Link

Created in 2009, Owners Link is the newcomer to the exchange option market and very effective closing tool, because for the technology the closer is able to show to the customer live samples in the table. Owners Link does bring with it a combined 40 years of experience in leisure, technology and vacation ownership industry alliances. Due to its extensive international network of these alliances it has created an online member program that has been designed to provide its members with a first-rate personalized experience by offering the following benefits:

- ❖ Joint venture.
- ❖ Share your weeks in to the Owners Link platform with no upfront cost.
- ❖ Thousands of members can see your weeks on rent and make an offer.
- ❖ No exchange fees.
- ❖ Cruises with exclusive rates for Owners Link members.
- ❖ Flights – Through the Owners Link website, members can browse different flight schedules and price of any flight, then book and pay for it online.
- ❖ Travel Concierges
- ❖ Go online and search and book at any of the thousands of Hotel's offered to members at discounted rates
- ❖ Rental Cars at member only pricing – book and pick up your car where is convenient airport for you
- ❖ Sports Travel Packages – fully customized travel packages to over 10,000 of the most exciting games and events in the world
- ❖ Destination Activities from scuba diving to Disney... book your activity before you leave
- ❖ Skiing and Snowboard Destinations including lessons, lodging, rentals and more
- ❖ Find a Golf Course on any of the thousands listed – beginner level to tour level

❖ You can use Owners Link on your iPad, iPhone, Blackberry, Androids, Tablets or desktop
❖ Owners Link offers multi-lingual services to its members

Owners Link offers **JB (Just Book) Weeks** which will give members the maximum flexibility and range to have total worldwide access at privately negotiated rates. JB Weeks are the number of weeks you can include within a membership to be used on the Owners Link site in over 40,000 hotels, resorts, villas and condominiums in 150 countries worldwide from Members can also use JB weeks to stay on any day of the week and broken into 3, 4, and 7 night segments. There is no maximum usage per year. Weeks start from USD$199 per week but the average price of a 7 night JB weeks is USD$699.

In addition to JB Weeks, members also have their last minute **ASAP Specials**. As the name implies you have a selection of quality accommodations to select from within a 5 to 45 days of your anticipated check-in date. Use of the ASAP Specials has no impact on JB Weeks or your Resort's week's allotment and is fully transferrable to friends and family. Special can start as low as USD$199 per week.

Owners Link is also privately held company, is a member and member of the American Resort Development Association (ARDA) and the Mexican Association of Tourist Developers (AMDETUR) (CRDA) and among others.

Again, check to see if your resort offers Owners Link as a membership benefit.

IMPORTANT NOTE:

The alternatives mentioned above are just some of the many **OPTIONS** that may be available to timeshare owners, IF your resort has an affiliation with them. However, RCI or Interval International cannot and will not arrange any of these options for you.

Well, that about does it for exchanging. I hope that I have been able to solve the Exchange Mystery for you. It really is very simple to exchange.

One more exchange story:

In 1984 I made an exchange to Hawaii trading the two-bedroom that I mentioned in the lock-off story. Because my spouse and I were traveling with another couple we needed at least a two bedroom. Upon check-in, I was told there were over-booked on two bedrooms available, and as I was about to protest, the receptionist asked me, "would a four bedroom be okay?" It turned out to be a great unit with four individual suites with our own swimming pool, BBQ and maid. It looked like something out of Architectural Digest. Since we were going to be there for four weeks, I made some calls and two other friends flew over and enjoyed our "four bedroom" upgrade.

HAVE A GREAT EXCHANGE VACATION!

Chapter 11

The Price of Ownership...

WHAT ARE THEY REALLY WORTH?

This is one question that I constantly hear from owners and skeptics alike. Are they worth what I paid? Did I get value for my money? Price and value: Price is defined as the amount of money you pay for something, and value as the amount of money, or something else that is of importance to you.

You, the buyer, determine the VALUE of a timeshare. If you believe what you are buying is important and will benefit you and your family - emotionally, spiritually and physically - then it is worth whatever the price you pay.

The PRICE, on the other hand, consists of the many variables. Remember, back in the chapter on exchanging your weeks, we talked about the importance of location. Well, the price of a timeshare is based on much the same premise. Buying a week in a popular Caribbean resort could command twice the price of a small, older, more remote location. Regardless of the size of the unit you buy, location is one of the determining factors.

Other factors that determine the price of a timeshare are:

- ❖ The quality of the resort
- ❖ The amenities offered by the resort and within the local area
- ❖ The seasonal designation
- ❖ The size of the unit
- ❖ The number of weeks you want
- ❖ Exchange demand
- ❖ Local market conditions

If you choose to buy the least expensive option that the resort offers, you will most likely get the least value from it. Why? Because if you are constantly experiencing problems with use, exchange, or even rental, then it is of no benefit and whatever price you paid was too much. Now, I am not saying you should never consider the least expensive option, but if you can live within the limitations and restrictions then go for it.

The price of ownership is directly proportional to the amount of *use* you get from it.

WHAT A WEEK SELLS FOR

To say specifically what a week sells for is impossible. The average price worldwide, for a timeshare interval is US$18,600 and in the United States, the average price is $18,723 which reflects that there is not the huge price discrepancy as there was when I first published in 2006. Also as I mentioned above, many variables and factors influence the price. All prices in this chapter are quoted in US dollars.

CASH OR FINANCED?

Once you have decided to buy a timeshare week you then need to determine how you are going to pay for it. Are you going to pay cash or finance it? This, of course, depends on your personal financial position and what you can afford at the time of purchase.

If you are able to pay **CASH** pay cash. You will most likely receive a 5, 8 or 10 percent discount off the price quoted because the resort will not have to carry the paper. Paying in full at the time of purchase can be done either in actual cash money, on a credit card, a wire transfer between your bank and theirs or a personal check (where permitted). Checks are generally only accepted in the United States and Canada. Elsewhere, ask your salesperson.

Worldwide, 34 percent of buyers pay cash at the time of purchase. In the United States it is approximately 25 percent, while in Canada it is around 15 percent. There are, however, many countries in Asia and Europe where more than 50 percent of the buyers pay cash. This could be because the initial price is lower than the $18,600 average that makes the cost of financing such a small amount unreasonable. In the past few years, the industry is seeing a trend towards more consumers paying cash or cashing out suggesting a more affluent buyer with more disposable income.

FINANCING your timeshare purchase can be done in one of two ways. The first way is the **seller financing** the purchase. 94 percent of timeshare projects offer some form of financing options. Two, five, seven and ten year terms are available to buyers, with each term offering a different interest rate. Remember that the term and interest rate are all based on the amount of the down payment.

Interest rates, on average, are about 14.5 percent after a 25 percent down payment. Interest rates may vary from 10 percent to as high as 18 percent, depending on the resort and location. Tropical locations tend to offer the higher interest rates as they carry more buyers financing.

The industry is also seeing a trend where more buyers are going to longer financing terms. This is due to more buyers making lower down payments at the time of purchase. In the United States, for example, 80 percent of developers offer a minimum down payment requirement of only 10 percent, exclusive of special financing packages. This ability to buy for as little as 10 percent down, and over a seven or ten year financing term, now makes a timeshare week a viable option for those in a lower income bracket. From the 10 percent down payment minimum offered in the United States to the 45 percent minimum I paid in the Caribbean, offer what you can honestly afford at the time, and work out the terms later. Confused? Simplified, the more money you put as a down payment, the lower the monthly payment.

The second method is **personal financing**. This means you borrow the money to pay out the resort for your purchase. In other words, you take the 30 or 45 day option that the developer offers as a pay out period, go home and make your own financing arrangements.

If the purchase price is under $10,000, and you have a great relationship with your bank or credit union, you may qualify for a personal loan. Most credit unions will finance the entire amount of your timeshare purchase through a personal loan or a line of credit. While many credit unions do offer very competitive member interest rates, banks may charge you 1 percent or 1.5 percent higher. If the purchase price is more than $10,000, you may consider the option of refinancing your home mortgage or taking out a second mortgage with your bank or mortgage holder.

Should you personally borrow from family and friends to buy a timeshare? Only you can answer that. If your family has the available funds, consider a loan agreement with terms, just like a bank. Everyone will benefit from this arrangement.

If you are considering any financing option, here are some examples based on borrowing $10,000 after the down payment. The percentage you put down is not relevant.

Interest Rate	Financing Term	Monthly Payment	Total Interest
12.75%	24 months	$ 474.24	$ 1,381.98
12.75%	36 months	$ 335.74	$ 2,086.69
12.75%	60 months	$ 226.25	$ 3,575.48
12.75%	84 months	$ 180.56	$ 5,167.76
Interest Rate	**Financing Term**	**Monthly Payment**	**Total Interest**
12.75%	120 months	$ 147.84	$ 7,741.48
14.5%	24 months	$ 482.49	$ 1,579.97
14.5%	36 months	$ 344.21	$ 2,391.72
14.5%	60 months	$ 235.28	$ 4,117.28
14.5%	84 months	$ 190.17	$ 5,975.00
14.5%	120 months	$ 158.29	$ 8,995.40
Personal Loan[12]			
7.5%	24 months	$ 450.00	$ 800.01
7.5%	36 months	$ 311.06	$ 1,198.40
7.5%	60 months	$ 200.38	$ 2,023.05
Mortgage [13]			
6.9% ($20,000)	120 months	$ 231.19	$ 7,743.73
6.9% ($20,000)	300 months	$ 140.09	$ 22,028.57
6.9% ($20,000)	360 months	$ 131.73	$ 27,424.02

If you take the developers financing option, you will be asked to sign a **Promissory Note** for the amount borrowed, just like any lending institution. You are obligated by law to make payments. Should you choose

---

[12] Banks tend not make personal loans for more than 60 months or 5 years.

[13] This $20,000 would be the amount refinanced to your existing mortgage.

not to pay the lender, they will send your contract to a collection agency, which may have an adverse affect on your credit score.

There are some projects that do offer a **walk away clause**. In the event you do not, or cannot, make the payments, the resort will take back the week. You will, however, forfeit any moneys paid to that point. Walk away clauses are similar to a foreclosure, except the bank or collection agency will not come after you and it will not affect your credit rating.

One last thing before I leave the financing issue, 36 percent of developers do sell their financing to a lender. So, if your monthly payment stubs show a different name than the one on your contract, this is why. If you have any questions or concerns, contact your sales representative or the resort accounting office.

PAYING IT OFF BY CASHING IT OUT?

I have heard so many owners say that they were not aware they had an option to cash out in their contracts. In all the timeshare weeks I bought there was always an **option to cash out** available. Now, some resorts may not tell you about this option. This is because they want you to continue making payments so they continue to make their money on interest. Reputable resorts will not only tell you, but also encourage you to pay it off when you possibly can. Cash out discounts can be up to 10% off of your promissory note if you cash out prior to your first monthly payment. Their reasoning for this is if it is paid off, you will never miss a payment, therefore cutting down on their future collection costs. It also gives resorts the ability to use that money sooner and/or cuts down on the discount paid to a financing company.

The cash out option is available at any time during your financing period and can be done without any charge. You will be responsible for the balance of the promissory note and you may or may not receive a discount, that will depend on your resort´s finance department. Obviously if you can cash it out before the end of your contract you will save money on the interest.

ANNUITY OPTIONS

Some Developers also offer a guaranteed deferred annuity option when purchasing. Similar to an investment annuity that is primarily used as a means of securing a significant payment during retirement years; these annuities may be offered as an incentive to purchase.

These annuities are fixed investment products which are designed to accept and grow funds, providing a one-time return to the owner upon maturity depending on the length of the contract. There is an upfront cost to the purchaser to set up the annuity which may be up to 20% of the contract purchase price, however the return upon maturity is promised to the original purchase price. Some annuity options may include coverage for the contract terms maintenance fees, but remember you will have to pay the initial annuity set up. There are a number of companies which underwrite the annuity, but not all properties offer them at the point of sale.

Should you choose the annuity option at the time of purchase; you will be contacted by the Annuity Company within 30 - 60 days of your purchase. At that time you would pay the annuity cost and then sent an investment confirmation with the signed certificate and full printout of the terms and conditions. Be certain to read them through carefully, and to keep the certificate in a secure location. You usually have one year after this type of annuity matures to collect the funds.

INSURANCE PROGRAMS

In the past year there are an increasing number of resorts, especially in Mexico, which are now offering insurance coverage for their new purchasers that have promissory notes. This insurance is based on a percentage of the loan but covers new purchasers for job loss, disability as well as having a death benefit. Should a member need to make a claim, the payout is made, in all cases to the company that is the holder of the promissory note. The insurance is underwritten by MetLife© a major player in the insurance industry, and although available only in limited resort areas at the current time, I expect that in the new few years it will become a staple in the industry in that resort developers will not have to worry about collection of debts when a new member loses their job or god forbid, dies suddenly. Cash sales or loans which are paid in full do not qualify for this option.

DONATING TO CHARITY AND/OR TAKING A TAX DEDUCTION

YES, you can take a tax deduction. Hold on, before you run right out and buy a timeshare, you should want one for no other reason than you want to use it. The tax deduction is the bonus you get after you have bought. Also, not all countries allow you to take a deduction, so you should check with your federal taxation department or an accountant familiar with timeshare.

In the United States, the Internal Revenue Service (IRS) does allow for deductions in the following areas:

- ❖ Writing off purchase costs, finance charges and maintenance fees
- ❖ Any mortgage interest paid while financing (second home qualification)
- ❖ Renting our your timeshare (portion)
- ❖ Taking a loss on the sale of a timeshare
- ❖ Charitable donation deductions
- ❖ Corporate business expenses

To deduct more than US$500 as a charitable donation, you must show the IRS the following:

- ❖ Your purchase contract (how you acquired it and when)
- ❖ Cost of your Timeshare
- ❖ Receipt from the person/charity showing their name, the date and location of the contribution as well as a description of what you donated which will support fair market value.

To deduct more than US$5,000.00 the IRS will need all of the above and a certified market appraisal.

I am not going to quote the IRS tax code regarding each of these areas because they are long, dry and written in legalese. In Canada, some corporate deductions are allowed for under Revenue Canada Taxation laws. If a tax deduction is important to you, contact your accountant, or local IRS or Revenue Canada office for specific information. There are also books available both online and in bookstores on tax advantages for timeshare owners. Check with your local bookstore or check online.

MAINTENANCE & OTHER FEES

After you have made the initial purchase, you are obligated to pay an annual maintenance fee to either the Developer or the Home Owner Association. This is the last mandatory cost of owning a timeshare. Maintenance fees help to maintain the quality and future value of your property. All the owners share these maintenance costs equally. The amount of the fee will depend on the size, location and amenities of the resort and are assessed annually by the Home Owners Association.

Do maintenance fees go up every year? Yes, maintenance fees can increase every year. On <u>average</u> maintenance fees increase between 3 percent and 10 percent per year but there are properties where fees have gone up in excess of 25 percent. Resorts with large fee increases are not common, but it does happen from time to time depending on the resort's financial situation. I own in a resort where the fees have not risen in ten years and at another one, where every year, I consider selling before I go broke paying the increased fees.

How much should the fee be? The average weekly maintenance fee, world-wide has increased in the past ten years from a modest $325 to over $600. The United States average is $822, Mexico is $685, where as in Africa it is $573. These are only averages so do not panic if you pay more (or less), you more than likely own in a superior location. I pay almost $600 per week for a one bedroom in the Caribbean and only $250 (Canadian dollars) for a two bedroom in Canada. Ah, location, location.

So, where exactly does your maintenance money go?

- ❖ Property taxes
- ❖ Property insurance
- ❖ Resort administration
- ❖ Wages for the all the resort personnel
- ❖ Reservations services
- ❖ Laundry
- ❖ Garbage collection
- ❖ Utilities: gas, electricity, water, sewer
- ❖ Furniture repair and interior maintenance
- ❖ Exterior maintenance
- ❖ Lawns and landscaping
- ❖ Parking and resort vehicles
- ❖ Room supplies
- ❖ Outdoor lighting
- ❖ Appliance repair
- ❖ TV and cable service and maintenance
- ❖ Telephone service and maintenance
- ❖ Reserve Management Plan or Contingency Funds
- ❖ Resort amenities: tennis courts, pools, spas, fitness centers, chairs, towels, umbrellas, etc. and their respective maintenance and/or replacements

What is an Assessment or Special Assessment? These are fees over and above the fixed annual maintenance fee and are charged per week of ownership. Assessment fees are charged for extraordinary expenses that the resort incurs in a particular year that there are not sufficient monies available in the reserve or contingency fund. Assessments can also be the result a natural disaster such as earthquake, hurricane, fire or flood and again, not sufficient funds in the reserve fund, or insurance coverage, to cover the repairs or rebuilding effort.

Assessments may, or may not, have been specifically included in the written contract but resorts are within their rights to charge them providing they are not unreasonable in nature. Other rare situations where assessments are given are when a resort does extensive renovations are done to their units. The costs are then broken down and divided among the owners based on the size of the unit owned. For example a studio owner would pay less than a two bedroom owner.

For example, I own on the island of St. Maarten and after being hit with consecutive hurricanes, I was charged an assessment fee to help the rebuilding effort. The Reserve Fund did help, but as the cost of rebuilding was enormous, the owners all had to chip in through the assessment fee. Assessment fees are not an every year occurrence. I have owned for over thirty years and only paid assessments four times in two different properties. By the way, my St. Maarten assessment was a $450 additional expense, per week, over my $600 maintenance fee that year.

These numbers are not meant to scare you. They are real and an ongoing reminder that you own a timeshare. Reminder, you bought a timeshare to save money on vacation and, even including the maintenance fee, you ARE saving money.

If money is a serious concern for you, consider buying a week jointly with a friend. You can use the week alternately, share the expenses and both reap the benefits of ownership.

BUYER'S REMORSE

I would not be doing justice if I covered everything about the timeshare industry except how to cancel. **Can I really cancel if I change my mind?** Ah, this is one of those questions nobody wants to honestly answer but yes, you can cancel if you change your mind, however you should be aware of a few things.

The first, and most important thing, is that you were shown on the contract a **rescission clause or liquidated damages clause.** Then, you would have initialed or signed next to that clause indicating that you are aware of your right to cancel within the stated rescission period.

Whether it is called a rescission period or a "cooling off period," the time you have to change your mind after purchasing varies almost as much as the seasonal designations. Every state, province and country offer different time periods for handling buyer's remorse. Some states offer as little as twenty-four (24) hours. Other locations give you three (3), five (5), seven (7) or even ten (10) days to cancel. In Europe you have up anywhere from 15-30 days to cancel the sale. Specific cooling off and/or rescission periods are covered in more detail Chapter 15.

Despite your being aware of this clause, you will be asked by not only the salesperson, but also the financial person, why you want to cancel. You must decide if is it truly, 100 percent, monetary related, or is it the fear of making a mistake? The financial aspect is understandable. You said yes too quickly and then realized that you really do not have the money. If money is truly the issue, you may be offered some financial options which would work better for you and you could end up keeping what you purchased. Every resort will work with purchasers to help them afford their purchase or refinance loans in an effort to make it a win-win for everyone concerned, remember ask for help if you need it!

On the other side, the fear of making a mistake is normal. However, it is not something that should prevent you from making a good decision about your life. Realistically, when we buy something, in which we are not 100 percent confident in our decision, we suffer from a malady known as buyer's remorse. In Chapter 7, I covered why people are afraid to buy, but should you find yourself in a position of extreme buyer's remorse, here is what you can do.

How can I cancel?

Trust me, nobody, especially the salesperson wants to hear the words "I want to cancel," especially when it means their commission just flew out the window. If you feel as if you made a big mistake, or there is another valid reason you should cancel, tell everyone concerned and they will try to resolve it. This is especially true if you have more questions that you were afraid to ask during the sales presentation.

Remember, everybody's goal is to come out in a win-win situation. If you cooperate with the salesperson, financial person or the manager, you may still keep your week, but under different terms.

It is important to understand the cooling off period varies from state to state, province to province and country to country and will be noted in your contract paperwork usually under a cancellation or liquidated damages clause.

However, should you really, really want to cancel, the chart on the next page will show you what your options available:

	Within the Cooling Off Period	**After the Cooling Off Period**
HOW TO ADVISE THE RESORT	Verbally advise the salesperson or resort of cancellation. Cancellation notification in writing If the resort fails to honor your notification you can contact the government office responsible for consumer protection to assist you in getting your deposit back and the sale canceled.	If you failed to advise the resort during the cooling off period, you cannot do so now. You can try to cancel the sale but since you have passed the time period allowed by law, you have no direct recourse for cancellation.
YOUR DEPOSIT	100 percent Refundable upon cancellation	Not Refundable
YOUR CONTRACT	Cancelled	Still in effect
YOUR OPTIONS	Work with the resort to re-finance or provide alternative ownership options (Smaller unit).	Work with the resort to re-finance or provide alternative ownership options (Smaller unit).
RESULTS	Peace of Mind	Enjoy what you bought and either rent it out or sell it.

Credit Card Cancellation

Then, there are other buyers who will try to cancel their sale via the back door. They will call their credit card company and ask them to cancel the "deposit" saying they were scammed or some other reason not related to buyer´s remorse. Since the majority of deposits are charged to a credit card, people believe that if they contact their credit card company and tell them they want to cancel, it will be canceled. Well, that is not exactly the case.

First, the credit card company will ask you submit a cancellation request. This will consist of answering some questions <u>and</u> a copy of the written cancellation notification you sent to the resort and deposit receipt.

Some of the questions you could be asked by the credit card company are:

"Did you advise the resort of your intention to cancel the deal?"
"Did you advise them orally or in written form?"
"When did you advise them of your intention to cancel?"
"Do you have a letter or credit receipt?"

What happens next all depends on "when you cancel." If you are within your rescission period, they will ¨cancel¨ your Charge and advise the resort of the cancellation by way of a credit card dispute. The resort will challenge the dispute based on your having signed contractual paperwork and in some cases, you may lose the dispute and be responsible for the charge. If you are past your rescission period, they may not consider a refund because they consider your contract now binding with the resort; however some credit card companies will ¨dispute the charge¨ for you; however you will more than likely lose the dispute.

One last reminder if you try canceling the sale using this method. Each credit card company has a time limit on how long after the sale they will give you a refund or credit. If you are not sure, ask.

If you still wish to pursue canceling your purchase then my only suggestion is to retain legal counsel and expect to pay more in legal fees than the price of ownership. Then you have to ask yourself, "is this really worth it?"

So, when you are signing all the paperwork, remember that you were told about the rescission clause. If you find yourself truly suffering from buyer's remorse, cancel within the rescission period and save everyone the hassle. Remember, there is no excuse for waiting.

On a personal note I would like to say that buyer's remorse is an immediate feeling. It is not something that you experience a month, six months or a year after you buy. I was amazed to find out that people will wait up to a year to "decide" to cancel their sale because they have "changed their mind." Let me ask you this, "Do you wait a year to return your new car, that shirt or dress that you bought?" If you find yourself in financial trouble call the resort and make arrangements to either re-finance or restructure your membership.

In the next Chapter I cover how to RENT YOUR TIMESHARE. So, if the rescission period is past and maintenance fee is an issue, look at rental income. You will then have no direct expense for that year and may even have made money on a tax deduction. Think about that.

Do not let the following be the story of your life:

AGE 21 - 30 -- I CANNOT SAVE NOW. I am young. There is plenty of time. Wait until I start making a little more. Then I will save to do this.

AGE 30 - 45 -- I CANNOT SAVE NOW. I have a growing family on my hands. It takes all I make to keep them going. As soon as they are a little older, it will cost less and then I will save.

AGE 45 - 55 -- I CANNOT SAVE NOW. I have two children in college. It is all I can do to pay their expenses. I cannot save a penny. Wait until they are out of college and on their own and then I can "salt it away."

AGE 55 - 65 -- I CANNOT SAVE NOW. I know that I should but things are not breaking like they were. It is not easy for a person of my age to step out and get a better job. Maybe I will be able to save later.

AGE 65 -- I CANNOT SAVE NOW. We are living with my son and his wife. My social security does not go that far. I wish I had started saving years ago but I cannot save now because there is no income.

I will leave you with these three quotes to ponder:

"It costs twice as much to own something cheap."
"Nothing of value comes cheap."
"There is no price we can put on our health, happiness or family."

Chapter 12

For Rent, One Timeshare...

Another comment I hear from owners everywhere is, we cannot use our timeshare this year, what can we do with it? My response to them is RENT IT. Yes, you heard me correctly. You can rent out your timeshare, but it takes patience, initiative and hard work. If you think that someone will walk right up to you and say, "hey, can I rent your week," forget it, it rarely happens. Be realistic in your expectations, because until you get the hang of renting, it will be very frustrating experience.

Rental provides timeshare owners with an alternative to home resort use and exchange. For renters it provides an opportunity to experience, first hand, the benefits of ownership at a reasonable rate. You may end up being surprised and your renter may even turn into a buyer, what a bonus!

Once you have decided to rent out your week you then need to choose how you are going to rent it. Below are options available to you. Use the one with which you feel most comfortable and confident. For first time renters you may opt to use your home resort rental program, but whichever method you use, just remember, be patient.

Oh, by the way, the most important thing you need to do before you line up the renters: **pay the maintenance fees for that year**. If there are any outstanding fees for the week(s), you will not be able to use your week(s) in any form.

USING YOUR HOME OWNER'S ASSOCIATION OR VACATION CLUB

If your home resort offers its members a rental program, use it. This is your simplest and easiest option and most resorts offer this option on their member websites or have toll-free numbers to call and deposit your weeks into rental programs.

The first thing that you need to do is to deposit your week(s) in the rental pool. Do this as early in the year as is allowed. Some resorts do allow for deposit into the rental pool when the maintenance fees come due and are paid. The club or resort will then send a rental release that needs to be signed. There is no guarantee that they will rent your week in that particular year, but they will carry the week(s) forward to the following year if you agree. Should you change your mind about renting; some resorts will permit you to retrieve the week(s) from the pool, at no cost, provided they have not been rented.

Once your week(s) has been rented you be sent a check for the rental LESS any commissions that they take. Yes, there are commissions. I own at resorts that charge as little as $45 per week up to, and including, one that charges 45 percent of their asking rental price. The industry average is around 35 percent. This commission or fee is spread around into advertising, administrative costs, a cut for the resort or hotel and a cut for the developer. Most rental programs do operate on a non-profit basis, but do not be too surprised if yours does not.

Rental programs will charge whatever they feel they can get for your week(s) or on a per night basis. This is based on size, location (if fixed unit), season and the local competition. Some programs will guarantee that your maintenance fee is covered, others do not. Each resort operates their rental programs differently so do not be surprised if you own in two different locations and they each have different programs.

For example, you own a one bedroom in high season and your maintenance is $250 per week. They may charge $400 for the week or rent two nights out at $200 per night. You get your $250 back, plus possibly a small percentage more, and the rest is divided to cover their cost.

Having a good, solid rental program is one of the most powerful tools that a resort can have. It can maintain good property value and create owner satisfaction for the long term. Owners that do not have to reach into their pockets for maintenance money every year will continue to use the rental program which benefits everyone.

USING A RENTAL COMPANY

Your second option is to use a company that specializes in renting out timeshare weeks. Most rental companies also sell timeshare and will use your week to interest a potential buyer. Remember that there are also some unscrupulous rental companies out there. You should be careful when choosing a rental company. Many are reputable but, many are not. Ask people you know who have rented a week through a rental company what their experiences were and would if they recommend that company. Ask people for referrals and listen to them.

Timeshare rental brokers can get you the most exposure, but remember you will have to pay for it in some manner. **You should NEVER have to prepay for this service upfront.** If the company is legitimate and reputable, they will take their costs from the amount collected in rental income. Payments will be for either an advertising charge or a commission after the sale.

Following are some questions you should ask the rental company BEFORE you consider giving them your week(s) to rent.

1. Are you a licensed timeshare broker in your state/country?
2. How many weeks did you rent in the past year?
3. Do you keep enough weeks available for rental?
4. How long has your company been renting weeks?
5. How long, approximately, do you think it will take to rent my week(s)?
6. How do you advertise the rental weeks?
7. How long do I have to exercise my rental option?
8. Can I get my week(s) back if I change my mind?
9. Can you provide me with references?
10. What is your total rental commission? What does it include?

Make sure that you actually follow through with checking references or search complaint websites for any complaints or issues regarding the company.

I did not the mention the most obvious question: How much will you be charging as rent? Rental prices, like sale prices, depend on many factors. The size, season and location will determine the rental price. Remember, that other units of similar nature, that are for rent in your location may affect what you receive. Expect to pay commissions from 15 percent to 50 percent of the rental price.

One last thing about rental companies, do not telephone them constantly to ask if they have rented your week(s). It will only frustrate everyone involved. Calling once a month is not too bad, every other month is better. If they offer email, use that to keep in touch. Once they have rented your week(s) they will contact you personally or send you a check. Never give them your bank information for them to deposit payment, always request a check.

Timeshare rental companies can be located through most timeshare projects, referrals from other owners, trade publications and the 1000 plus Internet websites. As with any business transaction, deal only with a reputable company.

RENTING IT YOURSELF

This option is not for the faint of heart. If you have patience, perseverance and the time, it will reap its rewards in the end. What I am about to pass along to you is a method I have used for years and works. Remember for all the hard work you do in the beginning, the easier it becomes in the following years. Who knows, you may then find yourself traveling on a Getaway or Bonus Vacation and renting all your use weeks like I do.

Maintenance Fees

Ensure all your fees are paid in full, including any assessments or taxes. If you are renting for future years the maintenance fees **must** be paid in advance.

Which Week(s) will you Rent?

If you own a fixed week(s) this is not a problem. If you own a **floating week or a points system**, you need to secure a specific week within your home resort for the week(s) you want to rent. You can make this choice yourself or let your rental prospect tell you. Floating weeks have more flexibility for your renters, however they must tell you far enough in advance for you can make the arrangements. Remember that not all resorts allow floating weeks to be put into their rental programs. Ask before you pursue this.

Pricing your Week(s)

Your goal should be to recover your maintenance fee and any other costs applicable to the week at the very least. This may include any rollover charges or "potential yearly increases." Potential renters may be buyers looking for a bargain so price your week accordingly.

Second, always remember to add on the Guest Fee charge to your rental amount if your resort or club charges this fee to allow someone other than the member to use the resort.

Third, decide a reasonable and realistic rental amount per week, or per night. Following are some options to consider in helping you determine a rental rate:

- ❖ Ask twice (2x) your maintenance ($375 x 2 = $750) plus Guest Fee (if applicable)
- ❖ Ask for the maintenance amount and a percentage above ($375 x 20 percent = $450) plus Guest Fee (if applicable)
- ❖ Ask for 50 percent of a comparable hotel room, per night, in your timeshare location
  ($150/night divided by 50 percent = $75/night then x 7 nights = $525) plus Guest Fee (if applicable)
- ❖ Determine a rental price by dividing your maintenance fee by seven (7) nights
  ($375 divided by 7 = $ 53.60/night then consider
  Renting for $75 /night = $ 525)
  plus Guest Fee (if applicable)

Collecting the Money

Deposit: Prospective renters should pay at least 50 percent **up front** when they make their reservation. This is important. If you do not collect at least 50 percent at the very beginning of the transaction, they may change their mind and not bother to tell you. Fifty percent ensures that, should they change their mind, they will call you and try to get their deposit back.

Balance of the 50 percent is due 15 to 30 days before the rental period. After I have received the final payment, I send an information package to them.

Cancellation Policy:

> 120 days prior to use - Full refund less $50 charge
> 60-120 days - Full refund less $150 charge
> Less than 60 days - No refund.

The penalties for canceling are obvious. You have had to take this week, or unit, out of "your rental pool," which could be rented by someone else. Even if they had made a deposit on a vacation package with a travel agent, they would have to pay a cancellation fee.

The method of **Receiving Money** is up to you. Certified check, money order and PayPal are all acceptable and guaranteed methods of getting your money. Cash is fine if the renter lives nearby. Taking uncertified checks or doing a wire transfers (giving out your personal banking information to a stranger) is a gamble in any transaction, so use your judgment.

If you own your own company and have the ability do credit card transactions, this method will make it easier for all concerned.

Damage deposit: This is an area no one, particularly a landlord, wants to face. However, it is important that you make some arrangements to cover any damages made by your renter. If you do not, your resort will charge you personally. Make whatever arrangements you need to protect yourself against a bad renter.

I provide my prospective renters with a damage waiver form that they must sign. This form includes their credit card number, which will be given to the resort in case any damages are incurred. This protects you against damages caused by your renter.

Advertising your Rental

Advertising your week may be as simple as word of mouth or as complicated as using the Internet, the choice is yours. I have been lucky because my weeks have been rented through the word of mouth, but I know others that have achieved success from their lunchroom bulletin board.

When advertising your week(s) for rent, make it as creative or as simple as you want. If you are going to use some form of print media, the cost of the ad could be a limiting factor. Do not forget to include advertising costs in your rental fee.

Below are some suggestions for you. Use as many of the following methods as you feel are necessary. If you have an opportunity to use free classified advertising space, definitely take advantage of that.

- ❖ Word of mouth
- ❖ Friends and family
- ❖ Facebook, Twitter, Linked In, Blogs and other professional and personal social media sites
- ❖ Business associates - this is where the majority of my renters come from
- ❖ Internet - anyone of the thousands of free websites
- ❖ EBay
- ❖ Bulletin board(s) where you work - all of them
- ❖ Local or neighborhood newspapers
- ❖ Metropolitan newspapers
- ❖ Association or Club magazines and newsletters

Paperwork

As with any business transaction, paperwork is important. The old days of doing business on a handshake may initially seal the deal, but it is the paperwork that binds it. You will not need a lawyer to draw up any complex contracts, so long as you keep things simple. I have, over the years, created sheets and forms so that there are NO misunderstandings between parties.

I also provide my renter's with an **Information Package,** which contains the following three things:

1. **Resort Information** sheets that contain the following information:
   - ❖ Where it is located - name, address telephone and facsimile numbers
   - ❖ Google directions on how to get there, including a map if within driving distance
   - ❖ Unit size and what are included - appliances, TV, DVD, iPod station, stereo, dishes, etc
   - ❖ What amenities are offered at the resort - tennis, golf, pool, beach, etc
   - ❖ What facilities are offered at the resort - spa or gym, laundry, shopping
   - ❖ What facilities or amenities that are offered nearby
   - ❖ What local transportation is offered, and cost - bus, taxi, car rental, etc
   - ❖ Map of area - if available from your local tourism board
   - ❖ Name, address and numbers of you, the owner in case of emergency

2. **Rules and Regulations Sheet:** This sheet can be photocopied from the one provided with your membership. If your membership package did not include these, make up simple rules that you know are enforced at your resort.
3. **Comment Sheet:** These help you keep track of what is happening at your resort. They also provide valuable comments from your renters. Do up a sheet similar to one from your last exchange.

Remember, you are renting something that you own. Just as if you were renting your house, take all the precautions necessary to insure that your risk is minimal. Just because people sound great on the telephone does not necessarily mean they are trustworthy and reliable. The reverse applies as well. If you treat your renters fairly and honestly, they will respect your property and may, quite possibly, become regular renters or even buyers.

Should you have a renter who wishes to rent for future years, follow the same steps as if they were just renting from you for this year. Take a deposit (50 percent) of whatever you will charge for those weeks. As you have to pay your maintenance fees in advance, this money should cover them, plus a little more for yourself. In the case of future rentals, I suggest you do a simple contract outlining the terms, monies paid and when the balance of the money is due. This will insure that no confusion or misunderstanding occurs. I have a number of renters on contract where it not only works well but also eliminates worry about the coming year(s).

Renting to family and friends is always a good way to go. Yes, I did say renting. If you choose to give your week away to family and friends that is one thing, but if you need or want the money, rent it to them. So long as you cover your maintenance fee, it is still an inexpensive way for someone you care about to vacation.

Remember, rent only if you cannot use or exchange your week. Finally, never give up your use week unless you get reasonable compensation for it.

Following are some samples of paperwork I use for my rentals.

HAPPY RENTING

RESERVATION REQUEST FORM

Name:_____   Telephone:(___)_____

Address:_____   Email:_____

City:_____   Zip/_____ Cellular:(___)_____

Number of people traveling?_____

Unit that sleeps: □ 2 □ 4 □ 6 □ 8 □ More
When would you like to travel? (Chose 3 date options)
Choose your location?[14]
    □ 2 Bedroom -- Fairmont Hot Springs, BC Canada
    □ 1 Bedroom -- Las Vegas, NV USA
    □ 2 Bedroom -- Las Vegas, NV USA
    □ 1 Bedroom -- St. Maarten, Netherlands Antilles
    □ 1 Bedroom -- Puerto Vallarta, Mexico[15]
OR Where would you like to travel? (Chose 3 locations)[16]
Can you travel within 60 days? □ No □ Yes
Short notice weeks are available in select locations, are you interested?
    □ No   □ Yes
Is location important to you? □ No □ Yes, explain:_____
Are there any Handicap restrictions? □ No □ Yes, explain:_____
(Not all resorts are handicap accessible)

Payment and Cancellation Terms:
1. A deposit of 50 percent is required upon your reservation request. Return this form with payment.
2. The balance of payment is due 15-30 days before rent period. If you fail to pay the balance, this will result in forfeit of your deposit and use of the week.
3. Cancellation Policy:
   - 120 days prior to use -- Full refund less $50 charge
   - 60-120 days -- Full refund less $150 charge
   - Less than 60 days -- No refund
4. If you make a reservation for a week within 60 days and cancel there is NO refund.

Please Scan and email back to abcsmtih@yahoo.com

---

[14]   These units are fixed weeks but may be changed with sufficient notice.

[15]   These units are floating weeks available on first-come, first-served basis.

[16]   These would be exchange weeks utilizing one of the above locations, with sufficient notice.

RENTAL RECEIPT

DATE

YOUR NAME   Telephone:123 - 456-789
123 Villa Blvd.   Cellular:234 - 457-891
Boston, MA10000   E-mail:_____

Received from:_____ Mr. Renter _____

    Address   Telephone:
    Address   Work Telephone:
    City, State or Province   Cell:
    Zip Code   E-mail:

The amount of $ (600) for the rental of: (1 Bedroom) Condominium located in Puerto Vallarta, Mexico for the week(s) of____(date)____to____(date)____ inclusive.

Payment of $_____□ Certified check □ Wire Transfer □ PayPal
OR
    Credit card charge:_____□ VISA □ MasterCard   □
    Other:_____
    Name of Cardholder:_____Expiry Date:_____
    Card Number:_____
    Issuing Bank:_____

I do hereby authorize (your name) to charge to my credit card the sum of $_____Cardholder Signature:_____
Deposit of $_____Paid:_____(date)
Balance of $_____Due:_____(date) or □ Paid
Deposit is non-refundable if cancellation notification not received by:____(date)
For cancellation terms refer to reservation request sheet.

DAMAGE DEPOSIT WAIVER FORM

I, (We)_____(All Renter's names)_____understand that we are renting a_____(studio, 1, 2, 3 bedroom)_____condominium unit at_____(Resort name)___for the period of_____week(s) from_____to_____inclusive. I (We) also understand that any damage to the condominium unit, or its= contents, will be our responsibility entirely.

Should the condominium unit require any repairs or maintenance upon check-in, I (We) will advise the manager of the resort so that the necessary repairs can be made. This will be done without charge to either party as it is the responsibility of the resort to maintain the unit.

I (We) understand that any damage to the unit will be subject to payment by me in the following manner:

Pre Payment or Deposit in the amount of $_____

□ Certified check □ PayPal

OR

Credit card charge: □ VISA □ MasterCard □ Other:_____

Name of Cardholder:_____Expiry Date:_____

Card Number:_____

Issuing Bank:_____

I do hereby authorize (your name) to charge to my credit card the sum of $_____Cardholder Signature:_____

This form will be SIGNED and RETURNED with the Reservation Request Form.

Chapter 13

For Sale, One Timeshare...

Okay, so you want to sell your timeshare for all the right reasons. You are financially strapped and can no longer come up with the monthly payment or the annual maintenance fees. There should be absolutely NO other reason for wanting to sell it.

You think that there might be a good reason. You do not want it anymore, you do not like it anymore, and it does not work as promised or just because you think you made a mistake in buying one in the first place. Any of those reasons, though rational, is more than likely due to problems you may have met with since buying.

Unfortunately resales have created a big black eye for the timeshare industry. Industry experts state that resale's have become the nemesis of the industry. Resale issues are one of the biggest problems, and are the prime factor in limiting the growth of the industry. Until this issue is resolved, the image of timeshare will suffer.

Not only is the resale issue affecting the public perception of the industry, it is also responsible, indirectly for the difficulties in selling new units. When an owner cannot sell their week they get disgruntled and tell someone, who tells someone else or worse, post negative comments on social media. This then propagates the theory "bad news travels faster than good news." How do you think those pre-conceived ideas and negatives spread so quickly?

How many people want to sell their weeks? Actual hard numbers are limited and industry surveys have found out that 12 percent of owners were trying to sell their weeks. Worldwide this would be approximate 800,000 owners. Is this a large number? Yes, relatively speaking it could be. However, we have to remember that there are almost seven million timeshare owners throughout the world so this 12 percent is a very small number proportionally. Statistically, a large number of people have thought about selling their intervals, but, not surprisingly, price was the only motivation.

WHY DO YOU WANT TO SELL?

Why would you want to sell a lifetime, or perhaps 30 years, worth of great vacations? Before you decide to sell what you own, think back to the excitement and emotion you felt when you bought that week. What has caused you to lose that good feeling? On the surface, financial considerations are the number one reason for owners wishing to sell. While there are other valid reasons, such as illness, divorce or quite possibly that you need a much larger or smaller sized unit, the main reason, I believe, is the lack of owner education.

Why would anyone want to sell a future of great vacations? With all the options available through the exchange companies - vacation any time, anywhere; discounted airfares; rental cars; cruises; golf; skiing; shopping and much more - why would you want to sell? Primarily, if the timeshare owner does not know how to use what they own, or understand the benefits or features, available to them, the easiest way out is to sell.

According to a recent industry survey, the number one reason that people gave for wanting to sell their timeshare: it did not work for them as promised. When asked in more detail why, owners responded primarily that they could not get the exchanges they wanted. Again, this reflects the lack of owner education.

If I had any doubts about initially writing this book, this section dissolved them. Even before I was doing timeshare sales, the most common complaint that I heard from owners was - it does not work! When asked why, owners eventually confessed that they really did not understand how to make an exchange or use the benefits properly. Chapter 10 covered making the most of your exchanges and benefits so now you should be willing, or trying, to give your timeshare another chance. **Before** you decide to sell, try using the information given you. If, after using the options I have outlined in previous Chapters, you still are unhappy, then of course, SELL IT.

This balance of this Chapter will provide you with any or all the information that you will need to sell your timeshare. Like a resale company, I cannot and do not guarantee you will sell yours, but at least it will give you the right information to will increase your resale chances considerably.

HOW LONG WILL IT TAKE?

One thing to remember when selling your timeshare week - PATIENCE IS A VIRTUE. Yes, it is an old cliché, but true. Where your home may sell in a couple of weeks or months, your timeshare may take longer, and always a lot longer than you think it should. If you are not in dire financial straight, then time is your friend and you can wait to get a fair price. If time is your enemy, remember patience is a virtue.

From the date you start actively marketing your week, or giving it to a resale company, anticipate waiting from twelve to eighteen months if you own a prime week, or points, in a premium location. If you own an off-season week or points in a low demand area it could be much more than eighteen months before you get an offer.

WHAT PRICE SHOULD I ASK?

That is the million-dollar question. You may not want to hear this but all of those vacations that you took by owning your timeshare have paid for themselves tenfold during your ownership. Typically timeshares will resell anywhere from 35 - 55 percent of the developers pricing structure with some areas in the world may selling for less.

Ask a fair and reasonable price. Take into consideration how many years you have owned it and what you paid for it. The total maintenance, assessment, exchange and membership fees you have paid then, HONESTLY, compare it with what those vacations would have cost you doing it your "old way."

Here's a little calculator for you:

Purchase price (or financed price):_____
Exchange fees paid during term of ownership:_____
    Maintenance fees paid during term of ownership:_____
    Assessment fees paid during term of ownership:_____
                      TOTAL $ Paid_____
      Divide by:
          Number of year's ownership:_____
                  TOTAL $ per year_____
      Divide by:
          Number of persons who vacationed per year_____
          TOTAL $ per person per year_____

If you have traveled to far away lands and taken advantage of all the benefits available, take those into consideration. One European vacation can cost as much as owning one week. If you owned for five years before selling, you have saved a considerable sum of money. Alternately, if you have never left your home state or gone anywhere other than Mexico, you may have broken even.

You may think that I am full of BS saying this, but that's okay. I do realize if you own a two-bedroom condo on the beach in St. Maarten it may take ten years worth of ownership to break even, but you will still come out ahead.

What is a fair price? Use good old-fashioned common sense. If you have broken even over the years, ask a reasonable price. If you have come out ahead with the benefits, ask a more reasonable price. If you honestly believe that you have lost money, be realistic and ask a reasonable price and write off the difference as one of life's sweet ironies and take an IRS tax deduction, if you are eligible.

THE TRUTH ABOUT RESELLING YOUR WEEK

1. You will **never** get what you think the week(s) are worth.
2. Resale is controlled by Supply and Demand where YOUR timeshare is located.
3. Resale falls into several areas that will affect your price:

   Standard: Generally about 95 percent of timeshares can be realistically resold.

   Resale pricing is typically 35 to 50 percent of developer's new price.

   Tropical: This generally depends on the location, whether beach front or not, and the time (years) remaining on the right-to-use.

   Resale pricing is typically 30 to 40 percent of developer's new price.

   Premium: These properties include Four Season, Ritz Carlton, Disney, Hilton, Marriott, Fairfield and others that may include a membership program in which the owner receives credits. These programs are similar to frequent flyer or hotel type programs.

Resale pricing runs typically 70-90 percent of developer's new price. There are rare instances of getting what was paid, plus a little bit more.

Cheap Stuff: These are locations where demand is low or non existent for exchange purposes. These are most likely off season weeks and hotel efficiency units.

Resale pricing: Take whatever you can and "get the hell out of Dodge." Otherwise have someone just take over the payments, maintenance fees and give you a buck to make you feel better.

Points: As you will see in the next chapter on points, not all points are created equal and depending on the resort where your points are located your resale options may be limited. However, current owners of points are your best resale source. For example, if you own Disney points you should look for another Disney point's owner who wants more points.

Note: Some points programs, when resold to a non-family member revert to the resorts most basic membership, with no transfer of the benefits that came with the original membership. This is usually noted in the Rules & Regulations under transfers.

Resale Pricing: Some Points based programs can sell for close to the original purchase price, however for the most part expect anywhere from 30 to 45 percent of developer's new price.

4. Check internet resale sites to compare prices on your resort and unit size as well as comparable locations and unit sizes. Resale prices can vary from one end of the spectrum to the other for your unit and location.

5. When using a resale company keep in mind the following things are taken into consideration before they determine a price. These are: the size of the unit, age, season, the location and pricing of similar properties in the same area.

WHAT ARE MY RESALE OPTIONS?

Selling it Yourself

This involves talking to as many people as you can and becoming immune to the negative responses you will undoubtedly hear. With thick skin and perseverance you will do just fine when selling your week(s). If you are shy, however, I would highly recommend using any one of the following options.

Striking up a conversation with someone regarding traveling will usually get around traveling methods. This then ultimately leads you to utter those frightening words, "I own a timeshare." If the person you are talking to is interested, they will ask questions and well... that could lead to just about anything. I have run into people who have sold weeks on a bus tour in Hawaii, sitting under a palapa/umbrella in Puerto Vallarta, over coffee in the company lunchroom and in a bar at happy hour. There is no set time, place or circumstance that occurs, other than just being in the right place at the right time.

A couple of things to remember if you are considering selling your week(s) yourself:

- ❖ You are responsible for any transfer fees associated with the sale. This will make it easier on the buyer. You can build this cost into your sales price if you want or just ask the buyer to pay it.
- ❖ Decide how you are going to handle the transfer of any moneys - both the deposit and final payments. Possibly consider using a PayPal account as a means of making payments rather than give out confidential banking information.
- ❖ Have all of your documentation associated with property all together in one place. At the end of this Chapter is a resale checklist to assist you in gathering what documentation you should have. If you do not feel comfortable doing the transfer yourself, ask your vacation club or Home Owners Association to assist you.

Should you finance a sale? Only you can answer that question. If you feel that you can trust the buyer to make the payments on time, go ahead. Do up a simple contract outlining the sale amount, the down payment and payment terms. These days you can find all types of contract formats on line so find one that works for your situation and use it. You should also include some means in which to repossess or take back the week if payments fail to be made. Have both parties sign and notarize it.

Should you use a lawyer? Again, only you can determine that. If you do, select one who specializes in real estate or timeshare law to assure that nothing is overlooked. If the sale is a large one ($20,000+), I would suggest that you retain a lawyer and put any deposit moneys into an escrow account until the transactions are completed.

Another important point to remember, if you do not price your unit realistically ... no one will ever be able to sell it, including yourself.

Resale Companies

Just as mentioned under rental companies, as there are bad timeshare sellers out there, remember that there are also unscrupulous RE-sellers out there. You should be careful when choosing a resale or transfer company. **You should NEVER have to prepay for this service upfront.** Many are reputable but, many are not. Ask people you know who have sold a week through a reseller or transfer company what their experiences were and would if they recommend that company. Ask people for referrals and listen to them.

Timeshare resale brokers can get you the most exposure, but remember you will have to pay for it in some manner. Payment will be for either an advertising charge or a commission after the sale.

10 Questions to Ask the Resale Company

1. Are you licensed to sell real estate in your state and/or country? By whom?
2. How many listings does your company have?
3. How many sales did you have last year?
4. How will you sell my property?
5. How long does it take to sell a property on average - based on my location?
6. Who pays for the transfer of property?
7. Can you provide me with the names of some sellers for references?
8. Can you provide me with a list of recent sales - including the price?
9. What is the commission structure? Paid when?
10. Where do you advertise?

Precautions when using a resale company

1. Companies must provide FULL disclosure on:

    ❖ Any fees, commissions and any other costs payable by the consumer for the service;
    ❖ Any fees collected must be placed into a trust account on behalf of the owner. These fees must be used for the benefit of the owner only and used for services promised;
    ❖ The terms of the listing contract;
    ❖ What methods will be used to sell the timeshare and how it will be advertised; the average amount of time that passes, expressed in weeks, months or years, before the company locates a resale purchaser who completes a resale transaction;
    ❖ Disclosure of successful resale's within the most recent calendar year if asked;
    ❖ They **must** state that a price CANNOT be guaranteed;
    ❖ They **must** disclose that is NOT possible to guarantee that a sale will occur within a specific period of time;
    ❖ They **must** keep records of the number of inquiries made by prospective buyers for any listings that they hold;
    ❖ They **must** maintain a permanent address, phone number and keep regular business hours.

2. Find out how you can receive regular updates on the status of your timeshare.
3. As the salesperson to send you written materials regarding their resale process.
4. Be leery of companies offering gimmicks "guaranteed sale in two weeks."
5. Do not make immediate decisions regarding listing with the resale company if you have any hesitations regarding their reliability. Do not agree to anything over the phone until you have had a chance to check out the company.
6. Ask if the resale company is licensed in its home state. Check with the real estate commissions to verify the information.
7. If you can investigate the company's background and history of resale success.
8. If you experience any difficulty or problems contact the Better Business Bureau, state and local real estate commissions, consumer protections agencies, consumer reporters or the state/province's Attorney General.
9. Do not give any up front money to a Resale company to sell your week(s) if you do not feel comfortable working with them.

10. For your piece of mind ask if they are members of ARDA and do they follow ARDA's Code of Standards and Ethics. If they do, use them. Though ARDA does not endorse or recommend any particular resale company, they do regulate the timeshare industry as a whole.

Using your Home Resort's Resale Department

No, do not rush to the telephone and call your home resort unless you are SURE that they have a resale program for the members. If they do not, you will only become frustrated with the person on the other end of the telephone. Then they become irritated and you will ultimately end the call with a sour taste in your mouth for your resort.

Although some resorts DO HAVE resale programs, it is not the norm in the industry, yet. This is because most developers would rather sell their inventory first before reselling member intervals. Second, once they have sold out their properties, it is usually not worth their time or effort to operate a resale program. Only about 37 percent of mainly older, more established timeshare resorts have member resale programs, and only 13 percent have any plans to add them in the next five years.

The resorts that have resale programs have learned that it is better to keep good, happy members than to create future problems by not first offering to resell member weeks. These resorts, know that in buying back their members weeks will keep up the value of their resorts, rather than disgruntled owners failing to pay maintenance or assessment fees that could lead to future problems. Newer, smaller resorts find it too costly from a financial and legal basis to operate a resale program.

Personally, I believe all resorts, once they have sold out, offer a member resale program for that very reason, keeping up the value of the property. Developers need to understand that members will, at some point, want to sell what they own and should be doing whatever they can to assist in the process. Second, a strong resale market will become even more important as the baby boomer generation ages. As owners get older, more and more wish to sell their weeks rather than utilize them. The third, and most important, reason for resale programs, it will clean up the industry's black eye.

If your resort has a resale program, use it. Ask the right questions and ask a fair price. Just because the resort is selling your week does not necessarily mean that you will gain sudden wealth. Also be prepared to pay a commission to the resort for selling your weeks. Commission rates do vary from 10-35 percent of selling price.

Friends, Relatives or Independents

Using friends, relatives or independents to sell your weeks is fine if they are familiar with the timeshare industry. For example, asking a friend who knows nothing about cars to sell your old faithful Camaro will most likely lead to frustration. If anyone asks them a question regarding its performance or mechanical status they would be continually calling you for the information, thus becoming a go-between rather than selling it for you.

Now, do not get me wrong, you can use friends, relatives and independents to help spread the word that you are looking to sell your week(s). The more people that know you are selling will greatly increase your chances. Should a prospective buyer have any questions, provide each person with a single, typed information sheet. You can choose to include the price or not on the sheet. Make sure to include all contact names and numbers on the information sheet. Remember, be patient.

If a friend, relative or independent person provides a buyer for your week(s) give them a commission. It will make selling anything else for you in the future much easier. Usually 10 to 15 percent of the sale price is appropriate as a commission.

Alternatively, if that friend, relative or independent wants to buy your week(s), work out an acceptable price, take the cash and sign it over to them.

The Internet and Social Media

If you are able to surf the web and use social media you can place an advertisement or notice on your Facebook page, Tweet about it, put it on eBay or Craigslist or with any one of the 200 plus Internet Resale companies. Remember to use the same precautions that you would when choosing a non-Internet resale company or broker. If you are not computer literate, but your children or a friend is, ask them to place an advertisement or notice on the web or on a Facebook page. If your family has their own website, list your timeshare there as well, the more exposure the better.

Internet resale company web sites do contain sections called FAQ's (Frequently Asked Questions). I would recommend that you read these carefully before choosing to do business with any company. Resale companies that do not charge any UP FRONT FREE will advise you on their home pages. Companies that do charge a fee should explain their fee very clearly within their web site and you should think twice about prepaying for a service that has not been provided.

Post as many advertisements as you can on the FREE Internet sections that will allow you to do so. Many web sites do offer free classified ads. Online services such as AOL and Prodigy and others all have free or low cost classifieds.

You will also see advertisements from companies offering to ¨resell your timeshare¨ appear as pop-up advertisements on a number of sites. This is especially true if you Google search timeshare resale companies which lead to these pop-ups to appear as it was something you had searched for online.

eBay

Yes, I did say eBay. eBay Real Estate is now involved in both the timeshare resale and rental business. Since eBay has a global user base of over 322 million[17] user registered users it has become the largest marketplace in the world it provides a welcome platform for skeptics and bargain hunters alike the opportunity to buy, or sell, their timeshare or vacation ownership property. Although eBay does not directly sell timeshares or vacation ownership property they do offer developers and resale brokers the opportunity to make their properties available. So before you rush to log on and list your timeshare, you will need to register your week(s) with a resale broker who is currently part of the eBay Real Estate consortium. For more information, contact eBay Real Estate. Rentals can also be done on eBay.

Craigslist

Craigslist is not specifically setup to give their any real estate listing national exposure. It is more designed for selling items a washer or furniture items to people in your local area. Remember, Craigslist makes it nearly impossible to sell a timeshare or any item where you need nationwide exposure. For example, you live in Seattle, WA and your timeshare is in Hawaii. Should you list your timeshare on the Seattle section or the Hawaii

---

[17]   Ebay Company Profile 2014

section? If you advertise your timeshare only in your local section, then only people living in your area going to see your listing. If you put your ad in the Hawaii section, then only people living in Hawaii will see it. Think about it, would someone in Hawaii want to buy a timeshare in Hawaii? If you think that Craigslist can help you resell your timeshare, give it try, but remember there is no national exposure.

Print Alternatives

Print advertisements should be placed in your local newspapers for as long as you can afford it. If you live in a small community it might be more advantageous to place the advertisement in a major metropolitan newspaper. Trade magazines are also available for advertising.

If you belong to any association or clubs with a newsletter or monthly magazine this could also provide an alternate source of advertisement. This is because newsletters are sent to a wide variety of people throughout your town, state or the country.

Make your advertisements easy to read and eye catching. Use your imagination. Try to picture what would attract you to an ad and write it that way. Push all the benefits that space allows, or write something eye catching enough so that people call. Please remember, if you are trying to sell a Green week in East Texas, you will have to use a considerable amount of imagination when writing the advertisement.

Sample: Want to be a world traveler? Opportunity exists to experience world travel for a fraction of cost.

Timeshare for sale in (location). $XXXXX. Do not want to part with it, but have to.

If your local telephone company provides a reasonably priced, temporary, 800 numbers for personal use, get one and make it easier for people to call. Remember, people hate to spend their money, even if it looks like a bargain.

SHOULD I BUY A RESALE WEEK?

This is your choice. There are many things to take into consideration when buying a resale week. Here are some tips to think about before you leap into that great deal:

- ❖ If it looks to good to be true, it probably is - look for the catch;
- ❖ Be aware that there may a lien against the interval if there are any taxes or maintenance fees owed by the seller;
- ❖ Verify with the resort what, if any, the current owner obligations are;
- ❖ Verify with the resort exactly what it is you will be purchasing against their records - remember it is their records, not the owners that determine the above two items;
- ❖ Do a Title search for outstanding liens against the week (fixed or deeded ownership) if you doubt the seller's words;
- ❖ Purchase title insurance and use a company known to the resort if this is important to you;
- ❖ The seller should pay for transfer fees;
- ❖ If the price is reasonable and terms can be agreed to, go for it.
- ❖ Use common sense, or a lawyer, if you do not posses any of the former.☺

RESALE CHECKLIST

Whether it is your home, vacation home or a timeshare, all the same steps are involved in selling real estate. Before selling your interval, make sure that you have all the paperwork involved together in one file folder. This insures that the buyer has everything necessary to take over ownership.

Use the following checklist to help you gather what you need.

- ❖ ALL contact information, including any e-mail addresses for the resort and your membership club
- ❖ The deed, right-to-use contract or any other membership agreements
- ❖ Any financing, contract or lien agreements (if you are still paying for it)
- ❖ Any release documentation if property is paid for in full
- ❖ Any Title of Insurance policy documentation
- ❖ All information that identifies your membership in the resort
- ❖ Any documentation you have relating to your exchange affiliation (membership numbers, catalogues, newsletters, etc.)
- ❖ Documentation showing the amount and date of maintenance or assessment fees
- ❖ Documentation showing the amount of any real estate taxes (if paid separately)
- ❖ Any newsletters pertaining to your resorts vacation club or Home Owner's Association

- ❖ Name of contact within the vacation club or Home Owners Association
- ❖ **The <u>most</u> important thing to remember is to know whether or not your vacation interest is legally classified as real estate or personal property**

The following pages list some questions you should have the answers to if you are planning to sell your timeshare, by any means. The others are just to find out which areas you are unhappy with and, maybe with a little more knowledge, can use if effectively and not need to sell it.

Good luck and it may soon be…

Sold, One Timeshare

RESALE QUESTIONNAIRE

1. **Why do you want to sell it?** □ Can't Use □ Can't afford it
   Elaborate:_____
2. **Did you ever exchange with it?** □ Yes   □ No   □ Sometimes
   How Often? □ 1   □ 2-5 □ 6-10   □ 11-20 □ More 20 times
3. **RESORT INFORMATION**
   Name of Resort:_____
   Address:_____
   State/Province:_____ Country:_____Zip/Postal Code:_____
   Telephone: (___)_____ Facsimile (_)_____
   Contact Person:_____ Position:_____
   E-Mail: (if known)_____ Other:_____
   Contract and/or Membership Number:_____
   Year Purchased?_____
   What size of unit do you own?   □ Hotel Studio/Efficiency
       □ 1 Bedroom □ 2 Bedroom   □ 3 Bedroom
       □ Other
   Does it have a lock off?   □ Yes □ No □ Can't Remember
   Number of Weeks Owned: □ 1 □ 2 □ 3   □ More 4 How Many____
   Season or Week Numbers:_____ □ Fixed □ Floating
   Check in Day: □ Friday   □ Saturday   □ Sunday
       □ Any Day
   Name of your HOA or Vacation Club?_____
   Is it Points or a Coupon Based Program: □ Yes □ No Total Points
   Exchange Company Affiliations: □ RCI   □ II   □ Other:
   Membership Number(s): RCI_____ II_____
   Is your Resort a member of the American Resort Development
   Association or Equivalent?: □ Ye □ No □ Don't Know

   HOA or Vacation Club

4. Have you had any problems with them? □ Yes □ No
   If yes, elaborate:_____
5. Are you unhappy with the management of your resort? □ Yes □ No
6. Were you promised things during your sales presentation that did
   not happen?   □ Yes   □ No_____
7. Has your unit become   □ Too big □ Too small for your use?
8. Did you buy during □ Wrong season?   □ Wrong week?
9. Are you able to get the exchanges you request?   □ Yes □ No
   □ Sometimes
10. Which fees do you think are too high? □ Exchange □ Maintenance
    □ Membership
11. Did you purchase during your □ 1st □ 2nd or more Sales Presentation?

155

12. Would you rather own a timeshare closer to home? ☐ Yes ☐ No
13. Has your resort ceased operations? ☐ Yes ☐ No ☐ Don't Know
14. **Status of Ownership:** ☐ Paid in Full ☐ Still Making Payments

What did you pay for it? _____

Balance owing? _____

If making payments, How much per month? _____

Term of Financing? (months) _____

Interest Rate? _____

How long before paid in full? _____

Title Insurance: ☐ Yes ☐ No ☐ Don't Know
15. **Maintenance Fees?** ☐ Paid to Date ☐ Outstanding

How much per week? _____

What date are fees due? _____

Assessment fees? ☐ Paid to Date ☐ Outstanding

What date are fees due? _____

How much will it cost you to transfer the membership? _____

16. What do you think a realistic asking price would be now?

Chapter 14

Points, Coupons and/ or Vacation Clubs?

To this point I have covered everything you ever wanted to know ad nauseam. By this chapter you are either interested in the concept enough to attend a sales presentation or have only persevered to this point to find out "who" did it. Just Kidding! Seriously, I would not be doing my job if I did not cover something about the alternatives to tangible ownership: point systems, coupon systems and vacation clubs.

Tangible ownership is referred to as ownership of real property. You can touch and feel it. You have a deed or right-to-use, fixed or floating week ownership. This is where your contract refers to a specific week of ownership within the resort that you can claim a right to in future. Points or coupon systems are intangible alternatives - currency as it were - that can be traded and used to vacation.

Vacation clubs, points or coupon-based systems provide a very flexible use of accommodations in multiple resort locations. Here's why...

POINTS

In all my early years of ownership I knew very little about the points and coupon side of the industry. For the first publishing of this book, to get the correct information on what point systems really were and what they can really do for you; I spent considerable time talking to both exchange companies, people who owned points systems and salespeople who sold them. I also talked with resorts and developers who have been involved in their development and growth.

One very important fact - Not all points systems are created equal, but whether the program offers 10 points per year or 1000 points per year for your ownership interest, they all do the same things and exchange basically the same way. The differences are in the vacation clubs that promote them.

Points based systems are almost as old as timeshare itself. Started in the Switzerland in 1963 by a group of European developers they caught on throughout the world. They were touted as a more economical means of buying a vacation package. They have grown into a flexible vacation alternative. They came to the United States in the 1970's, and in 1989 Trend West created its World Mark properties with a few locations in the Northwest. Today, point based systems are now an integral part of the hospitality industry. Disney, Marriott, Hilton, Westin Vacation Club, Fairfield, Royal Holiday Club, Shell Vacations and others are providing consumers with programs offering travel related services for point redemption, such as airline tickets and hotel stays, either within their system or comparable alternatives. At present, 22 percent of new resorts offer a point based system, whereas 28 percent of older projects offer points. Points programs have become so successful that 43 percent of all new timeshare purchases are at points based resorts.

Rather than buying a set number of week's ownership, the consumer buys a certain number of points or a form of ownership that is valued at a specific number of points that provides them access to resort accommodations and amenities for a specific term of ownership. Ownership can range from as little one year, (campground type systems) to deed in perpetuity. Points are an exchange program based on the traditional week-based exchange system. The difference is that it creates a flexible infrastructure so that point's owners may opt for the more familiar week for week exchange or covert their points to shorter or longer stays, cruises, airfare discounts and other options.

Cost is determined by the number of points bought or the specific unit purchased or the number of points that are required for a week's vacation at that location or "home resort." The consumer will buy a certain number of points each year or a specific unit type based on what they feel will meet their needs: A specific sized unit, season, and number of nights, number of units, room orientation, resort location or other amenities available.

In other words, owners receive the right-to-use a package of points or a specific unit type however they prefer either within their club or after depositing with an exchange company. For example a program of 1500 points for a one bedroom can possibly be used as follows:

- ❖ 1500 points - One week in a one bedroom during high season at your home resort
- ❖ 1500 points - Two weeks in a lower season in a lower demand area in a larger unit
- ❖ 1200 points – One week vacation, high demand area, holiday season in a studio unit
- ❖ 800 points – Four day weekend stay in a high demand area, but not holiday weeks
- ❖ 2500 points – One week cruise in Caribbean (bringing forward or drawing points)

The number of points needed is based on the location, season, and the size of the unit and number of nights that you wish to stay. For those owners who wish to take a number of mini-vacations points systems given them flexibility and options not widely available to a traditional timeshare owner.

Some programs do allow members to **save points** to the next use year or **borrow points** from a future use year so they can get a bigger unit in their home resort, take that cruise, go to Europe or use a four-bedroom condo in Hawaii in February. Each program varies the number of years that can be carried forward or drawn on. If this is a critical feature for you, ask specifically during the presentation.

There are also some resorts that will allow you to **buy additional points** to upgrade a particular year's vacation requirements. For example, you normally travel with your spouse but one particular year you wish to take your large extended family skiing and need something more substantial than your "studio point" package. Cost for buying points varies from program to program. The industry presently ranges from approximately US$.75 to upwards of $62 per point.

To **utilize points** for timeshare exchange with either RCI or Interval your resort must first deposit a timeshare week with the exchange company.

Oh, the final thing, YES there is an annual **maintenance fee**. Just because you own points you still have to pay to maintain your "home resort." Fees run parallel to traditional timeshare locations near or where you own.

In the past fifteen years, especially since 2006, point systems, rather than the sale of weeks, have come to be the standard for new resorts and developments looking to expand their sales options and give buyers increased flexibility. Older resorts are converting what inventory they may have not sold to point based programs in order to keep up with the changes in the industry, so it was no surprise that both exchange companies created points based exchange options to give everyone more flexibility.

RCI points™

To exchange members exchange options, RCI created its RCI Points program in 2000. The program was designed to be a global system choosing when, where and how you want to vacation. Points based owners have a choice of not only utilizing their current RCI membership and exchange options but all the benefits and advantages of the Points program.

First, your home resort must be an RCI Points affiliate. Not every resort is affiliated with RCI Points and you should contact your home resort to find out if they are affiliated. If they are, you have the option of becoming a RCI Points member. If your resort is not affiliated you will need to purchase timeshare in a resort that has the RCI Points affiliation.

Do RCI Points differ from other Points Programs?

As mentioned earlier, points based clubs or resorts self-determine how many points they will offer buyers and set their own internal valuations. RCI Points are assigned by RCI based on your resort's location, quality, and its level of amenities and the size of the units. If they add amenities, such as new pools or tennis courts, the point value will likely go up. Standard developer points do not offer this benefit. It is important to remember that RCI points are NOT backed by real estate, as developer points are. RCI points are just an evaluation process.

Unlike other points programs, RCI points will be automatically carried forward to the next year if not used in the current Use year however they will not be carried forward for more than two years.

You can save and extend, or borrow points from your next use year if you wish to use a benefit that requires more points that you currently have for a given Use year. Most points program will allow you to return the borrowed points to the appropriate year if for some reason you need to cancel your reservation. You should however check with RCI for more details.

You can also rent additional RCI Points if you find yourself short for a particular vacation destination.

What do RCI Points do for me?

RCI Points allow you the flexibility of:

- ❖ Choosing how many days you want to stay at a either your home resort
- ❖ or another affiliated resort
- ❖ Choose what size unit you want or stay in any season
- ❖ Staying at your home resort if you prefer
- ❖ Save, rent or borrow points to create special vacations
- ❖ Use a portion of your points to exchange for discounts on airline tickets, rent cars, take cruises plus
- ❖ many other options at RCI's Points Partners

As an RCI Points member you also have access to the Weeks exchange program giving you access to any one RCI's nearly 4,500 affiliated resorts worldwide. You can choose to exchange to a location in RCI's Directory of Affiliated Resorts. You can request either a full week exchange at an RCI affiliated resort or you can break your vacation shorter periods at an RCI Points affiliated property.

Your reservation procedures do not vary that dramatically from the Weeks program, except that your standard reservation period is extended from 10 months in advance to thirteen months. RCI Points members have a priority period at their home resorts where they can book as early as thirteen months in advance of their check-in dates. To make a reservation at a resort within your home group of resorts, you may reserve a unit as early as 11 months in advance of your start date. Members need to be made aware there may be reservation fees required to make a reservation at your own resort.

If you are an RCI Points member your Points Membership Fees do include access to the Weeks exchange program.

Examples of using RCI Points (60,000 points)

A. A long weekend at a California Beach Resort in August
(3 nights in a one-bedroom and a discount on a 3-day car rental)
and
A Ski trip to the Rockies in December (7 nights in a one-bedroom unit)
B. Discount on a 4-day Caribbean cruise
C. Discount on a two round trip airline tickets to your choice of hundreds of destinations

If you already own at an RCI resort and wish to become an RCI Points Member, call your home resort and find out about converting your existing ownership to Points if it is affiliated with the program.

Whether you already own at a resort affiliated with the RCI Weeks program or the RCI Points program you can customize your vacation needs and take advantage of the opportunities and flexibility of vacation planning. If you are not a point owner, and wish to become one, there are many programs out there and hopefully I have helped to understand how they work.

Club Interval Gold

Club Interval is an exclusively designed points-based exchange service. The program allows Club Interval Gold members to deposit your fixed and/or floating resort timeshare week with Interval in exchange for Club Interval Points. Club Interval Gold members can redeem points for a seven-day vacation at any of Interval´s resorts, or stay a few days, or use toward a cruise, spa, golf, or tour vacation. Members can also combine and save points toward a future vacation. To be eligible to participate in Club Interval, members must own or purchase an eligible vacation interest in a resort or development that is enrolled in the Club Interval program.

Interval created the program in 2009 in order to provide members with the ultimate in travel flexibility. The possibilities within the program are almost endless, for example, you can:

* use your points for a weeklong vacation
* use your points towards a ShortStay Exchange, for vacations of one to six nights
* any of the Interval Options
* trade up for a larger unit to accommodate more people
* take smaller units, turning one deposit into multiple stays
* make one week into a series of shorter breaks
* combine points from future weeks for even greater trading power

Examples of using Club Interval Points (70,000 points)

A. Traditional week-based exchange
B. A long weekend at an Orlando Resort (55,250) plus 3 nights in the Poconos (12,909)
C. A week in Las Vegas (40,000) plus 2 nights in Palm Springs to golf (10,400) and still use 15,000 points towards a cruise

The best news, you can keep any of your unused points and they can be applied toward future exchanges.

The number of Club Interval Points that will be allotted to the member will be based on their deposit of a unit week and their choice to convert it to Club Interval Points.

Club Interval Weekly Points Values* are as follows:

TDI Range	4 Bedroom (Sleeps 10 privately)	3 Bedroom (Sleeps 8 privately)	2 Bedroom (Sleeps 6 privately)	1 Bedroom (Sleeps 4 privately)	Studio (Sleeps 2 privately)	Hotel Room (Sleeps 2 privately)
135-150	123,750 to 165,000	101,250 to 135,000	78,750 to 105,000	67,500 to 90,000	45,000 to 60,000	40,500 to 54,000
115-130	103,125 to 137,500	84,375 to 112,500	65,625 to 87,500	56,250 to 75,000	37,500 to 50,000	33,750 to 45,000
90 - 110	82,500 to 111,000	67,500 to 90,000	52,500 to 70,000	45,000 to 60,000	30,000 to 40,000	27,000 to 36,000
65 - 85	61,875 to 82,500	50,625 to 67,500	39,375 to 52,500	33,750 to 45,000	22,500 to 30,000	20,250 to 27,000
50 - 60	41,250 to 55,00	33,750 to 45,000	26,250 to 35,000	22,500 to 30,000	15,000 to 20,000	13,500 to 18,000

* The points are based on the Club Interval Weekly Points Values Chart, which was established by Interval and may be modified by them from time to time as industry needs change.

One last thing on be aware of with Club Interval Points - once you have deposited your home resort week as points it cannot be withdrawn.

Points have come a long way so this option may be something that if you do not already own, will consider as a very viable option to getting the most from your vacation dollars.

VACATION CLUBS

Resorts that have vacation clubs usually, but not always, involve dual or multiple location accommodations. Simplified, this means that the resort owns more than one property in locations throughout the country or world. These other locations are available for home resort use or on an internal exchange basis with either little or no charge. At present there are more than half of all resorts with some form of vacation club membership.

There are a number of vacation club programs that also consist of other services or products that, in many forms, resemble frequent flyer programs or frequent guest programs. For example, if you stayed in an affiliated hotel for a few days and rented a car you will acquire points that can be applied to your "vacation ownership" program. Conversely, your "vacation ownership" points may be converted into other alternatives. You will see this type of membership with the major hotel chains that offer a timeshare product.

Vacation clubs should not be confused with a Home Owners Association. A vacation club offers travel options, the Home Owners Association is responsible for your home resort and this is who you normally pay your maintenance fees to each year.

Vacation clubs may also offer their member's access to other types of lodging. Campgrounds, condominiums or trips on cruise ships - the choices are varied.

COUPONS

Coupons work almost similar to a point based system and has been around for about 20 years and are found in smaller, more intimate locations.

Cost is determined in much the same way as with points, based on the size of unit, season and the length of stay as well as the location of where you want to buy. They can be accumulated to upgrade your vacation or broken down to take mini-vacations to suit your needs. Coupon programs are normally sold in batches - for example 10, 20 or 50 coupons with pricing according to the package purchased.

Maintenance fees are lower due to the smaller nature of the resorts that do not require extensive staff or upkeep costs. Exchanges are made by securing a seven-day assignment from your home resort and depositing with the exchange company.

So Which System is Better?

Regardless of which type of system that you chose to use, there are pros and cons associated with your choices. Vacation Clubs are an extra program offered by resorts to travel between resorts with little or no charge or give other ¨perks¨ resembling frequent flyer points which can be used for other travel options.

Coupons are for those who do not think they would travel very much and purchasing the option of only ten visits is more appealing than a long term ownership commitment.

As I mentioned above, points based systems are coming into their own and offer members considerable flexibility when it comes to planning their vacations and expanding their membership options. Below and on the next page is a quick summary of the positives and negatives of point-based ownership.

Last, but certainly not least, just remember, the most important thing is not whether you own a fixed week, floating week, split week, deeded, right-to-use, fractional, points, coupons membership, etc. it is how you **choose** you to **USE** it.

On the POSITIVE side ...	On the NEGATIVE side ...
As lifestyle changes, points can be adapted to accommodate changes.	Developer must hold reserve inventory to accommodate point owners.
Offer new marketing or sales opportunities to buyers	Higher maintenance fees.
Equitable exchange opportunities	Higher purchase prices in high demand locations.
Allows a developer to blend unit types to meet specific member needs.	Requires larger and more technically qualified reservation and exchange staff.
Split week, day and weekend usage.	Additional use-cost to owners.
Eliminates decision of unit size.	Can create limited unit availability to members.
Easier to sell points to existing points owners.	No guarantees to owners of holiday or high demand week availability.

Little or no internal exchange costs.	Reduced point values in off or low season.
Use not limited to standard seasonal week designations.	No guarantee of season or unit size for owners.
Ability to "buy" points to upgrade.	Potential inventory problems due to overselling.
Vacation flexibility.	Harder to exchange externally.
Good resale market, especially to existing Points owners.	Regulatory concerns.
	Unproved track record.
	Intangible ownership. Not considered a real estate investment.
	No recognized uniformity within programs.

Chapter 15

What are My Rights? Am I Protected?

In the early years the words "caveat-emptor" or "buyers beware" were the prevailing philosophy in the timeshare industry. In today's market, to quote old song lyrics, "times they are a changing," Consumers are no longer the misinformed, naive, trusting souls of yesteryear. They are now very well versed with the term's misrepresentation and lawsuit. Because societal and consumer expectations are changing, so must the timeshare industry. This chapter will cover the legalities of who is doing what to look after your best interests.

Although you feel confident in what you own, you may still have concerns about...

WHO IS LOOKING OUT FOR YOU?

Is there some government body, or some rules, regulations and legislation that ensures that I am protected against unscrupulous timeshare sellers? Yes. It seems, lately, that each day brings some new legislation to the floors of government's looking to regulate timeshare. Are there so many problems occurring, that I need to worry about what I own? No. The legislation is to define and refine how the industry must operate in today's market by attempting to solve the problems of the past. In other words, the industry must deal with the outstanding issues that affect it, and lay down new legal guidelines for the future of it.

In the beginning there were few laws or regulations, and governments created those that did exist. Legislators, pressured by constituents, began to re-evaluate the distinctions between what was consider legal or illegal. Suddenly, the largely unregulated timeshare industry found themselves the target of attorney generals and legislators faced with an overwhelming number of consumer complaints. So, minimum standards were established, often by the governments themselves. In 1982, Florida rewrote its timeshare statutes that have since become the industry landmark for change. The rewrite contained tough provisions for change and resulted in a much cleaner industry where developers and marketers can flourish on an even playing field.

First we should start with your ...

Home Owners Association (HOA)

Initially projects are controlled by the developer. However, when a timeshare resort is close to being sold out or completely sold out, a Board of Directors is elected by the owners to manage the property. The day to day operation of the resort is then taken over from the developer.

What exactly is a Home Owners Association? A good, strong HOA will provide caring management of your property in absentia. It is their job to keep the property in good repair to retain the quality and value expected by all the owners. This is done by way of the maintenance fees that are assessed each year by the HOA. Any extraordinary expenses are evaluated as they occur and if necessary, billed separately as an assessment fee. Maintenance and assessment fees were covered in Chapter 11.

In the United States, Home Owners Association's are regulated by Condominium Acts from the states in which they are located. A HOA is governed by the laws of the state where the association is located, not the individual owners. The state of Florida was the first to get on the bandwagon, so to speak, by legislating owners' associations. Florida's Condominium Act, the Not for Profit Association Act and the Florida Vacation Plan and Timesharing Act set forth statutes and provisions for establishing standards for Home Owners Associations. Many states and some countries are now following Florida´s leadership in this particular area. Canada also has fairly strict condominium and strata regulations, both national and provincial, which must be followed by any HOA - timeshare or otherwise.

Outside of the United States, each country has laws and/or regulations on how condominiums or owned multi-occupancy residential units are established and what rules and provisions must be included. If you HOA is situated outside of United States, or Canada you can research this information on the internet to ensure that your applicable HOA is indeed following the established guidelines.

What does a Home Owner's Association do?

A HOA <u>must</u> have a Board of Directors, which are considered to be the "managing entity" of the timeshare plan. It is the Board's function to provide the following:

- ❖ Manage and maintain all accommodations and facilities constituting the timeshare plan.
- ❖ Collect all assessments for common expenses.
- ❖ Provide to all purchasers an itemized budget that includes all estimated revenues and expenses for the association.
- ❖ Bill each owner/member annually for a pro-rated share of common expenses, based on the projected annual budget.
- ❖ Maintain all books and records concerning the timeshare plan so that they are reasonably available for inspection by any purchaser.
- ❖ Arrange for an annual independent audit by a certified public accountant of all books and financial records of the timeshare plan, according to generally accepted accounting procedures. In some states it is required that a statement of receipts and disbursements be sent to the state escrow accountant for review.
- ❖ Provide for inspection, any books and records, upon request by the Board of Directors.
- ❖ Schedule the occupancy and maintenance of the timeshare units and/or weeks if the resort offers flexible or floating unit weeks.
- ❖ Perform any, and all, other functions and duties necessary and proper to maintain the accommodations and facilities as provided in the purchase contract and as advertised.
- ❖ Maintain a complete record and list of the names and addresses of all purchasers and owners of timeshare units in the timeshare plan must be maintained. This list must be updated at least quarterly.
- ❖ Provide adequate notice of board meetings and grant owners the right to attend and speak out about any item on the agenda. The board may reasonably adopt reasonable rules governing the frequency, duration and manner of owner statements.
- ❖ Mail a meeting notice, and copies of the proposed budget, to the owners at least fourteen days before the meeting to consider the budget.
- ❖ Send each owner a complete financial report of the receipts and expenditures for the previous year, or a complete set of financial statements for the preceding fiscal year. Both prepared according to generally accepted accounting procedures.
- ❖ The Condominium Act requires that any written complaint filed by an owner must be done by certified mail and the board has thirty days to reply in writing. The reply must respond to the substance

of the complaint. If legal advice is required by the board, they have ten days which to respond to the complainant and 60 days to respond to the complaint.

❖ **IMPORTANT** - Your HOA should have a sound Reserve Management System program in place. It is the HOA´s fiduciary responsibility to individual owners that the property will be maintained and refurbished as needed. Each state/country has guidelines and requirements of what is required in a reserve management plan and how often it should be done. Regardless of these laws, a good reserve management system or plan ensures that owners are not over or under assessed and that reserve funds are available when needed. In some areas, it is called the Contingency Fund.

<u>Do I have a say in how my HOA is operated</u>? Many owners ask if they really do have a say in what goes on with their resort. Yes, they do if they so desire. By being active in your Home Owners Association, you do have a voice in how your maintenance and assessment fees are being spent. Owners are encouraged to attend annual meetings, speak out and suggest methods by which the resort could or should be maintained. If you have an active HOA, participate in it.

Unfortunately, most owners could not care less what is being done for them. It is not uncommon for owners to complain about everything that is being done on their resort, but are unwilling, or not wanting, to participate. Another significant area most owners overlook is the newsletters sent out to them. They do not bother to read about what may be happening on their resort. If your HOA is not active, find out why and do something about it.

A large part of the HOA mandate is to ensure owners pay their maintenance and assessment fees, and on time. This is essential, because even if they experience a 5% delinquency rate, something on the property will deteriorate. If your resort cannot be maintained properly, the value and quality will decrease, your ability to exchange will definitely decrease, which ultimately leads to owner dissatisfaction and bad mouthing of the industry. You have paid hard earned dollars to be proud of what you own, do whatever you can to assure you are getting your money´s worth.

By the way, if there is any final inventory available, it is offered at fire-sale pricing, so the HOA does not have to carry any of the sales or marketing costs.

Aside from your HOA, one of the first steps towards Federal or Industry self regulation was the establishment of...

The American Resort Development Association (ARDA)

The American Resort Development Association (ARDA) is the Washington D.C.-based trade association representing the vacation ownership and resort development industries (timeshares). ARDA has almost 1,000 corporate members ranging from privately held firms to publicly traded corporations with extensive experience in shared ownership interests in leisure real estate. The membership also includes timeshare owner associations (HOAs), resort management companies, industry vendors, suppliers, and consultants—as well as owners through the ARDA Resort Owners Coalition (ARDA-ROC).

ARDA and its members subscribe to the highest standards of professionalism and ethics in resort development. The association assisted in the development of a code of ethics that is strictly enforced among all members. This code of ethics is the most comprehensive in the hospitality and real estate industries. ARDA also provides educational forums for its members and plays a major role in establishing state and federal consumer protection laws.

This code of ethics started to move the industry towards self-regulation by focusing primarily on solicitation and sale practices. The code has four sections: (complete code of ethics can be found at http://www.arda.org/ethics/)

I.   **The Preamble**: This requires ARDA members and those who use ARDA services to conduct themselves honestly, fairly, and with integrity, dignity and propriety.
II. **Definitions**: This provides definitions of the terminology utilized in the code.
III. **Ethics Requirements**: This is the heart of the code. This covers both on- and off-site sales and marketing practices. This section requires that all information, descriptions and disclosures be "accurate, clear and complete." Information must be true and never misleading. Areas that historically had been misrepresented—such as resale, rental, exchange and reciprocal-use programs—are all specifically cited. Additionally, there is a section on solicitation that forbids deceptive practices and a detailed section on sales requirements that mandates disclosure policies and rescission rights.
IV. **Administrative Procedures**: This section defines the administrative structure and describes policies for handling complaints. It also covers penalties and sanctions.

In addition to enforcing the code of ethics, ARDA promotes the growth and development of the timeshare industry through a variety of initiatives.

Advocacy: ARDA monitors regulatory issues that affect timeshare by engaging in lobbying efforts focused on the establishment of a legislative environment that enhances consumer confidence and protection.

Networking: ARDA offers industry professionals educational and networking opportunities each year through the ARDA Annual Convention and Exposition.

B2B Partnerships and Bridge-Building: ARDA pursues business and growth opportunities through alliances with organizations in related and complementary industries in the U.S. and overseas.

Outreach: ARDA keeps its members updated with the latest industry news.

Knowledge: ARDA shares market intelligence and keeps its members informed of industry trends and events through a variety of informational tools, including Developments Magazine, research, webinars, and www. arda.org.

Professional Development: The ARDA International Foundation (AIF) offers professional and educational development through publications covering the industry's ethical, legal, regulatory and operational intricacies; study courses; and tests that assess industry knowledge.

Consumer Product Knowledge: www.vacationbetter.org is ARDA's consumer-facing website that provides non-branded information about the value of vacationing with timeshare. The website is an educational, transparent resource to help new owners reaffirm their product purchase with tips on how to make the most of their timeshare vacation, to provide non-owners with information about product type and variation and to share vacation stories, quotes and testimonials from real owners with vacationers in general.

ARDA Resort Owners Coalition (ARDA-ROC)

ARDA's Resort Owners Coalition (ARDA-ROC) is a tax exempt, nonprofit alliance for over one million vacation ownership owners, developers and managers who advocate for public policy positions that protect the interests of individual vacation ownership owners, preserve the integrity of vacation products and enhance the vacation purchase. The concept of ARDA-ROC is simple—owners across the country join together to gain collectively what they are unable to achieve on their own. With unity comes strength!

As a timeshare owner, you can participate in ARDA-ROC legislative efforts. Your voluntary contributions are used to protect owners, like yourself, from federal, state and local government attempts to raise revenues at the expense of timeshare owners.

ARDA-ROC is supportive of consumer protection for timeshare owners and has been active in establishing and supporting the system of state timeshare registration laws, which has been very effective in regulating developers and forcing unscrupulous developers and sellers out of the industry for over 29 years. ARDA-ROC continues to defend against potential timeshare tax legislation for owners all across the country. Additionally, ARDA-ROC supports the implementation of cost and timesaving measures with respect to non-judicial foreclosures to save time and money for associations and owners.

ARDA-ROC's main goal is to improve vacation ownership for the future by defending owners on many issues. Over the past few years, ARDA-ROC has been successful in protecting owners from the following:

- ❖ Attempts to limit or eliminate the second home mortgage and/or timeshare deduction;
- ❖ Attempts to impose state sales taxes on timeshares;
- ❖ Attempts to tax owners of timeshares as transient occupants (that is, hotel guests);
- ❖ Attempts by the IRS to tax timeshare homeowner associations' capital reserves (part of your maintenance fee) as income;
- ❖ Attempts to tax your annual assessment through a state food and beverage tax provision.

In August of 1997 Legislation, H.R. 1350, which was supported by ARDA-ROC, was included in the Balanced Budget Agreement signed by President Clinton. Also known as the "Homeowners Association Clarification Act," the new law generally permits timeshare associations to elect Section 528 of the Internal Revenue Code. Under Section 528, most timeshare HOAs will pay higher tax on investment income. However, prepaid and excess assessments, as well as capital reserve accounts, will be clearly defined as tax exempt.

Contact your home resort or ARDA if you are interested in participating in ARDA-ROC.

Okay, you have your HOA, ARDA, the ARDA-ROC but who else is looking out for your best interests?

Well, there is...

Federal Trade Commission (FTC)

Timeshare is largely regulated by the Real Estate Commissions in the state in which the timeshare property is located and, indirectly, by ARDA. The Federal Trade Commission acts mainly as an overseer to ensure that everyone is doing business in a fair and equitable basis. They watch closely to see that no unfair trade or labor practices occur between the businesses associated with the timeshare industry, and arbitrate any conflicts that do arise. The FTC also participates in, or oversees, any sting operations needed to stop, or prevent, bad or illegal business practices.

In Chapter 17, I also show how the FTC takes an active approach in trying to bring those perpetuating any type of frauds or scams on timeshare owners to justice.

The Federal Trade Commission also publishes guidelines for buying and reselling timeshare intervals. These are available either by calling or writing the FTC or by using their Web site.

State Legislation

ARDA also monitors all state legislation and rules governing timesharing, subdivided land, real estate licensing, property management licensing, telemarketing, general marketing and promotion, and taxes (sales, property and occupancy) that affect its members.

Most of the legislation centers on amending state real estate laws, licensing requirements, telemarketing practices and taxes. Florida still remains the front-runner concerning timesharing legislation, with Illinois and Hawaii coming close behind. Georgia, on the other hand, just recently deregulated timeshare due to the state´s lack of problems with the timeshare industry and insufficient funds to regulate if there were problems.

In 2000 Florida again became a front-runner when it was the first state to enact legislation that permits transactions, and signatures to be done via the Internet. For more information, contact your state legislative office or write to them requesting copies of the bills if you are interested. For further information refer to the Timeshare Address Book at the back of the book.

As almost states now have timeshare projects, most have active legislation, either passed or pending, regarding timeshare, timesharing related activities and Home Owner Associations. On the table below are the states t with either a yes or no, indicating if state legislation has been passed or may be pending and the timeshare rescission periods.

STATE	LEGISLATION	RESCISSION PERIOD[18]	STATE	LEGISLATION	RESCISSION PERIOD[12]
Alabama	Yes	5 Calendar Days	Mississippi	No	7 Calendar Days
Alaska	No	None Listed	Montana	Yes	3 Calendar Days
Arizona	Yes	7 Calendar Days	Nevada	Yes	5 Calendar Days
Arkansas	Yes	5 Calendar Days	New Hampshire	Yes	5 Calendar or Business Days
California	Yes	7 Calendar Days	New Jersey	Yes	7 Calendar Days
Colorado	Yes	5 Calendar Days	New Mexico	Yes	7 Calendar Days
Connecticut	Yes	5 Calendar Days	New York	Yes	7 Business Days
Delaware	No	5 Business Days	North Carolina	Yes	5 Calendar Days
District of Columbia	No Data	None Listed	North Dakota	No	None Listed
Florida	Yes	10 Calendar Days	Ohio	No	5 Calendar Days
Georgia	Yes	7 Calendar Days	Oklahoma	Yes (Limited)	10 Calendar Days (Discretionary)
Hawaii	Yes	7 Calendar Days	Oregon	Yes	5 Calendar Days
Idaho	Yes	5 Calendar Days	Pennsylvania	Yes	5 Calendar Days

---

[18]   Rescission Periods are based on Information provided by ARDA State Government Affairs Office in December 2012 from the ARDA-ROC website. Please consult legal counsel or the applicable state statue for current information. Same Calendar and Business rescissions days are not specified.

Illinois	Yes	5 Calendar Days	Rhode Island	Yes	5 Business Days
Indiana	Yes	3 Business Days	South Carolina	Yes	5 Calendar Days
Iowa	Yes	5 Calendar Days	South Dakota	No	7 Calendar or Business Days
Kansas	No	None Listed	Tennessee	Yes	See Statutes
Kentucky	Yes	5 Business Days	Texas	Yes	5 Calendar Days
Louisiana	Yes	7 Calendar Days	Utah	Yes	5 Calendar Days
Maine	Yes	3 Business Days	Vermont	Yes	5 Calendar Days
Maryland	Yes	None Listed	Virginia	Yes	7 Calendar Days
Massachusetts	Yes	3 Business Days	Washington	Yes	7 Calendar or Business Days
Michigan	Yes	9 Business Days	West Virginia	Yes	10 Calendar or Business Days
Minnesota	Yes	5 Calendar or Business Days	Wisconsin	Yes	5 Business Days
Missouri	Yes	5 Calendar or Business Days	Wyoming	No	None Listed

If you live in Canada, or own a timeshare in Canada, there is...

The Canadian Resort Development Association (CRDA)

In 1980, the Resort Time-sharing Council of Canada (RTCC) was formed to help regulate the timeshare industry in Canada. After a number of years with little or no activity, it was re-established in 1987, as the Canadian Resort Development Association. CRDA is affiliated with other organizations, such as ARDA and GATE, and participates internationally in reporting on Canada´s role in the worldwide timeshare industry. The association is regularly consulted on all matters that could affect both resort development and the almost 200,000 Canadians who are currently timeshare owners.

The CRDA's code of ethics is based on the ARDA Code and in 1996 was strengthened to assist members to deal with specific situations and responsibilities. As with ARDA, CRDA members pledge to uphold the CRDA code of Standards and Ethics.

The CRDA is also involved with education, research, seminars and publication of general timeshare booklets for public inquiries. CRDA also distributes a newsletter at regular intervals to their membership. This newsletter informs all those related to the travel industry, of any new developments, growth, trends and research that are relevant to the Canadian Resort, Interval Ownership and Vacation Club industries. Newsletters are also sent to the government and media.

Aside from the CRDA, some of Canada's provinces are establishing their own timeshare regulations. Ontario recently proposed a 10-day cooling off period that would allow buyers to reconsider their purchases. Currently Ontario has no legislation for timeshare directly but is also proposing that timeshare sales be accompanied by a disclosure documents that meet requirements that are to be set by regulation.

Moving south from Canada and the United States we come to....

Mexico

It is no surprise that the majority of buyers in Mexico are Americans and Canadians. Why is that? Except for Alaska, Mexico can be reached within a few hours by airplane so getting away for a three, four, seven or more day vacation is easy, and affordable and warmer!

SECTUR, Mexico's Tourism Ministry, recognizes that tourism is an important producer of foreign revenue and a vital sector of the nation's economic growth. Accordingly, the timeshare industry constitutes one of the most important aspects of investment in tourism. For the industry to continue to grow in Mexico, it must offer potential buyers a high degree of security and guarantees.

To achieve this, the timeshare industry in Mexico is governed by a federal standard called Normative Elements of Time Share Services (called norma in Mexico). Established by the Ministry of Commerce and Industry Promotion (SECOFI), they require the Consumer Protection Agency (Procuraduría Federal de la Republica para el Consumidor, or PROFECO) to enforce its provisions with a "program of verification and vigilance."

The result of continuous and rapid growth of tourism development in Mexico and the need for a single common front to seek consultation and joint work between the authorities and the private sector to regulate criteria and define an appropriate regulatory scheme that would boost the tourism industry in Mexico real estate, AMDETUR was created in 1987. It was formed by a group of eight founding members and Tourism Developers Association of Promoters of Puerto Vallarta Timeshare, Bancomer, Costamex Group ICA Group, Interval International, Lexes Enterprises, Resort Condominiums International, Shell Remic Sponsor. Now AMDETUR is made up of over 250 members in Mexico which are made up of Interested Investors and Developers, Industry Distributors, Resort, Properties, Exchange Companies, Law Firms and Legal Consulting entities. The Board is composed of the President, Secretary, Treasurer, Resort Members, Committees and Chairmen of Local Associations.

Thanks to the support of its founding members AMDETUR now represents 90% of the Real Estate and Timeshare Developers and include Golf Courses, Marinas, and different models of Vacation Ownership. Members who fail to follow the designated rules and/or regulations are given notice and fined.

From 1993 onwards, these standards have acted as the framework specifically relating to commercial pre-sales and sales operations of providers of timeshare services. However, since this framework was created, multi-destination and point-based systems have flourished. The developers of the multi-destination and point-based systems now argue that this framework does not apply to them because it was designed exclusively for traditional timeshare operations. Due to this the government is trying to revise the timeshare standard to now include these new types of ownership. With PROFECO's provisions for consumer protection (five day rescission period), Mexico is leading the Latin and South American market in assuring developers and consumers alike are protected.

From Mexico, we continue south to....

Latin America

Uruguay, Dominican Republic, Chile, Costa Rica, Brazil, Columbia and Argentina all have Timeshare Associations and are represented by LADETUR (Federación Latinoamérica de Desolladores Turísticos, AC) collectively.

Then from Latin America we move even further south to explore...

South America

The South American market today is very similar to what the United States market experienced in the early 1980's. They are struggling to keep up with the increasing development as well as fighting against insufficient capital and financing. For many years South America has been characterized by the media as being dangerous, having outrageous inflation, considerable poverty, high unemployment, serious human rights violations and governments that feed off protection and bribery. What is never shown is the magnificence of the Andes, the mystery of the Amazon, the great waterfalls in Argentina, the casinos in Uruguay and the old historic cities of Colombia. What is not mentioned at all is the incredible warmth of the Latin people. Because of South America's diverseness: politically, economically, culturally and physically, it has been difficult to implement any continent wide legislation.

In the past years, the impropriety of several developers has damaged the sales potential in some markets. This has affected the honest developers who believe South America is a gold mine for future timeshare development. Because of the discontent amongst the developers, and a huge outcry from consumers, legislation has been proposed in Brazil, Colombia, Venezuela and Argentina. While these regulations may be new and lack some "teeth," they are moving towards fixing problems that would otherwise kill the timeshare industry.

An ongoing effort by ARDA and Interval International is being made to develop resources in other countries like Paraguay, Uruguay, Bolivia, Peru and Chile to encourage economic and political reforms. The future for the South American market is very ripe for growth however the government's need to establish regulations to provide more consumer confidence and protections.

As I stated before, should you want to buy in one of South America´s beautiful countries, check with the local consuls or government consumer offices for more information.

Before we leave the America´s and move over to Europe and beyond, I just want to briefly mention:

GATE (Global Alliance For Timeshare Excellence)

GATE was established in 1999 by the leaders of the major worldwide timeshare associations to promote the timeshare industry around the world. Each association keeps its own identity, but as a group these associations seek to cooperate on issues of common concern in order to advance the growth of the timeshare industry, the interests of their members, and the consumers they serve worldwide.

The founding associations were the American Resort Development (ARDA), the Canadian Resort Development Association (CRDA), Australia (ADHOC) Latin America (AMDETUR/LADETUR), Europe (OTE now RDO), Middle East (AIRDA) and South Africa (VOASA).

As the timeshare industry continues to mature and expand around the world, GATE is working closely with RCI, LLC and Interval International (II) to promote legislation to protect the consumer globally.

In Europe, the timeshare industry is represented by...

European Timeshare Federation

For many years the European timeshare market was a hornet=s nest. Most countries that sold timeshare did what they wanted, while countries like Spain and Portugal were notorious for their solicitation and sales techniques. Then in 1983, Portugal implemented legislation that virtually banned off-premise solicitation and gave buyers a fourteen-day cooling off period. This legislation soon led to even more chaos in the European industry. Then, in October of 1994, to create a level playing field for the European timeshare industry, while also providing consumer protection, the European Parliament formed the **EU Directive**. In April 1997, the legislation was enacted with all countries concerned to be compliant by the end of 1998. This piece of legislation was passed to protect buyers from unsavory marketing and sale practices and to provide those protections throughout the European Community.

The Directive contains thirteen articles and an annex outlining contract requirements. Each member state must enact the legislation providing at least as much consumer protection as the Directive.

The Directive seeks to regulate the sales and marketing of timeshare and the contracts into which the purchasers enter. One important area is that certain information be disclosed to prospective buyers. There must be a detailed disclosure document on the resort produced, and must be supplied with any advertising regarding the property. The price of the product must be accurate and disclosed in advance, however they do not preclude additional discounting during the sales process. Any, and all fees involved with the sale, must be disclosed. Other required disclosures are an accurate description of the property, the location, the services provided, common facilities, cancellation rights and how further information can be obtained.

The Directive also states that timeshare contracts must contain certain information, plus the required information from the disclosure document. Everything must be in writing and any information that changed from the original disclosure to final contract must be noted and specifically excluded from the contract. Contracts should also be written so that they are easier to understand.

The language of the contracts must be provided in the official language of either the buyer's home or nationality if it is an official language of the European Union. A certified translation of the contract must also be provided in the official language of each member state where are a resort property is located. For developers who have projects in multiple countries, this can become quite burdensome. Contract changes also provide a problem concerning translations because companies that operate in several countries must reproduce all the certified translations each time a change is made. Due to this process, it can take several weeks to get translations to all parties concerned.

Initially Cooling-off periods were changed to a <u>minimum</u> of ten (10) days. Buyers have the right to cancel within that period of signing the contract. This right <u>must</u> be explained to the buyer. When the buyer enters into a finance agreement with the resort, its agent or a third party referred by the resort, the agreement is automatically canceled, without penalty, when the sale is canceled. The cooling-off period can be extended up to three months if proper disclosures were not made. In the last few years a new cooling-off period for timeshare contracts was initiated, it is now:

1. The right to contract cancellation within 14 days for any reason without penalty
2. If the seller has not provided the required information, the contract cancellation (cooling-off) period is extended to one year plus 14 days.

The most controversial requirement of the Directive was to ban advance payments by buyers to the sellers during the cooling-off period. Deposit payments have always been a major part of the industry because they show the buyers commitment to the sale. Some countries, like Germany, believe that an "escrow" or "third party trust" account should be used to place deposit monies into, showing good faith intent by the buyer. Other countries, like the United Kingdom, have refused the idea of third party or escrow accounts. It comes down to the fact that if a potential buyer cannot put money down and has the right to cancel, why would you provide them with anything less than total disclosure. It is a complete waste of everyone´s time and money.

Has it become a level playing field? That is hard to say at this point. If each of the fifteen countries implements the Directive, but enforces it differently, will there still be a hornet's nest? Only time will tell. Although the Directive is posing significant changes to the European timeshare market, the expectation is that it will improve public relations and industry growth. Willemien Bax, secretary general of the European Timeshare Federation commented, "It's important to our image and to our future success."

The fifteen countries that are affected by the European Union Timeshare Directive are: Austria, Belgium, Denmark, Finland, France, Germany, Greece, Ireland, Italy, Luxembourg, the Netherlands, Portugal, Spain, Sweden and the United Kingdom. Although Norway is not an EU bound country, it has recently enacted timeshare legislation.

RDO (Resort Development Organization)

As a result of the EU Directive, in February of 1998, The Organization for Timeshare Europe was created by the European Timeshare Federation, to essentially follow the same mission as ARDA by joining all of the member nations into one European organization. Although its name was changed to the RDO or Resort Development Association in 2009, it originally had no formal connection to its US counterpart; its mission will be to coordinate lobbying efforts on behalf of the industry. The RDO also acts as a voice in unifying the vacation ownership industry across Europe, encompassing a number of usage types including timeshare, fractional interests, private residence clubs, condo hotels, destination clubs etc, all aimed at providing holidaymakers with quality holiday accommodation through various concepts of use.

It represents over 130 members from all sectors of the timeshare industry including resort developers, exchange companies, management and marketing companies, trustees, finance houses and resale companies. The RDO works with all its fourteen member countries legislative bodies in to create fair and equitable rules and regulations that protect the consumer and create a positive image for the industry as a whole. Consisting of a board of directors and executive committee, there will also be five councils: legislative, communications, education, membership and ethics.

Other European timeshare agencies are: The Timeshare Council, now called TATOC, which is located in the United Kingdom and the Association Nacional de Empresarios de Tiempo Compartido (National Association of Timeshare Developers) in Spain. In 2001 Spain's regulations on off-premise contacts was enforced which now requires them to show identification, wear a uniform and avoid aggressive methods when approaching prospects. They are also banned from working near public buildings. Spain is the only country in Europe having regulations that have imposed almost total control over the way timeshare can be sold. The RDO now works in conjunction with the other worldwide timeshare associations in an effort to try and ensure that the rights of all purchasers are protected.

RDO members represent the best in European vacation ownership and are committed to high service standards and integrity. They are bound by a code of conduct and an independent arbitration scheme, providing levels of protection beyond those required by law. The following countries have direct RDO affiliation:

- ❖ RDO UK (The Timeshare Council - TATOC)
- ❖ RDO Spain (ANETC)
- ❖ RDO Germany (RDO Redaktionsbüro Berlin)
- ❖ RDO Malta
- ❖ RDO Greece (Greek Timeshare Association, GTA)
- ❖ RDO Nordic Regions (Finnish Timeshare Association)
- ❖ RDO Hungary

Continuing eastward we soon reach...

India

In India, you will find the All India Resort Development Association (AIRDA) which is an independent, non-profit advisory dedicated to the timeshare and vacation ownership industry in India.

In 1998, the increased demand for timeshare development in India, and of course, some form of regulation to monitor the development and promotion of these properties, a visionary group of resort developers and RCI decided to create an independent body. This association mandate and agenda would keep in mind the timeshare growth in the country and the constructive role that could be played by developers to grow the industry. More importantly, it was set up to work hand-in-hand with both promoters and consumers. This was how the foundation was laid for the All India Resort Development Association (AIRDA).

AIRDA's key member segments include timeshare developers, exchange companies, marketers and other participant stakeholders. In addition to playing catalyst for the vacation ownership industry, AIRDA also assumed the role of an overseer - ensuring that the promoter-consumer relationship is ethical, fair and value-based.

Promoter members commit to adopt and abide by a code of ethics that reflect fair practices and set the stage for strong, sustainable and profitable businesses. The code also seeks to protect that most important link in the value chain - customers. India has a ten working day cooling-off period.

Africa

Of the 230 timeshare properties in southern Africa, 178 are actually located in South Africa, the remainder are spread between the following countries; Zimbabwe, Réunion, Mauritius, Namibia, and Swaziland. There are only a few countries in Northern Africa that have timeshare properties (Egypt, Morocco and most of them are overseen by the European Resort Development Association (RDO) as mentioned above.

In 1990, South Africa established the Vacation Ownership Association of South Africa (VOASA). It was previously known as the Timeshare Institute of Southern Africa, which was an organization representing the interests of the respective timeshare development companies with its primary objective being to "create, maintain and develop an environment within which the long-term viability and growth of vacation ownership through shared vacation ownership can be optimally ensured."

VOASA´s fundamental existence is its ability to self regulate and control the industry in such a manner that the national authorities, via the Department of Trade & Industry, maintain confidence of its ongoing ability to manage and deliver a mature industry that instills confidence within all stakeholders and is positively perceived by the consumer at large.

As we continue to venture eastward from Europe, I regret to say that I could find no specific information regarding legislation in the Middle Eastern countries. If you want to buy in one of these locations, I would suggest checking with the appropriate consul or government offices before you buy to get reliable information.

Australia, New Zealand And Asia

Although timeshare has been around for many years in Australian and New Zealand, the emerging markets in the Asian sector are gaining significance. Because of the very fact that they are emerging markets, they tend to lack any substantive regulations. Both ARDA and RCI believe that there is a need to develop strong trade associations for everyone involved in the timeshare markets operating in that region. There is a strong desire to create a code of ethics having "teeth," besides getting local governments to recognize the need for timeshare regulation.

In 2010, at an Alternative Ownership conference, held in Thailand, it became apparent that there is a need for a Pan-Asian timeshare association in the region. Although associations had already been formed in Malaysia, Singapore, Indonesia, Hong Kong, the Philippines, Vietnam and Thailand, these associations are weighing the need for legislation and regulation within their native countries.

In 1987 New Zealand formed the formed the New Zealand Holiday Ownership Council (NZHOC) and in 1994 and Australia formed the Australian Timeshare and Holiday Ownership Council (ATHOC). Both associations primary goal is to work with all sectors of the timeshare industry including resort developers, exchange companies, management and marketing companies, trustees, finance houses and resale companies. Stringent laws were enacted in the late 1980's after considerable timeshare sales and marketing abuses were discovered. New Zealand has a seven day cooling-off period while Australia has a ten day cooling-off period.

In 1996 the Fiji Timeshare Association was formed and currently has nine participating members. The cooling off period in Fiji is seven days.

The following is a list of the cooling-off periods that applies to each country[19]:

- ❖ New Zealand - 3 days
- ❖ Australia - 10 business days
- ❖ Malaysia - 10 days
- ❖ Singapore - 3 business days
- ❖ Indonesia - 7 days
- ❖ Hong Kong - 5 business days
- ❖ Philippines - 15 days
- ❖ Vietnam - 0 days but legislation is currently being drafted to incorporate a time frame
- ❖ Thailand - 7 days

---

[19] All Cooling-off periods mentioned above are valid at the time of printing and may be subject to change by the laws in each country.

Again, if you want to buy timeshare in the Asia-Pacific region please read your contract carefully and look for a cooling-off or rescission period in the contract. Otherwise you can contact the local consul or consumer office for current regulations and information.

From the Far East, we cross the Pacific to reach... well home I guess if you live in the US or Canada... and we have now come full circle, so to speak, regarding who is looking out for you around the world. Every day, somewhere in the world, new timeshare legislation or rules are being established for the protection of consumers, especially in the internet-Google age, where so there is no reason to not be able to find out what laws are in effect.

The one last thing that I wanted to cover is...

OWNING OR BUYING A TIMESHARE IN A FOREIGN COUNTRY

Well, since I owned timeshare in four countries for a long time, I personally, would say that foreign ownership has worked out just fine.

Of the other 6,700,000 plus timeshare owners, from 174 countries, owning in 100 plus countries, foreign ownership has many different meanings. For example, if you are an American and own in Lake Tahoe, to you foreign ownership might mean Mexico or the Caribbean. To an Englishman, it might mean owning in Scotland or Spain. If you were from South Africa you may think that anywhere in North Africa is a foreign property. Whichever meaning you personally have, many owners of timeshare who originally may have bought in their home country are discovering that foreign ownership is not as scary a proposition as it once was.

More and more people are traveling on exchanges to foreign countries. They are falling in love with people, scenery, cultures or something that just makes them feel good and, as such, are now choosing to own there.

Before you chose to buy and own in a foreign country here are a few questions for you to consider:

1. Is the country relatively politically stable?
2. Is the timeshare project or developer registered in any way, with any government agency? (Not all foreign timeshares are registered in the United States)
3. Does the developer have other resorts? If yes, where are they? How long?

4. Is the developer credible and in a good financial position?
5. What type of ownership will you receive? <u>Right-to-use</u> will be the most common (Right-to-use can also be much less expensive to buy and maintain.)
6. If the contract provided is Right-to-use, how many years are or available or left on it?
7. What type of membership will you receive? Fixed, Floating, Fractional, Points, Coupons or   other?
8. Is there Title Insurance available on the timeshare resort or project?
9. Is there a USA membership or contract office? Who are they? (For Americans or Canadians)
10. How will the maintenance fees be paid, and to whom?
11. Is the timeshare resort exchangeable?
12. Which of the exchange company's are affiliated with - II or RCI?
13. If the resort is pre-construction, have you seen it? When will it be finished? What is my guarantee on completion?
14. If I finance, who will be carrying the financing? Where are they located?
15. What is the rescission or cooling-off period?
16. Do I get contracts in my official language, or in the language of the country where the timeshare is located?
17. At some point that I choose, can I make changes to my membership?
18. Will I be able to rent, resell or bequeath my timeshare interval?

If you feel that all of your questions have been credibly answered, go ahead and make your foreign purchase. There is definitely a risk when buying anything in a foreign country, but if you feel confident in the developer and the price is right then the risk is definitely worth it.

One last reminder, "caveat-emptor" or "buyers beware" still does apply in whatever, or wherever you choose to buy. **Remember, the only person most responsible for looking out for your best interests is <u>you</u>**.

One last thing that many people do not like to think about, but needs to be covered is...

WHAT IF I/WE DIE? - WHO GETS OUR TIMESHARE?

The subject that no one wants to talk about, but still happens every day... what if you should die? What happens to your timeshare?

When you purchase your timeshare, you can either have your beneficiaries put on the contract or ask to list beneficiaries just in case something happens to you. If you chose to have your beneficiaries actually named as contract holders, most resorts will require that the beneficiaries actually be present to sign both the contract and any promissory notes to cover the legalities relating to who is going to be responsible for any payments (loans or maintenance fees). If your designated beneficiaries are not travelling with you, you can list them as beneficiaries; however they may be subject to transfer fees and/or lose benefits depending on their relationship to you.

The simplest way to ensure that your favorite child, person or charity gets your timeshare is to specifically bequeath them the timeshare in your Last Will & Testament. This document can also be used to avoid any confusion at the resort with who will become the new owner(s). In any case, your Executor, lawyer or family member will have to send the resort a copy of the death certificate for their records to process any change in ownership. If you and your spouse own co-jointly, the right of survivorship does apply and most resorts only need a copy of the death certificate.

An important thing to remember regarding the death of a contract holder is that the timeshare still is valid and payments and fees must be paid, whether by the surviving contract holders or family members. Death does not automatically cancel any timeshare contract, unless the deceased is the only person listed as the contract holder and again, documentation must be provided to the resort in order to process the cancellation.

If you want to find out about your resorts process regarding the death of a contract holder, refer to your resorts or vacation clubs Rules & Regulations where this information is usually stated quite clearly or you can contact your resort or vacation club for clarification.

Chapter 16

Now that You Have Had Time to Think About It...

In the beginning you understood, or knew, very little about timeshare or vacation ownership. You believed all the bad stuff you had heard and avoided presentations like the plague. Maybe, you bought a week and are trying to sell it because it did not work for you. Well, I hope that by this chapter you have come to realize that timeshare, or vacation ownership, are words that no longer need to be spoken in whispers. Vacation ownership, when used correctly, can do many wonderful things for yourself and your family.

Do I believe that everyone should own a week or two? Most definitely! Should you have "more money than God," certainly continue to vacation in your present lifestyle. If you have no money, you should not even be thinking about vacations in any sense. However, for those of us who are in–between, vacation ownership can provide:

- ❖ Physical, mental and spiritual rest, relaxation and rejuvenation;
- ❖ Better family communications - both during and after vacations;
- ❖ More quality family time;
- ❖ A wider range of travel experiences and destinations;
- ❖ A reason to take a vacation;
- ❖ The ability save money on your future vacations;
- ❖ The opportunity to meet new people;
- ❖ The encouragement to learn new sports or activities;
- ❖ More quality accommodations;
- ❖ Something to leave your children;
- ❖ Pride of ownership;

189

- ❖ Fun, excitement, happiness, pleasure and adventure;
- ❖ A more positive impact in our lives.

You have discovered that all those terrible things you have heard may, or may not, be justified. You have know learned how easy it is to exchange and rent and, even, God forbid, resell you week. You have discovered you really can afford it and that there may even be a few tax advantages. You became aware that "big brother," is truly watching out for you, wherever you choose to buy.

So, I will ask you again, do I think that everyone should own a week? **What is your answer, now that you have had time to think about it....?**

TEN TIPS ON WHY OWNERSHIP MAKES SENSE

1. The single most important tip of all: **It will enhance the quality of your life**.
2. You own your vacations, rather than rent them.
3. You guarantee the cost of your vacations for the future, rather than wondering what next year's hotel prices (or package deals) will be.
4. You are guaranteeing the quality of your accommodations by staying in fully furnished condominiums rather than small, cramped hotel rooms.
5. You have fully equipped kitchen facilities to save money on meals rather than dining in restaurants all the time. (Remember that mini-bar!)
6. You have the ability to exchange your ownership week(s) and travel throughout the world.
7. You can choose to rent your ownership week(s) if you cannot use it for a particular year.
8. You can make donations to charity, or give it to a loved one for a birthday, Christmas or honeymoon gift.
9. You can take advantage of all of the benefits and discounts available to owners through the exchange companies.
10. Even if you own only one week, you have the ability to travel on extra weeks for very little additional cost to you or your family.

TEN TIPS FOR BUYING A WEEK (OR TWO)

1. Most important tip of all: **Buy for use, not for an investment**.
2. If you can afford it, buy in a prime season. It has better exchangeability and flexibility.
3. Buy in a high demand area or location. It also has better exchangeability and flexibility.
4. When buying, look for a reasonable maintenance fee and fee history.
5. Ask about Reserve Funds. Does the maintenance fee include them? If not, why not?
6. When buying, ask about the management. Make sure they are doing a good job. Look around the resort to see if it is being well maintained.
7. If you can stay in the location first, do it. It will help you form an honest impression.
8. Talk to at <u>least</u> five other owners if you can. Ask them if they are happy with what they bought and why, or why not? Some people may always be positive or negative, while five will give you a better survey.
9. If you can, read the newsletters or ask a lot of questions so you understand the terms and conditions before you sign.
10. Make sure the resort is affiliated with an exchange company and is in good standing.

**It must be AFFORDABLE and fit your
LIFESTYLE. Let me repeat that.
It MUST be AFFORDABLE and fit YOUR PERSONAL lifestyle**.

One last thing and then I promise we are done.

TRIAL MEMBERSHIPS

This is only for those people who truly cannot afford to buy a week in a high demand location, but would very much like to own in one. If you have the funds available to buy a regular timeshare interval at the point of sale, do it. Trial membership is not your alternative.

If you have thought about it and <u>want</u> to own, but money is a very definite problem at the point of sale - ask the salesperson if the resort offers a trial membership. Increasingly high demand resort locations are now offering trial programs for people with limited funds. They would rather prospects get their foot in the door, so to speak, for very little money than miss the opportunity to experience all the advantages of ownership. This is because once people have experienced the advantages and benefits of ownership it is much easier to say yes in the future.

Trial programs usually run for twelve, eighteen or twenty-four months. During this time you can use the resort's facilities as well as experience the benefits and discounts offered by an exchange company. Some programs allow for a one week stay at the resort during that period to help you choose full ownership. Other resorts offer the use of Bonus weeks to help prospects make their decisions.

Pricing for trial memberships can run <u>from as little</u> as US$500 to US$5,000 depending on the length of the trial period. This money is due immediately at the point of sale. Some resorts will finance fifty percent (50 percent) of the trial membership if money is really an issue, but not normally longer than thirty days.

Another great advantage to trial membership is that some resorts will allow this dollar amount to be deducted from the down payment when a regular timeshare interval is bought. This method is becoming very successful. Prospective buyers then need only the balance of the down payment, not the full amount.

An example of converting a trial membership to full ownership:

Price of timeshare interval:	$10,000
25 percent Down Payment:	2,500
Trial Membership Cost:	$ 1,000
Balance of Regular Down Payment	
Due at Purchase:	$ 1,500

In all trial programs, if you do not buy a regular week during, or after, the trial period ends your "trial membership" also ends. Resorts will not allow you to continually buy trial memberships to avoid buying a regular week.

More resorts now offer some form of trial programs, and as these programs have become more popular, and an effective was to entice new buyers.

Having been a timeshare owner for over twenty years, I can honestly say I have never regretted my purchase decisions. Oh yes, do not get me wrong, I have had some problems over the years, but who has not. You must remember that I have owned during the entire growth of an industry. I have survived all the ups, downs, misinformation, dubious exchanges, maintenance increases and other changes during all of those years. This also includes listening to all the BS and negativity from friends, family, acquaintances and strangers. If I can live with the past, then I am reasonably sure that you can handle the future.☺

In conclusion, now that you know the truth about the industry, choose a vacation ownership package that suits you. Do not let anyone else tell you what, when or how you should buy, and that includes me. Do what is right for you, your family and your peace of mind. Just as food, water and air are needed to keep us physically alive, vacations are essential to keep our mental and spiritual selves alive.

Remember, there is no trial run for our LIFE -- it is the real thing – learn to appreciate every little bit of it. Waiting until ... another day ... well, you may not get the chance.

So, I will ask you again, what is your answer, now that you have had time to think about it**?**

MAY YOU *and* YOUR FAMILY
HAVE MANY HAPPY YEARS OF SEEING THE
WOLRD USING VACATION OWNERSHIP

Chapter 17

Buyer Beware -
Timeshare Scams & Frauds

Back in chapter 4 I said that I would be neglectful not to mention that there are also a wide assortment of timeshare scams and frauds which have surfaced in the past five years, especially since the collapse of the real estate market in 2008. The media is full of stories about some form of fraud or scam that is perpetuated each and every day. From the emails saying you have won a trip but all you need to do it call or email your credit card information for them to guarantee your flights to those ones requesting you send money overseas to release a relative from a foreign jail. They are not limited to any specific type of demographic; no one is safe from being approached from some form of scam, especially in this new world of social media. Instead of the telephone calls of the old days, scams now also come by email, websites, posts on Tweets, Facebook etc and only limited to the criminals imagination.

The fraudsters usually set up a ¨boiler room¨ concept and hire specially selected individuals to work telephones or social media and emails to contact people on lists that they may have purchased, stolen or hacked. Their only aim is to ¨collect the money or credit card information¨ and then change locations or leave town, shut down that particular website, cancel and change telephone numbers or change their name and start over, sometimes the next day. In many cases, the same company will have ¨set up¨ offices in different states with corresponding telephone numbers and if searched correctly, and a bogus address. For example, a company is using an address of XYZ Building, 15 Hill Avenue, Suite 1105, Somewhere, FL 33033. But if you check online the real building only has 6 floors, so a suite #1105 is not real or they pick a room number which you cannot verify is real or not. Phone numbers are set up using routers or companies which sell US numbers for a monthly fee so that they can move them from ¨company to company¨ or ¨state to state.¨

In the United States, there are two groups, one, the FTC (Federal Trade Commission) and the American Resort Development Association (ARDA) which continually monitor and work with various state and federal law enforcement groups to clean up these scams and put those responsible for them in jail or fine them heavily. In Mexico, there is AMDETUR and ADEPROTUR, both government agencies which monitor timeshare activities and also work to clean up these scams. There are also agencies in other countries which monitor timeshare activities which were mentioned in chapter 15.

So what is a timeshare scam or fraud? It is someone who will tell you that they have a buyer or renter for your timeshare and then fraudulently take your money by saying that you need to pay an upfront fee of some type. In some cases they are only trying to get your credit card or bank account information so that they can perpetuate the fraud by making other charges to your account which then becomes difficult to trace.

How and why were you contacted? The how is an ongoing problem for any business organization, as we may remember from the 2012 Target credit card theft problem. Companies spend a considerable sum of money protecting their members/users privacy, however all it takes is one person who for some reason decides to steal this information - whether they work for the company or hack into their network to sell the information, money is always the prize. People get paid for taking the information and the fraudsters make a ton of money from taking advantage of unsuspecting individuals.

In the timeshare industry, the information obtained by the fraudsters is quite complete surprisingly. They know when you purchased, what you purchased, how much you paid, and your contact information to which exchange company you use to exchange. From that, you are put on a call or email list and the scam starts. What you do about it is up to you. Below I cover both telephone and email scams, but more importantly, I cover what you should do if you are contacted or a victim of a timeshare scam. Actually the suggestions would work for any other type of scam you may encounter. Specifically, all of the scams listed below are counting on either your desperation to sell or rent your timeshare or just on the plain old greed factor.

TELEPHONE SCAMS

Telephone scams in general have been around for a very long time, but as mentioned above have taken on the timeshare market these past few years. As of this printing there are five main scams listed below, with many variations, which keep rotating throughout the industry.

1. <u>Resale Scam</u>: You receive a telephone call from a company claiming to be a resale company telling you that they have a buyer for your timeshare and all you have to do is to pay a set transfer fee or tax percentage and then you will receive your money. They give you an amount which is anywhere from one and a half to three times what you paid for your timeshare as the extra incentive.

    For example: You paid $13,000 for your Studio unit - you will be told that there is a buyer willing to pay $25,000 for your week and all you need to do is pay 10% tax on the purchase price ($2,500) and once it is received you will have the $25,000 either deposited into your bank account (they ask for this information) or they will send you a check.

    A variation of this is scam is that they pose as a "legitimate timeshare association" stating that you may relinquish your membership rights through them, but in order to do so, must send a deposit to a specific account to cover the transfer costs. Both of these variants claim to already have buyers lined up to purchase your property.

2. <u>Rental Scam A</u>: You receive a telephone call from a company claiming to be a rental company telling you that they have a renter for your timeshare and all you have to do is to pay the reservation and guest fee and then you will receive your money.

3. <u>Rental Scam B:</u> This is one that is used in some sales rooms to convince you to purchase a timeshare from them. While you are still sitting on the table, the salesperson may put you on the phone with someone ¨from a company that the resort works with doing their rentals¨ and convinces you that they can rent your week for two or three times your maintenance fees so that you can pay it off sooner or make money (greed factor). All they ask of you is to pay an upfront fee starting from $399 to over $1,000 depending on the ¨company¨. If you decide to purchase and take this route, you will then be contacted by telephone from the ¨company¨ after you get home and then pay them the applicable fee. After you have been contacted and paid the fee, they charge your credit card and

after that, it is highly unlikely that they will be in touch with you. If you call to try and reach a representative, will be told they are busy and will call you back or just say they have no renters yet.

NOTE: This rental scam is NOT tolerated by any respected resort and usually creates cancellation requests and complaints which resorts do not want or need, so sales personnel responsible for these scams find themselves unemployed quite quickly or having their commissions withheld when these sales are cancelled. Social media and complaints websites are full of this owners complaining of this type of scam, however as long as some people are fueled by greed, they will continue to be around.

4. Lawsuit or Legal Scam: This fraud involves the same type of situation, in that you will receive a call from a supposed law firm or advocate stating that there is a lawsuit pending against your resort or club for something plausible and if you want to be involved you will need to pay part of the legal retainer or to be included in the lawsuit. A variation of this one - as an owner at your resort or a member of your ¨club¨ a lawsuit was won and if you provide bank account transfer information they will send your portion of the winnings.

5. Trial Membership Offer Scams: This scam involves you receiving a telephone call from a company claiming they called to offer you a trial membership program even though they already are aware than you own a timeshare product. They know this because they have access to the information which they purchased from a non-legitimate source and are operating out of ¨boiler rooms.¨

Once you tell them you are not interested in a trial membership because you already have one, they will then ask if you are interested in selling it because they can ¨get you a good¨ price for it. If you tell them that you are interested in selling, BEWARE, because this is where the scam starts. They will tell you that all you need to do then is to the pay a set transfer fee or tax percentage before they can start the process. They of course, want you to make the payment upfront and now the scam circles back to the scam/fraud I listed in number 1 above.

As a point of interest, usually one, if not all of the above scams are operated out of the same ¨boiler room.¨

EMAIL SCAMS

Similar to the telephone scams above, you may receive unsolicited emails from companies stating any one of the above telephone scams. You may, and can also receive, email follow ups to the telephone scams. These usually involve the ¨so called proof¨ of the company´s background, the buyers purchase contract, escrow funds validating the supposed deposit of the purchasers money, tax/fiscal or government paperwork and forms, wire transfer instructions and other things to support their claim and validate their position.

These companies rely on the fact that most people are not familiar with contracts, governmental or tax paperwork so they create almost ¨perfect¨ replicas of the real contracts, government and/or tax forms so if people do happen to Google that particular tax agency and/or the tax form, they will see something that ¨looks like¨ the one they were emailed and believe it to be real. They also include false or misleading email addresses with terminations like .gob instead of .gov and put on phone numbers, which when you call are answered as if the caller had reached that particular government agency. Based on this, they then send the requested amount of money and then wait... and wait... and wait...

Just in the past five years, as the Director of Member Services in several resorts, I have seen these ¨we have a buyer¨ telephone/email scams taking a huge toll of both the member's wallets and their trust. There are no exact numbers available as to how many timeshare owners have been taken advantage of on this particular telephone/email scam but I know of some people who lost tens of thousands of dollars paying the bogus transfer taxes and then receiving nothing in return.

WHAT SHOULD YOU DO?

First and foremost, when you receive an unsolicited telephone call or email stating that there is a buyer or renter for your timeshare **stop and ask yourself - did you actually list your timeshare with any company, website, or social media site?** If the answer is no, then you can be 100% guaranteed the call is a scam. If you have listed your timeshare for sale or rent, make sure that you are receiving a call or email only from that particular company.

In an effort to reduce these types of scams and frauds, your resort or club management works diligently to try and keep owner informed through newsletters, club websites and social media sites. If you are contacted (or worse yet, a victim) they want to know everything about the encounter so that they can proceed with legal action against these companies. They also advise any government agency that may assist in putting an end to this type of scam or fraud.

Here are some things that you can, and should do when you receive these types of calls or emails:

1. If called, say you are interested but you need <u>Contact information</u>: ASK FOR and KEEP:
   a. The full legal name of the company
   b. Where they are located - complete address
   c. Their telephone numbers - all of them
   d. The name of the company´s President/CEO
   e. The salesperson´s full name and extension number (even a cell number if you can)
   f. History of the company - how long in business, etc
   g. Do they have a website, Facebook page, Twitter account, YouTube, etc...?
   h. Are they members of a timeshare organization such as ARDA (American Resort Development Association); AMDETUR (Mexican association); CRDA (Canadian Resort Development Association) etc?
   i. Complete name of all defendants/law firms etc... if a ¨legal¨ case.

   NOTE: IF they refuse to give you any of the above information or say it is not available or confidential - take that as a true warning sign that they are not legitimate.

2. If you receive an unsolicited email to resell your week - contact them under the same premise that you are interested and get the above information.
3. Ask them to email you ALL the paperwork that will be necessary to complete the transaction, and I mean everything, so that you can read through it and possibly send it to your lawyer for review. The salesperson will offer a comment stating that a ¨lawyer may be expensive and why would you need one, these are just simple forms...¨ That alone should set off some warning signals that something may not be right. Some examples of paperwork would be:
   a. Offer to Purchase
   b. Escrow account information
   c. Their contract to authorize them to resell your week

      d.   Bank wire transfer information
      e.   Tax submission forms
      f.   State or provincial transfer forms
      g.   Copy of Lawsuit or filing papers

4.   Call every phone number on the paperwork and see if a real person answers. 99% of the time you will get a voice mail message asking you to leave a message and you will be called back by ¨Bob, Carol, Ted, Alice, Steve, etc...¨. If you pay attention to the voices on the messages you may find that it is the same female voice leaving all of the messages for the women and male voice for the men. This is especially the case with the same company using different names to pull the same scam in different locations.

    Short Story: I used this tactic to call seven different companies which had sent unsolicited emails to members and after the third voice mail message in as many states, I noticed that the voice was the same. I kept calling and sure enough it was the same female voice for the women and the same man´s voice on the men´s emails. How can six different people, in six different states have the same voice - what are the odds on that?

5.   Go online and do a little research. As mentioned above, Google search the address to see if it is legitimate. Google the Better Business Bureau (BBB) in that city. The company will most likely appear, but the date of incorporation is within the last six months to one year with no history. See if you can find the CEO or President by searching for them. Again you may find someone of the same name, but not in the same industry. It is quite common for these companies to use as much ¨real¨ information as they can to validate the scam.

6.   Go online and search for any complaints about these companies. There are a number of timeshare and general complaint sites that victims will post on to warn others. If you have been a victim, post something yourself. The more people who are aware, the less chance the scams will work.

7.   Send a copy of EVERYTHING that you receive and discover online to your Resort´s Club or Management with your concerns on HOW they contacted you. This is important to ask because some resorts may not know that their membership information has been compromised. Your resort will then follow through with their legal department to investigate the source of leaked information as well as work with any and all agencies to try and stop this type of fraud.

8.   Contact the Better Business Bureau in the state(s) they list and advise them of the attempted scam and send them copies of everything they request.

9. Contact your local Consumer Protection Agency and the Federal Trade Commission and send them copies of everything they request.

The worst case scenario - you are a victim of this type of fraud. Do not beat yourself up about it... get even... follow all of the steps I mention above and do not let it happen to you again. Yes, I did say that - do not let it happen again. I know of a couple of older members in a resort which were taken advantage of not once, but twice. The second company was so convincing that they told the members that they would launch a lawsuit at no cost to them, as well would reimburse them the value of their loss as a show of good faith. All they needed to do was pay the Mexican SAT tax on the ¨real¨ transfer and give them wire transfer information to send the money, rather than write a check, like the company that scammed them did when they asked for payment. The Tax form looked so real that they sent the money and never heard from the second company again. Unfortunately it took the second time they were scammed before they contacted their resort and told me about their situation.

Another story to show how to deal with these scams, I have another member who knew from the first call and emails that the approach was a scam, called me and after giving her the suggestions above, she decided to have a little fun with the company to see how far they would go to get her transfer money. She called them back and said she would not sell to them for $21,000 because she had another company which offered her $35,000, they countered with $40,000 and she said she would call them back. After a couple of days, she finally reached someone and said the counter offer was $55,000 and what could they give her? Well, can you see how ridiculous this is getting... with her pretense that someone else was interested she created a bidding war on money she knew she was never going to receive. The member told me she had a really hard time ¨keeping a straight face¨ as it were while talking to the salesperson on the phone but finally ended the charade with - ¨are you serious? Until I actually see the check, which I want sent by UPS tomorrow latest, I will not pay you anything¨. The salesperson said he would call her right back... my guess is that she is still waiting...or not!! If you are so inclined, have fun with them, make them crazy believing you are falling for the scam and then make a real demand for your money before you pay them anything. My guess is that you will never hear from them again and your name may be taken off future call or email lists.

SOCIAL MEDIA APPROACHES

Facebook, Twitter, Blogs, personal websites and whatever comes next.... all of the above scams and frauds can be sent through all of these types of social media so be careful how you set up your privacy settings or who you accept as a "friend", "tweet" with or who accesses your blog ... no site these days is safe from people who are trying to find a way to relieve you of your hard earned money. If you receive any unsolicited "to good to be true" notices, think twice and follow the procedures I outlined above.

My last suggestion is to NEVER, EVER send, or give, any money upfront to any person or company for any rental, resale, lawsuit or membership transfer, especially with the promise of them sending you money at some later date. Remember, you should never have to pay upfront to have a legitimate company sell or rent your timeshare property.

In summary, you will not be scammed if you remember what I said earlier in this chapter - when you receive an solicited telephone call or email stating that there is a buyer or renter for your timeshare stop and ask yourself - did you actually list your timeshare with any company, website, or social media site? If the answer is no, then you can be 100% guaranteed the call is a scam.

Chapter 18

Tips for the Savvy Traveler

We all like to believe that when on vacation we are savvy when it comes to dealing with most problems that arise. As a frequent traveler I have come across a number of situations over the years where common sense and calm deal very effectively with the problem. However, there are a few instances where help, in any form, in welcomed and appreciated. So, if you are a frequent world traveler, this section might be redundant for you, however if you have only traveled a few times you may appreciate and welcome the basic information provided.

THE BASICS

❖ Use common sense when dealing with any situation, in any country. Stay calm and cool. Getting angry, irritated or upset only leads to more trouble - anywhere you are.

❖ When walking about sightseeing, be observant and look around you from time to time to see who may be lingering around. A suspicious person should be reported to someone in authority if you feel you are being stalked, watched or uncomfortable. If this is not possible, get on some form of public transportation or take a taxi and leave the area for somewhere else. Better to avoid a potentially dangerous situation than encourage it.

❖ Take a picture with your phone of your ID, passport, credit cards, prescriptions and tickets and email them to yourself in the case of theft or loss. These days you can access your email account from anywhere and then you have the information available if you need it. You can also list the serial numbers of your electronics on a piece of paper and take a picture of that and add it to your email.

❖ When using your ATM access card to get money, be smart. Do not give others the opportunity to see what you are taking from the cash machine. Only withdraw what you need for a short time. Better to make more trips for smaller amounts, than one trip and either lose it or have it stolen. In many countries you will receive money in local currency and there may be a daily limit of cash that can be taken from ATM's, so do not get angry if you only get a couple of hundred dollars in <u>local currency</u>.

❖ Credit card frauds still exist so when using credit cards, use common sense. Make sure it is in your possession when you leave the store and you have the receipts. Only travel with what credit cards you feel you will absolutely need in case of an emergency. Traveling with every card that you own, is not only foolish, but should your wallet be stolen, becomes a pain in the neck. In this new electronic and digital age, be careful when using your credit cards around someone using a cell phone as there have now been instances of pictures of cards taken with the new "camera phones" and then the information from the picture is used for fraudulent purposes.

❖ DO NOT walk around flashing large wads of bills as you will only make yourself a target for robbery. When going out for the day or evening, take only what you think you will need and leave the rest in your hotel safety deposit boxes.

❖ The use of safety deposit boxes is a good idea. More and more resorts and hotels have them in individual rooms where you can use your own combination. Use them. If there is no safe in the room, use the hotel´s safe option - they all have them. Put all of your valuables into them. This includes Passports, debit or credit cards, tickets or any jewelry you are not wearing at the time. The lines at Consulate offices get longer each year replacing the Passports stolen from purses, bags, fanny packs and backpacks.

❖ Even though most hotels and resorts have electronic keys, you should not needlessly display your room keys in public or leave them on restaurant tables, at the swimming pool, on your beach chair or any other place where they can be stolen. Hotels provide many options to guests to secure their regular keys - from chains worn around the neck to returning the key to the front desk when leaving for the day. Check with the hotel you are staying in for the best option. In most European countries you may have to leave your hotel key at the front desk when leaving the hotel, for any reason. Also remember if you have an electronic room key, do not put keep it near your cell phone as it will demagnetize. The last thing you want late at night is to have to go to the front desk to have them reactivate it or give you a new key.

❖ Do not answer the door to your hotel, condo, and ship stateroom to anyone without verifying who it is. If a person claims to be an employee, call the front desk or Purser to verify that someone is supposed to have access to your room, for what purpose and how long.

❖ When returning late to your hotel or condo late in the evening, use the main entrance of the building. If you believe that someone is following you, ask a security person to walk with you to your room.

❖ Close the door securely whenever you are in your room and use the locking devices provided when retiring for the night.

❖ Check to see that any sliding doors, connecting doors or windows can be closed and locked securely. If your Buree or hut does not have windows, use the mosquito netting provided. I would not be too worried about anything other than the bugs.

❖ Use caution when inviting strangers to your room. This could lead to trouble.

❖ Earlier I mentioned to take pictures of all credit cards and documentation with you. You should also send a copy to a responsible person not travelling with you as a backstop measure. When I travel I always carry photocopies of everything that makes it very easy to replace anything in case of loss or theft and keep it in the safe. Just make sure you do not keep the copies with your documentation.

❖ Traveler's Checks. Although their use and acceptance has diminished considerably around the world they still do exist and are a safe alternative to money. Some people feel more comfortable using them as an alternative to carrying credit cards. Traveler's checks are still accepted in most countries now so buy the ones that are the most economical for you. For couples traveling together, but doing activities separately, consider using American Express dual traveler's checks. Have your spouse sign half and you sign the other half, which provide more flexibility and security. Again, take pictures of them and keep copies with you and leave a copy at home in case they are stolen.

❖ When buying from farmer´s markets, bazaars, street or beach vendors use common sense and courtesy. Bartering is common in many countries but should not be abused to the point where you are offering a price that is unrealistic or ridiculous. Be prepared to take some time for negotiations in large Middle Eastern bazaars. I once had to meet the whole family and have tea before I could even start bartering on some Turkish towels in Istanbul. Two hours later I had towels, doilies, slippers, pillow cases and new friends. My next stop, unfortunately, was the luggage stall to get the towels home and well, as they say, that is another story.

❖ Respect and obey the laws of the country that you are vacationing in. You should be aware that outside of the United Sates and Canada, Napoleonic Law governs most countries. This means that you are guilty until you can prove yourself innocent and you are not necessarily entitled to a telephone call.

❖ So, whether you are vacationing in your home-town, Vienna, Cancun or Marrakech - use common sense.

RENTAL CARS

❖ Not all rental car companies are created equal. Consider using the major rental car companies when looking for a rental car as they will be the most reliable. Use caution when renting from local companies as you may not have any recourse should anything happen while you are renting their car. The cheapest does not always mean the safest.

❖ Read all the information provided. Renting and driving a car in Mexico, Europe, or even Hawaii is much different from renting in your home-town.

❖ Decide if you are going to take the extra insurance. Many credit card companies do cover these additional charges but you might want to check first. If you do decide to take the extra insurance read very carefully the terms of these options as you may still find yourself paying out huge sums just for a scratch on the door. Remember that if you agree to a 10% deductible, you are still responsible for 10% of their estimated repair cost not what you think it would cost to fix the damage. Also be aware that they put a ¨hold¨ on your credit card for the amount of ¨their deductible¨ which may affect how much available credit you have left on your card for the rest of your vacation.

The Collision Damage Waivers (CDW) on rental cars varies considerably with not only the rental company but the countries you are driving in so ask before you rent. Many do have a specific limit on the insurance or damage waivers for which you could end up being responsible for any amount above that limit.

❖ Some countries may require a locally issued driver's license or an International Driver's License. Check with your auto club, travel agent or exchange resorts to see what type of license you will need.

❖ In some countries car rentals come with a standard gear shift, not an automatic shift. If you really want an automatic shift, check the price. It can be twice as expensive as a manual or standard shift.

❖ Study a map of where you are going and make note of important markers to help guide you to your destination. Knowing that you need to turn left after you see a particular sign or monument is much easier than trying to read and drive at the same time. It is also far less dangerous to you and your fellow drivers.

❖ Remember that not all countries drive on the same side of the road. It can be very disorienting to try to drive on the left, when you always drive on the right side of the road.

❖ Mileage is most countries are measured in kilometers not miles.

❖ Miles to kilometers: Multiply the miles by 1.6.
  • (5 miles x 1.6 = 8 kilometers)

❖ Kilometers to miles: Multiply the kilometers by .62
  • (5 kilometers x .62 = 3.1 miles)

❖ Obey all posted traffic and road signs. Despite the use of international signs some countries may use signs in their native language. Local maps do provide some help in this area.

❖ Gas may also be sold in liters, not gallons. Always fill the tank. It will save you many a headache over saying, "Just 10 gallons please" and run out of gas on a road in the middle of nowhere. If you plan on any long distance travel where services may not be available, take along a full, spare can of gas and a gallon of bottled water in case the radiator overheats.

❖ Lock any valuables that you have in the trunk when stopping to eat, take pictures, and go to the bathroom or whatever. Do not risk that 3 minute trip to the bathroom leaving your camera on the seat. It only takes 30 seconds for someone to break the window and go.

❖ Always lock the vehicle and take the keys when you are not driving it. Even for that 3-minute trip to the bathroom. How do you think cars get stolen?

❖ Toll Roads and Bridges. They exist everywhere in the world. Make sure you have enough local currency to pay them as some may not take credit cards. You should also make sure of where they are in your journey. If you do not, you had better be prepared for anything.

❖ Spot checks. These also exist throughout the world. Checking for everything and anything, you can be stopped by any form of authority. Remain calm - nervousness causes them to be more suspicious even if you have nothing to hide, they will search you for sure. Do not volunteer information just answer the questions asked, and especially do not make a point of aggravating them. Let them look if they want to and you will be on your way without too much trouble. If you are smuggling anything, be prepared to accept the consequences of that country.

❖ One last thing - make sure that you can take your rental car into another country if you plan to drive around the "continent" or elsewhere. For example, if you rent a car from some rental agencies, you may not be able drive it into Mexico, even for lunch. If this is in your plans, check with the rental agency about cross border accessibility.

THE MEDICAL STUFF

❖ Medical care varies from country to country. While all countries do their best to provide good medical care, there may not always be a fully equipped or have a 100% sterile hospital available. You may end up in a small country clinic or receiving first aid on a beach, miles from anywhere. In whichever situation you find yourself try to remain calm and rational. Sometimes the blood looks worse than the actual injury.

❖ If you are injured in an accident but are stable and transportable, you may want to fly back to your hometown/country for medical care. If you have just broken a bone, this can be plastered in a local medical facility. Should you require immediate emergency care, check with your local consulate office for their recommendation. If no other option exists other than the local hospital, have a family member do their best to communicate any information necessary for you to receive proper medical attention. If you need to, hire a translator to ensure the correct information is being relayed.

❖ One thing I have discovered in my travels is that the local remedies can be very effective on minor tourist ailments. Everything from bites, cuts, sunburns, headaches, stomach aches, diarrhea and nausea just to name a few problems tourists suffer from.

❖ Other than serious, hospital care, the following are a few commonsense tidbits:
Pack a light medical kit with you. Put in headache, stomach and anti-diarrhea medication first. Then add some Band-aids (assorted sizes), chapstick, cortisone cream and/or an antiseptic spray for small cuts and/or sunburns. Baby wipes (travel size), antiseptic hand clears, bug spray, safety pins, a small roll of gauze and 4 or 5 non stick gauze pads for miscellaneous cuts and scrapes. Put into a zip lock bag for easier packing and for carrying around with you in your day-packs. These few things will keep you prepared for most minor irritations.

❖ Keep an emergency contact list with you at all times. It is easier for medical personnel, the hospital or even the consulate, if they know who to call in case of emergency or if you are unconscious.

❖ If you take medication on a regular basis, take what you will need for your vacation PLUS an extra weeks supply. Should you be stuck anywhere, for any reason, you will have enough to last you.

❖ If you are on medication, take a picture or copy of your prescription(s) with you. Many countries may want to verify that you <u>need</u> to be carrying 50 tablets of a controlled substance for personal use. Even upon returning to the United States or Canada can be a problem if you use a specific drug and cannot show that you are legally entitled to be carrying it.

❖ The second reason - should you need to refill the prescription you can show a local doctor <u>exactly</u> what it is you take. Most countries <u>will not</u> refill a US or Canadian prescription for controlled substance medication. You will need to consult a local doctor who will write a local order for the medication using your original prescription as their guide.

❖ Many countries throughout the world do carry medications that are not readily available in Canada or the United States so take care when using over the counter medications. Just because your hotel clerk recommends something for your "stingray" bite, does not mean that you should run right to the pharmacy and buy it. Just because something may work for the local population, does not mean it would necessarily work for you. Please use commonsense and caution - read the labels, even if you have to have an interpreter read it to you.

❖ If you have never heard of a particular drug before, ask a qualified medical person for an explanation or a similar drug you know. Do not take anything that you do not know what the potential side effects will be. Always check the dosage.

❖ Do not take any foreign medication if you are on specific dosages of FDA approved medication. Many countries offer more highly potent dosages that may cause more harm than do good.

❖ If you suffer from allergies to anything - medication, foods, etc., write them down or take a picture of them and keep it the list in your wallet.

❖ If you have anaphylactic allergies or are a diabetic you <u>should</u> be wearing a medical alert symbol of some form. Available in necklaces, wrist or ankle bracelets, these are true lifesavers. Make sure that your allergy or required care in engraved on the back. In most countries the first places checked by trained medical personnel are neck, wrist and ankle. Some countries do check wallets, but if you are unconscious and the information is in your wallet, no one may think of looking there until it is too late.

❖ Travel with appropriate medication to deal with minor allergy attacks or carry prescriptions for certain types of anaphylactic antihistamines, EpiPens or Anakits. The last two items contain syringe filled epinephrine (which is a controlled heart medication) for extreme anaphylactic reactions. I have traveled the world with my medical bracelet and EpiPens for years. Fortunately, I only ever had to use them once which gave me sufficient time to get medical attention.

❖ Insurance policies: Check and make sure what your policy covers and how much it covers. If no, or limited, coverage is available BUY a travel insurance package. The cost weighed against potential emergencies is money well spent, even if you have never had a sick day in your life.

❖ If you have to pay for your local medical care, use the best option provided to you. If possible, use credit cards so as not eat up your cash on hand. Even US hospitals provide the option of financing your stay so as not to mortgage your family home to cover the cost.

AIRLINES: Airlines will do their best to accommodate any emergency in-flight. Call a flight attendant if any serious condition exhibits itself and they will advise the front-end crew who will determine the best course of action. I have had a number of allergy related incidents while flying and the airplane will land wherever and whenever they can to assist in the emergency.

❖ Airline medical kits do not carry much medication. They mainly carry aspirin and other items for minor passenger ailments. Some airlines do however carry snake-bite anti-venom. I find that quite bizarre, but what the heck, life is full of the bizarre.

❖ Airline personnel are not allowed to administer medication. They will give you water to take your medication, but will not inject you with your Insulin or EpiPen. Ask a family member or fellow passenger to do it if you cannot do it yourself.

CRUISES: If you are planning a cruise and need particular medical care, ask the cruise line if it is available.

❖ Ask your physician if there is any reason you should not cruise. Being away from full scale medical support may be a factor in your choice.

❖ Call the cruise line and ask about their infirmary or hospital facilities aboard the particular ship on which you want to travel. Be specific about what you need and what they have on hand. Ask if there is a licensed doctor and nurses and how many are aboard.

❖ Check with the cruise line as to their pharmaceutical offerings. If they do not have what you need, take it with you. Most normally stock the basics to deal with the everyday passenger ailments and may only have enough for stabilizing emergency care.

❖ If you have an emergency on board the cruise line will do whatever it can to get you to a facility where emergency care can be provided. However, if you are in the middle of the Indian Ocean, it may take awhile. Check with your insurance carrier to find out if they provide additional coverage in emergency situations.

❖ If cleanliness or sanitation is an issue for you, check with the Centre for Disease Control at www.cdc.gov. Cruise line's inspection reports are available on the Internet or by mail.

CUSTOMS AND HOLIDAYS

❖ Did you know that you can not take playing cards into Turkey? It is illegal to gamble there and they consider playing cards a gambling device. I witnessed a young man get hauled off to jail for asking store owners where he could buy cards similar to the ones to he was showing them. Some fast talking by the consulate saved him from life in a Turkish prison. Remember Midnight Express?

❖ Every country in the world has customs that we may not like or understand but we should HONOR them when we travel there. Just as we would expect a visitor from that country to honor our customs, we should do no less in theirs. **Respect is universal**. We have all heard the term "ugly American." Although not limited to just Americans, this came about because Americans spent more time looking out for themselves than respecting local people or their customs. Do not let yourself get labeled as an "ugly tourist."

❖ If you are traveling to a foreign land and not sure of their customs, buy a book that outlines the customs and restrictions. There is nothing you cannot find these days on the internet so Google the country-customs you are going to avoid embarrassing situations. If you cannot find what you are looking for contact the nearest consulate of the country or countries where you plan on going and they will be happy to provide you with information.

❖ Every country has their specific holiday, festival or celebration days. With color and fanfare these days are wonderful to be apart of, whether you are a local or a visitor. If you can participate in the local celebrations, do it - eat, drink and dance with the locals - you will have the best time of your life.

❖ Honor and respect the local holidays: These days are very important to the country you are visiting.

❖ Remember that whatever country you are in, during most major holidays ALL government offices, financial institutions and many stores will be closed for the celebrations. So, if you need to do some banking, do it either before the holiday or after the holiday. You would not want to find yourself cash poor over the holiday and the ATM out of service!

CURRENCY

❖ Use the local currency of the country that you are visiting. Not only do you get better treatment by the local people, you also will get a better price on most purchased items. If the locals have to keep converting your currency (example dollars) to Lira, Rials, Pesos, Bhat or whatever, you will be paying more for everything.

❖ Travel with a variety of payment options: Cash, debit and/or credit cards or traveler's checks.

❖ If you chose to pay by credit card you may be charged an additional fee by the vendor. Ask at the point of purchase. Many people like using credit cards because banks do give you the best inter-bank exchange rate when the purchase is posted to your account. An important point to remember is that most credit cards now charge a 3% foreign transaction fee so if you plan on travelling outside of your respective country, find a credit card that will not charge you this type of fee.

❖ Banks often offer the most favorable exchange rates. However, weigh the option of standing in a half hour line against using an exchange booth. Unless you are cashing thousands of dollars, the difference is usually not enough to make the wait worthwhile.
For example: in Mexico: 1 US$ to Peso: Bank - 13.00 pesos to 1 US$ or Exchange Booth - 12.70. On a $100 the difference is only 30 pesos or about $2.50 dollars. Is the wait worth it?

❖ If you exchange at banks, airports, train stations, bus stations, hotels, stores you may be charged a commission. Ask before you exchange your money.

❖ Before you leave you home airport buy a small amount of the currency for the country you are traveling to for your immediate needs on arrival – taxi's, tips, etc. Some cities do have independent foreign currency exchange houses which do offer respectable exchange rates, so if you have one near you it might be worth considering changing money there before, and after your trip.

TIPPING

- ❖ My philosophy on this is: Tip for good service or talk to the manager/owner about bad service. Remember that if you do not leave a tip, the waiter may just think you forgot or worse, that you are a cheap tourist.
- ❖ Tip as you would where you live. Whatever the bill is, take the percentage. Remember 20 percent for good service, 5 percent for lousy or bad service and 15 percent if it was okay. Tip more if the service was spectacular. Please do not use a calculator to convert to your currency and then back, it is a waste of time and you look silly. For example, whatever the local currency, if your meal cost you $100, leave 15 percent or $15 as a tip.
- ❖ Remember in all countries servers are paid minimum wage and live off their tips. Don´t be labeled as cheap, it leaves a bad impression. Should you ever want to eat at that restaurant again, service will most definitely be slower.
- ❖ Remember that service is proportional to tip anticipated. If you demand much attention or make many demands, tip the server for their time and attention to you. For all the attention they give you, they are neglecting someone else who may be a better tipper than you are.
- ❖ Hotel staff varies as to service provided. Consider a US dollar a day to your housekeeper or if you are staying a long time, tip each week. If special services are provided, like ironing (get your mind out of the gutter), pay separately for these services.
- ❖ Bell-hops usually get the equivalent of a US dollar per bag. It is worth it. Consider your back against their luggage dolly.
- ❖ Car Valets vary as to your own personal situation. I would rather tip a valet in Las Vegas to get my car, turn on the air conditioning, then bring it to me for a couple of bucks than walk across the 110^0F parking lot and get it myself.

Karen's Tipping Rule: Tip as you would want to be tipped, especially if that tip was your only means of feeding your family that day.

DATES AND TIME AND ELECTRICAL POWER

- ❖ Sounds silly perhaps, but not everyone expresses the date or time in the same way. For example, the **DATE**. I was born on October 10. Since the date, in either format is 10/10; I can never tell anyone which comes first - day or month. The format even differs between Canada and the United States. So, whether December first is written as December 1, 1999; 1 December 1999 or as 12/1/99 or 1/12/99, they all are the same. Remember, if number is greater than 12 you know it is a date not a month.

❖ **TIME** in many countries is expressed by using the 24-hour clock. AM times are indicated by the numbers 1 through 12 and PM times using the numbers 13 through 23. If you have trouble with the PM times, just subtract 12. For example: 21:30 - 12 = 9:30 pm. Midnight is 0000. Airline, train, bus, ship and ferry schedules all work on the 24-hour clock system.

❖ If you are crossing the International Date Line going from North America to Asia, add a day and/or vice versa.

❖ If you are still confused, ask the locals and they will always tell you what time it is. By the way, if you are on vacation, do you really want to know what the day, or time, is?

❖ **ELECTRICAL POWER** or voltage will either be 110v or 220v. Most modern hotels and resorts do accommodate 110v. Outside of North America 220v is more common. Check with your Exchange Company, resort or travel agent as to which type of voltage is used. Take an adapter for 220v. I always travel with a couple of adapters. Since they are so small, they fit in most luggage pockets.

DEPARTURE TAXES, TOURISM TAXES AND OTHER FEES

❖ Many countries charge a fee or a tax to leave or arrive in their country. So, be prepared to leave a few of your vacation dollars at your port of entry or exit. Taxes or fees vary from country to country so check with your travel agent or transportation provider on what the current rate is. Most tourism fees or taxes are mandated and regulated by the governments of the countries that you are visiting.

❖ Departure or tourism taxes can run from US$25 per person in Mexico, US$30+ in the Caribbean and more. If you are traveling with a large group it can add up quickly if you are not prepared. Arrival fees can range from US$20 in Mexico to more for Middle Eastern countries. Also remember that after September 11th, some countries charge security fees ranging from US$2.50 and up. Most of these taxes are included on airline tickets but if you are not sure, ask them.

❖ Many hotels and resorts also charge fees or taxes to guests and even timeshare exchange guests. It is not uncommon for there to be anything from a 2 percent to a 40 percent hospitality tax on your accommodation. Some timeshare properties the tax is incorporated into maintenance fees but owners/exchangers should check with your exchange company to verify if you will be charged, and what the amount should be.

❖ Your hotel or resort may also have other things that they charge for in addition to a hospitality or tourism tax. These may be a direct charge upon check in or check out, while others may be use a refundable deposit system. The latter will be returned to you upon departure or on return of the item in question. Cost of these additional items can be costly so if you are not sure, contact the resort.

Following is a list of things that you could be charged for, or they require a refundable deposit:

   ❖ Electricity and other utility charges
   ❖ Safe deposit boxes if in-room safes are not available
   ❖ Room keys (Especially lost keys or key cards)
   ❖ Beach or Pool Towels
   ❖ Beach or Pool Chairs
   ❖ Use of Spa facilities
   ❖ TV Remote Control(s)
   ❖ Maid service other than resorts normally provided service
   ❖ Security deposits for damage
   ❖ Parking (in high density locations)

❖ If you are a timeshare exchanger, the confirmation sheet that you receive from your exchange company should mention any charges or fees that apply to that particular resort. When you are budgeting for your vacations, whether a timeshare one or not, remember to take these additional costs into account.

❖ One last important tip: Whatever type of accommodation you choose to say in - timeshare, hotel, motel, Buree or cruise ship - you will be required to leave a deposit upon check-in. You may leave a signed credit card voucher or cash, but you will be required to leave one. Upon check out any charges will be billed to your credit card or deducted from the cash. Now when I travel I leave cash so that when I check out, getting back the cash is a nice perk. It makes me feel as if they are paying me for my stay instead of the other way around. In Las Vegas I especially leave a cash deposit, and then when I check-out I am actually leaving Las Vegas with money - it is kind of like a savings plan!!

All of these tips come from years of personal travel experience. If I have forgotten something just USE COMMON SENSE and ASK FOR HELP. People all over the world have helped me out of situations at one time or the other, so to all of you who helped me, my eternal thanks.

The most important tip of all –

BE POLITE, BE PATIENT, BE GRACIOUS,
BE RESPECTFUL and SMILE
and everyone will benefit from your vacation, especially you!!

Chapter 19

Terms Used in the Industry

Affiliated Resort: A resort that has a contracted agreement with an exchange company

ARDA: The American Resort Development Association that is based in Washington, DC

Agenda: Used to describe the steps of a presentation.

Assessment: A fee charged to owners for extraordinary expenses over and above a regular maintenance fee.

Biennial Membership: Ownership of a specific week for use every other year for a specified number of years.

Confirmed Exchange: This is hard copy confirmation from your Exchange Company for the week and unit that you agreed to accept as your exchange.

CRDA: The Canadian Resort Development Association that is based in Toronto, Ontario

Deeded Ownership: This type of ownership reflects a specific week and unit that comes with a deed indicating ownership in perpetuity.

Exchange Request: A request for three or four resort choices you would like to go.

Exchange Fee: This is the fee that must be paid to reserve or confirm an exchange.

Exchange Confirmation: The written notice that your exchange has been confirmed and that a vacation week has been reserved for you at one of your selected resorts.

FTC: Federal Trade Commission based in Washington, DC

FAQ: Frequently asked question(s).

FIT: Free and Independent Traveler

Fixed Time: These are timeshare or vacation ownership intervals that are sold using a system whereby the owner buys the same week in the same unit during each year of their ownership.

Flexchange^R: Interval International's short notice travel program.

Floating Time/Flex Time: These are timeshare or vacation ownership intervals sold using a system whereby the owner buys a variable unit or week during each year of their ownership. These types of owners must secure a fixed week from their home resort for deposit for exchange.

Fractional Ownership: The ownership of four or more interval weeks in the same location.

Getaway: These are Interval International´s short notice vacations for travel 59 days to 24 hours in advance.

Guest Certificates: These are Certificates purchased by the owner of a week which permit someone other than the owner to for the use their vacation interval. These are subject to additional fees.

HOA: Home Owners Association. This group oversees the management of your home resorts membership.

Home Resort: The resort that sold you your vacation interval or time. They will also assign a specific week or unit of use if you own floating or flex time.

Host Resort: This is the member resort that you travel to on an exchange.

Bonus Breaks or Vacations: RCI's spontaneous vacation weeks.

Lock Off Unit (Lock Out): These are units where a portion of the unit may be locked off from the main unit.

Maintenance Fees: Fees or assessments that you pay directly to your home resort for its maintenance, insurance etc. (please refer to Chapter 11)

Maximum Occupancy: The maximum many people are able to sleep in your unit.

OPC: Off Premise Contact.

OTE: Organization for Timeshare in Europe

Private (Minimum) Occupancy: Refers to the number of persons a resort unit may accommodate, based on two adults in one sleeping area and a private bathroom.

Resort Information Sheets: Information that is sent to you with your exchange confirmation about the resort you are exchanging to. This information describes the important details you will need while you are staying at that location.

Right-To-Use Ownership: Ownership of a specific week by way of having the right to occupy the property for a specific number of years

Start Date: The day or date in which you vacation interval beings.

Travel Dates: These are the starting and ending dates of a vacation exchange.

Triennial Membership: Ownership of a specific week for member use every third year for a specified number of years.

Unit Type: The basic configuration of a resort unit, such as studio, one-bedroom, two-bedroom, etc.

Chapter 20

Timeshare Address Book

In the following pages you will find contact information for some of the industry companies that I have included in this book. I have noted email addresses and websites, and if the company has a social media account I have added that as well. For obvious reasons, you would have to go the company websites to click on the social media links.

My apologies for not including every industry related company or publication dedicated to inform timeshare owners. If you would like, contact me at simplifyingtimeshare@yahoo.com and I would be pleased to include you in further editions

All information was current at the time of publication.

INTERVAL INTERNATIONAL
www.intervalworld.com
Facebook/Youtube/Google/Pinterest/Instagram

World Headquarters
(800, 888 & 877 Numbers are Toll-Free from
US, Canada, P.R. and U.S.V.I)
Hours are from 9:00 am to 11:00 pm ET Monday to Friday
10:00 am to 8:00 pm ET Saturday
10:00 am to 6:00 pm ET Sunday and Holidays

PO Box 431920
6262 Sunset Drive   Telephone: 305-666-1861
Miami, Florida 33243-1920

Membership Information,   Telephone: 800-843-8843
Renewal or Address Change   305-666-1884
PO Box 430960 Fax: 305-668-3423
Miami, Florida 33243-0960
Customer Service Email: CustomerService@intervalintl.com

Deposit and Exchange Request Telephone: 800-828-8200
PO Box 432170   305-666-1884
Miami, Florida 33243-2170   305-665-1918 (Spanish)
305-925-3013 (French)
                              Fax: 305-668-3423
Member Check-in Assistance   Telephone: 877-700-1154
                                            305-668-3411

Internet Support   Telephone: 877-784-3447
                                            305-668-3414
Fax: 305-668-3423
Email: CustomerService@intervalintl.com

Interval Travel - Airline, Hotel, Car Reservations
PO Box 4319020
Miami, Florida 33243-1920

Airlines, Hotel, Car Rentals	**Website**:	www.interworld.com
Cruises	Telephone:	800-622-1540
		305-668-3496
Cruise Exchange	Telephone:	888-801-0104
		305-668-3489

Interval Travel Customer Service Telephone: 888-801-0096
Email: TravelCustomerService@intervalintl.com

Getaways Reservations	Telephone:	800-722-1861
		305-666-3462
	Website:	www.interworld.com

Telecommunications for the Deaf Telephone: 800-822-6522
(Services available Monday through Friday 9:00 am to 5:00 pm - not on Weekends or Holidays)

Worldwide Main Offices:

Latin America Office:

Mexico: Tel: 052 55-5627-7300 Fax: 52 55-5627-7310

Languages Spoken — Spanish,
English
(Monday through Friday 9:00 am to 7:00 pm Local Time)

Asia/Pacific Office:

Singapore: Tel: 65 6318 2500 Fax: 65 6318 2511

Languages Spoken – English,   (Monday through Friday 9:00 am to
Cantonese, Bahasa Indonesia,   6:00 pm Local Time)
Bahasa Melayu, Japanese,
Mandarin, Tagalog, Thai

European Office:

United Kingdom: Tel: 44 844 701 4444 Fax: 44 844 701 7023
Languages Spoken – English, Dutch, French, Greek, Hebrew, Spanish
(Monday through Friday 9:00 am to 8:00 pm Local Time)

RCI

www.rci.com
Facebook/Twitter/Youtube

Hours of Operation:

RCI.com   24 hours a day, 7 days a week*

Click to Chat via RCI.com:

Monday through Friday: 8:00 a.m. to 11:00 p.m. EST
Saturday and Sunday: 8:00 a.m. to 6:00 p.m. EST

Emergency Check-in Assistance:

24 hours a day, 7 days a week including all holidays

Contact Center Hours of Operation

Monday through Friday: 8:00 a.m. to 8:00 p.m.
Saturday: 8:00 a.m. to 5:00 p.m.
Sunday: closed

Corporate Office	Telephone:	973-496-8687
9998 North Michigan Road	Fax:	973- 496-1977
Carmel, IN 46032		
Membership Information,	Telephone:	800-338-7777
Renewal or Address Change		317-805-8000
and	TDD Line:	800-982-4792
Deposit and Exchange Request Fax:		317-871-9335

WORLDWIDE OFFICES

Argentina 54 11 4711-2724

Australia 61 7 5588-9980

Brazil 55 11 4225-8300

Canada 416 515-7530

Chile 56 2 203-3737

Colombia 57 1 621-4939

Egypt 20 2 417-8323

England 44 1536 31-01-01

Finland 358 9 6937-9173

Germany 49 0 89 904753

Greece 30 1 8113800

Hungary 36 1 326-3424

India 91 80 558-7898

Italy 39 45 680-0466

Japan 81 52 211-1108

Korea 82 2 780-2841/4

Malaysia 60 3 209-4367

Mexico 52 5283-1000

Portugal 351 289 540400

Russia 7 095 258-6028

Scandinavia 54 33 322588

Singapore 65 223-4333

Spain 34 91 509-7800

South Africa 27 11 258-1000

Capetown 27 21 430-1160

GOVERNMENT & INDUSTRY ASSOCIATIONS

AMERICAN RESORT DEVELOPMENT ASSOCIATION

1201 – 15th Street NW, Suite 400	Telephone: 202-371-6700
Washington, DC USA 20005-2842	Fax: 202-289-8544
Facebook/Twitter/Google	E-mail: customerservice@arda.org
	Web sites: www.arda.org
	www.arda-roc.org
	www.vacationbetter.org

CANADIAN RESORT DEVELOPMENT ASSOCIATION

1240 Bay Street, Suite 807	Telephone: 416-960-4930
Toronto, Ontario Canada M5R 2A7	Fax: 416-923-8348
	Web site: www.crda.com
	E-mail: memberservices@crda.com

FEDERAL TRADE COMMISSION

Public Reference	Telephone: 202-326-2222
Washington, DC USA 20580	
Facebook/Twitter/Youtube	**Web site**: www.ftc.gov

UNITED STATES, FEDERAL

The Honorable (Name of your US Representative)

U.S. House of Representatives

Washington, DC 20515

Telephone: 202-225-3131 US House Operator, then Ask for your State Representative

E-mail: www.senate.gov/member/mo/ashcroft/general/termlimits/house.html

Internal Revenue Service (IRS)

Twitter   **Web site**: www.irs.ustreas.gov

UNITED STATES, Individual STATES

You can find out about your state legislature by clicking on the following website to direct links to your applicable state.

Website: www.ncsl.org/aboutus/ncslservice/state-legislative-websites-directory.aspx

WORLD TIMESHARE ASSOCIATIONS

The following associations are listed by region:

EUROPE

EUROPEAN TIMESHARE FEDERATION

Europees Centrum voor de Consument	Telephone:	+32 (0) 2 542 33 46
Hollandstraat 13	Fax:	+32 (0)2 542 32 43
1060 Brussels, Belguim		

Twitter **Website**: ec.europa.eu/consumers/ecc/consumer_topics/ timeshare_en.htm

RESORT DEVELOPMENT ASSOCIATION (RDO)

formerly the ORGANIZATION FOR TIMESHARE IN EUROPE

Head Office:	Telephone:	+ 44 (0) 207 554 8634
Hamilton House, Mabledon Place	Email:	info@rdo.org
Bloomsbury, London WIP 7FB		
Facebook/Twitter	**Website**:	www.rdo.org

TATOC - The Timeshare Association

Manchester House	Telephone: +44 (0) 845 230 2430
84-86 Princess Street	International Help: 0044 161 237 3518
Manchester, United Kingdom M1 6NG	Email: info@tatoc.co.uk
Facebook/Twitter	**Website:** www.tatoc.co.uk/

AUSTRIA - Osterreichischer Verein fur Timesharing und Ferienclubsysteme

Pannzuanweg 1	Telephone:	+43 663 85 63 68
5071 Wals	Fax:	+43 662 85 63 68 30
Österreich / Austria		

Facebook/Twitter/Google **Website**: www.unternehmen24.at/Firmeni nformationen/AUT/834855

BELGUIM   **Contact:**   RDO or TATOC

FINLAND - RDO NORDIC REGIONS (Finnish Timeshare Association)

Tasetie 8,   Telephone: +358 400 114 271
01510 Vantaa, Finland

                              Email: kirsi.valaja@
                                            suomenviikko-
                                            osakeyhdistys.fi
                              Website: www.suomenviikko-
                                            osakeyhdistys.fi

FRANCE   **Contact:** RDO or TATOC

GERMANY - RDO Germany (RDO Redaktionsbüro Berlin)

Schumannstrasse 9   Telephone: +49 30 884 601 14
10117 Berlin Germany   Fax: +49 30 884 601 11

                              Email: rdo.org rdogermany@
                              Website: www.rdo.org

GREECE - RDO Greece (Greek Timeshare Association)

10 D. Psarrou   Telephone: +30 811 3900
Polidrosso Amarousiou 15125   Fax: +30 10 685 9611
Athens Greece   Email: rdogreece@rdo.org
                              Website: www.rdo.org

HUNGARY - RDO HUNGARY

Pf. 184 H-2001   Telephone: +36 1 459 1104
Szentendre Hungary   Fax: +36 1 459 1107
                              Email: info@rdo.hu
                              Website: www.rdo.org

MALTA - RDO MALTA

The Penthouse   Telephone: +356 21347708
Ajiree Flats Testaferrata Triq Fax: +356 21347709
Ta'Xbiex
XBX1402 Malta   Email: rdomalta@rdo.org
                              Website: www.rdo.org

SPAIN - **RDO Spain (ANETC)**

Edificio Melior C/	Telephone:	+34 91 564 0 61
Diego de León 47	Fax:	+34 91 562 95 44
228006 Madrid Spain	Email:	rdomadrid@rdo.org
	Website:	www.rdo.org

SWITZERLAND	**Contact:**	RDO or TATOC

SOUTH AFRICA - VOASA (Vacation Ownership Association of South Africa)

3rd Floor, 3 High Street,	Telephone:	+27 (0)21 914 9693
Rosenpark 7530	Fax:	+27 (0)21 914 5202
Facebook	Email:	voasa@voasa.co.za
	Website:	www.voasa.co.za

CARIBBEAN

ARUBA - ATSA (Aruba Timeshare Association)

PO Box 672	Telephone:	+2978 79000
Oranjestad, Aruba	**Website:**	www. arubatsa.com/

BAHAMAS	**Contact:**	www.arda.org/caribbean

BARBADOS	**Contact:**	www.arda.org/caribbean

ST. MAARTEN - St. Maarten Timeshare Association (SMTS)

Welgelegen Road	Telephone:	+5995 26016
Little Bay, St. Maarten		
	Website:	www. timesharestmaarten.com/

MEXICO & LATIN AMERICA

MEXICO - AMDETUR

	Telephone:	**+**55- 5488-2028
	Email:	amdetur@prodigy.net.mx
Facebook/Twitter	**Website:**	www.amdetur.org.mx/ home/

LADETUR (Federación Latinoamérica de Desolladores Turísticos, AC) – See **AMDETUR** above

This group governs timeshare in Mexico, Uruguay, Dominion Republic, Chile, Costa Rica, Brazil, Columbia and Argentina

INDIA

INDIA - AIDA (All India Resort Development Association)

No 582, 1st Floor	Telephone:	+080 41255007
6th Cross, 11th Main	Email:	info@airda.org
HAL 2nd Stage, Near Indiranagar Club		
Bangalore – 560 008	**Website:**	www.airda.org/
Facebook/Twitter		

ASIA

AUSTRALIA - ATHOC (Australian Timeshare Holiday Ownership Council)

Suite 8, 3700 Bundall Road	Telephone:	+61 7 5526 7003
Surfers Paradise, Queensland 4217	Email:	info@athoc.com.au
	Website:	www.athoc.com.au

FIJI - Fiji Timeshare Association

Email:	www.fijitimeshare.com/contact.html
Website:	www.fijitimeshare.com/

INDONESIA - Timeshare Association of Indonesia

Website:	www.asita.org/

JAPAN - Japan Resort Enterprise Association Contact: TATOC

MALAYSIA - Malaysian Holiday Timeshare Developers Federation

Telephone:	+603-78771476
Website:	www.timesharemalaysia.org.my

NEW ZEALAND - New Zealand Holiday Timeshare Council

PO Box 1648	Telephone:	+64 003377 5888
Christchurch, New Zealand	Fax:	+64 003377 6116
	Email:	enquiries@nzhoc.org.nz
	Website:	www.nzhoc.org.nz/

Other countries are working on creating their own timeshare associations and legislation so that the ¨Rules¨ for all prospective buyers will be consistent the world over. As associations and governing bodies are created they most likely will create individual website, so until then, you can Google the country you are buying in, or trying to find out what their timeshare legislation might be and how it may affect you.

MAJOR VACATION CLUBS & HOTELS

DISNEY VACATION CLUB

Disney Vacation Dev. Inc.	Telephone:	407-566-3000
200 Celebration Place	Fax:	407-566-3333
Celebration, Florida 34747	Toll-Free:	800-500-3990
Facebook	**Web site**: www.disney.com/ DisneyVacationClub/	

MARRIOTT VACATION CLUB INTERNATIONAL

6649 Westwood Blvd.	Telephone:	407-206-6000
Suite 500	Fax:	407-206-6044
Orlando, Florida 32821-6090	Toll-Free:	800-307-7312
Facebook/Twitter	Email: owner.services@vacationclub.com	
	Web site: www.vacationclub.com/	

HILTON GRAND VACATION CLUB

6355 Metrowest Blvd.	Telephone:	407-521-3100
Suite 180	Fax:	407-521-3112
Orlando, Florida 32835	Toll-Free:	800-448-2736
Facebook/Twitter/Youtube	**Web site**: www. hiltongrandvacations. com	

HYATT VACATION OWNERSHIP, INC.

140 Fountain Parkway Ste 570	Residence Club: 727-803 9400
St. Petersburg, Florida 33716	
Facebook/Twitter/Youtube	**Website (Residence Club)**: www. hyattresidenceclub.com/hvc/en/ contactus.html

RITZ-CARLTON DESTINATION CLUB Toll-Free: 800-983-4234
Website: www.ritzcarltonclub.com/

FOUR SEASONS   Toll-Free: 800-343-0799
RESIDENCE CLUB

Website: residences.fourseasons.com/residence_clubs/aviara/

STARWOOD VACATION NETWORK (SVN) Toll-Free: 800-343-0799

Facebook/Youtube **Website**: www.starwoodvacationnetwork.com

Members of Sheraton and Westin Vacation Clubs under Starwood contact as follows:

Sheraton Owners: Toll-Free 888-786-9637 or direct at 407-903-4649

Westin Owners: Toll-Free 888-986-9637 or direct at 407-903-4635

WYNDHAM/FAIRFIELD - CLUB WYNDHAM Toll-Free:
800-251-8736

Wyndham Vacation Resorts   VIP Toll-Free: 888-884-4321

6277 Sea Harbor Drive
Orlando, FL 32821

Twitter/Facebook/Google/   **Website**:
Youtube   www.wyndhamvacationresorts.com/ffr/
                                  index.do

There are thousands of vacation clubs in the world - as many as timeshare projects and it would be impossible for me to list them all, however if you are looking for a particular club, just Google the name and go to the site.

MAJOR HOTELS

Hilton Hotels   www.hiltonworldwide.com
Facebook/Twitter/Youtube/Linkedin/Flickr

Hyatt Hotels   www.hyatt.com
Facebook/Twitter/Youtube

Marriott Hotels   www.marriott.com

Intercontinental Hotels   www.ihg.com
Facebook/Twitter

ITT Sheraton Hotels   www.starwoodhotels.com/sheraton/
Facebook/Twitter

Ritz Carlton Hotels   www.ritzcarlton.com
Facebook/Twitter/Youtube/Google/Instagram

Westin Hotels   www.starwoodhotels.com/westin/
                                  index.html

Facebook/Twitter

Holiday Inn Hotels   www.holiday-inn.com
Facebook/Twitter/Pinterest

Four Seasons   www.fourseasons.com
Facebook/TwitterYoutube/Google/Instagram/Pinterest

Starwood   www.starwoodhotels.com
Youtube

OTHER EXCHANGE COMPANIES

Here is the contact information for the companies covered earlier under Exchange options in Chapter 10, however there are others available and can be found by using Google to find them on the internet.

International Cruise and Excursions (I.C.E. Gallery)

Worldwide Headquarters	Telephone:	602-395-1995
1551 North Dial Boulevard	Fax:	602-395-6695
Scottsdale, Arizona 85260-2619		
	Toll-Free: US/Canada: 866-814-6295	

Additional Worldwide office locations can be found on their website.

Website: www.icegallery.com

Members Web site: www.myplatinumrewards.com

HSI (Holiday Systems International)

7690 Cheyenne Avenue	Telephone:	702-254-3100
Suite 200	Toll-Free:	US/Canada: 800-353-0774
Las Vegas, NV 89129	Email:	service@ holidaysystems.com

Additional Worldwide office locations can be found on their website.

Web site: www.holidaysystems.com

OWNERS LINK

Calle Bonampak, #29-01	Telephone:	+(52) 998-898-2634
Int. 307, SM 03	Toll-Free:	US/Canada: 888-806-9958
Cancun, Q.Roo, México 77500		

Email: memberservices@owners-link.com

Website: www.owners-link.com/menbersonly.aspx

DAE (Dial An Exchange)

7520 North 16th Street	Telephone:	602-516-7680
Suite 402	Toll-Free:	US/Canada: 800-468-1799
Phoenix, AZ 85020	Email:	infousa@daelive.com
	Web site:	www.daelive.com

Additional Worldwide office locations can be found on their website.

RENTAL AND RESALE COMPANIES

There are so many companies which offer exchange, rental and resale options I cannot possibly list them. I do not recommend, or endorse any company, so any decision on your part to work with them is your choice. If you wish to check online for companies that offer these services remember to check them out as thoroughly as you can before doing business with them. If they offer free listing services, this may be your better option.

Remember, NEVER EVER Pay any Rental or Resale company ANY MONEY up front, only when they deliver results.

TIMESHARE INFORMATION ON THE INTERNET

Due to space considerations I cannot possibly list all the timeshare or vacation ownership related Websites. If you would like to locate anything to do with timeshare or vacation ownership on the internet, use Google or any other search engine and type in timeshare or vacation ownership and you will be presented with many options.

I have included however, some of the more popular timeshare magazine and users group options. Again there are over thousands of sites, so find the one(s) that you like the best and go from there! I will also say that a number of timeshare resort properties do offer their members the opportunity to ¨blog¨ within their own member sites.

TIMESHARING TODAY - The Independent Voice of Vacation Ownership

140 Country Road, Suite 110	Telephone:	201-871-4304
Tenafly, New Jersey 07670	Fax:	201-871-4305
	E-mail:	Staff@tstoday.com
	Web site:	www.tstoday.com

TUG - TIMESHARE USERS GROUP (Largest Site dedicated to Timeshare Owners)

PO Box 1442	Telephone:	904-298-3185
Orange Park, FL 32067	E-mail:	tug@tug2.net
	Web site:	www.tug2.net

TUG BBS (Timeshare Users Group Forums)

Part of the Timeshare Users Group Site

Web site: tugbbs.com/forums/

The RCI Blog®

Facebook/Twitter/Youtube

Web site: blog.
rci.com/

The GATEHOUSE

1296 E Gibson Rd, Ste A #265	Telephone:	877-477-2900
Woodland, CA 95776	E-mail:	info@insidethegate.com

Facebook/Twitter

Web site: www.insidethegate.com/gatehouse/

Although Trip Advisor is neither a magazine nor a blog, it has become the primary source of information for all travelers worldwide searching for a vacation and/or find out about a timeshare experience. Trip Advisor also operates 23 other travel related sites. It encourages everyone to post about their experiences - good and bad.

TRIP ADVISOR

141 Needham Street	Telephone:	617-670-6300
Newton, MA 02464	Fax:	617-670-6301

Facebook

Web site: www.tripadvisor.com

Before I finish timeshare on the internet, I would not be doing justice if I did not include sites which allow the posting of complaints against resorts and/or negative experiences at resorts. Please bear in mind when you read these sites you are only ¨hearing¨ one side of any story and should be aware that when people are angry, upset or feel that they have been scammed or taken advantage of, they will post negative comments. I am not saying that the events they write about did not occur, however you should keep an open mind as one persons experience should not affect your consideration of purchasing a timeshare or any product - search for the good side as well and give them all a fair hearing and then make your decision.

American Resort Development Association (Complaints)

http://www.ardaroc.org/roc/resourcelibrary/default.
aspx?id=2781&libID=2801

**Federal Trade
Commission**

https://www.ftccomplaintassistant.gov/#crnt&panel1-1

Pissed Consumer.com   http://www.pissedconsumer.com/

**The Complaints Board.
com**

http://www.complaintsboard.com/bycompany/timeshare-a23086.html

**Timeshare Marketplace.
com**

http://www.timesharemarketplace.com/complaints

Consumer Bureau.com

http://www.timeshareconsumerbureau.com/news/
common-timeshare-complaints

Complaints List.com   http://www.complaintslist.com/timeshares/

Ripoff Report.com   http://www.ripoffreport.com/

About the Author

Karen resides in Puerto Vallarta Mexico, having moved there 20 years ago after a successful business career specializing in management, sales, finance and corporate restructuring. She continues to use those business and management skills in working with a number of resort and timeshare properties in Mexico. In 2006 she wrote and published the first Simplifying Timeshare, which was written to help timeshare owners in understanding and learning how to use their timeshare properties successfully. She also co-authored The Buying Curve, which was published in February 2014, which details the complete sales process and how to be successful in sales.

Lightning Source UK Ltd.
Milton Keynes UK
UKOW03f0706211014

240409UK00003B/177/P